"A HARD-HITTING, TRUE ACCOUNT OF HEROIC AMERICANS WHO FOUGHT THE VIETCONG ON THEIR TERMS."
—Al Santoli, author of *To Bear Any Burden*

"A SINGULAR CONTRIBUTION TO THE LITERATURE OF VIETNAM. . . . Of scores of books written about the Vietnam War, few if any bring the reader more powerfully into the thick of the conflict than this vivid, minute-by-minute account of one desperate, embattled day."
—Philip Geyelin, Columnist, *The Washington Post*

"AUTHENTIC DOWN TO THE LAST INSECT BITE. . . . Jim Donahue has captured the essence, the flavor, the thoughts of the man in combat . . . Donahue was there—you feel it, you know it. This is really the way it was."
—Francis J. Kelly, Colonel, U.S. Army

JAMES C. DONAHUE has received military awards that include the Silver Star, three Bronze Stars, the Purple Heart, two Air Medals, the Vietnamese Cross of Gallantry, the Combat Medical Badge, and American and Vietnamese Parachute Wings. After returning home, he earned a Bachelor's degree in Anthropology and a Master's Degree in Social Sciences, and worked for the U.S. Veterans Employment and Training Services. In 1976, he was one of six veterans honored by the national organization "No Greater Love" for "truly noteworthy contributions to their communities since returning from the war in Southeast Asia." He lives in Glenwood, New York, with his wife and two children.

No Greater Love

A DAY WITH THE MOBILE GUERRILLA FORCE IN VIETNAM

by

James C. Donahue

A SIGNET BOOK

NEW AMERICAN LIBRARY

A DIVISION OF PENGUIN BOOKS USA INC.

Copyright © 1988 by James C. Donahue

All rights reserved. For information address Daring Books,
Box 526, Canton, Ohio 44701

Published by arrangement with Daring Books

First Signet Printing, September, 1989

1 2 3 4 5 6 7 8 9

PRINTED IN THE UNITED STATES OF AMERICA

To
Sandi, Michael, and Sarah
and to
the Americans and Cambodians
who fought with the
Mobile Guerrilla Force

*Greater love hath no man than this,
that a man lay down his life
for his friends.*

—JOHN 15:13

Foreword

Southeast Asia is an ancient land of intense beauty that has been traversed for centuries by warring factions. It is a land whose appeal has been shattered repeatedly by moments of terror so brutal that its people have become like unwitting participants in a modern-day Greek tragedy. We Americans were also called upon to march through this mysterious land.

It has been some years since our hasty exit from the troubled lands of Indo-China. Since then, our society has attempted to come to grips with the nation's involvement in this costly war. A number of today's artists have attempted to capture on film and in literature the "true" nature of the war in Vietnam. This effort to adequately respond to our overwhelming fascination with the many puzzles of Vietnam may never be accomplished. In part, the war's legacy may be the crystallization of the perpetual conflict between soldier and citizen concerning "what it all meant."

Vietnam was a young man's war, fought in thousands of small-unit skirmishes across the country. It involved many cultures, soldiers, and civilians alike who were locked in a valiant struggle. For the vanquished there was death, for the winner only a promise of continued struggle until, perhaps, he too became the vanquished. This war was experienced, interpreted, and stored in the depths of the soldier's mind, to be truly recalled and reexperienced only from his perception. *No Greater Love* provides us with these perceptions—Vietnam as experienced by a soldier.

The common thread in this bloody environment,

which is woven into the experiences of all participants and is brought out in this chronicle, is the devotion, the attachment for one's comrade-in-arms, regardless of nationality. This deep-seated human response evolves from simple acts such as drinking from the same canteen to witnessing the self-sacrifice of a friend so that others would survive. Vietnam was a time of joy, of sadness, and of violence. Lillian Hellman said: "Most people coming out of war feel lost and resentful, what had been a minute-to-minute confrontation with yourself, your struggle with what courage you have against discomfort, at the least, and death at the other end, ties you to the people you knew in the war and makes for a time others seem alien and frivolous." The author of *No Greater Love* vividly expresses these mixed emotions as he shares with us one day of his war.

The reader of *No Greater Love* is encouraged to approach this book slowly, witnessing the sounds of the jungle, the nervous chatter of the characters as they engage with the enemy. Experience the variety of sensations that assault your senses as you crouch under fire with them beside fallen comrades. Allow your adrenaline, to flow in anticipation as the battle erupts around you. Only then can you develop an appreciation for what was endured by thousands of soldiers who fought in vain.

—Robert L. Jones
February, 1988

Bob Jones retired from the U.S. Army as a Major. His experiences included two tours in Vietnam and he was assigned to Airborne, Ranger and Special Forces Units throughout his career.

Jones is currently the Special Assistant for Employment with the Veterans of Foreign Wars (VFW) in Washington, D.C.

Acknowledgments

This book would not have been possible without the encouragement and assistance of my wife, Sandi, and my good friend, John Truax. I would also like to acknowledge the contributions of the following friends and agencies.

B. Kimball Baker—Editor *The National AMVET*

Stephen Banko—SGT, D Co., 2nd Bn., 7th Cav., 1st Cavalry Division

Aloysius Bartel—AMVETS National Service Officer

Anthony Cardinale—*The Buffalo News*

Robert Cole—SFC, Mobile Guerrilla Force, 5th Special Forces Group

James Condon—1st Lt., Mobile Guerrilla Force, 5th Special Forces Group

Francis Hagey—SFC, Mobile Guerrilla Force, 5th Special Forces Group

James Hartman—SGT, 6924th Security Squadron, U.S. Air Force

James Howard—M/SGT, Mobile Guerrilla Force, 5th Special Forces Group

William Kindoll—SFC, Mobile Guerrilla Force, 5th Special Forces Group

Warren Pochinski—SFC, Duc-Phong, 5th Special Forces Group

L. Brooks Rader—SSG, Mobile Guerrilla Force, 5th Special Forces Group

Roger Smith—SSG, Mobile Guerrilla Force, 5th Special Forces Group

Ernest Snider—SFC, Mobile Guerrilla Force, 5th Special Forces Group

Scott Whitting—SSG, Mike Force, 5th Special Forces Group

Steven Yedinak—CPT, Mobile Guerrilla Force, 5th Special Forces Group

Department of the Army, Research Assistance Branch, Alexandria, Virginia; Headquarters, 1st Infantry Division, Fort Riley, Kansas; John F. Kennedy Center for Military Assistance, Forg Bragg, North Carolina; National Personnel Records Center, St. Louis, Missouri; U.S. Army Center of Military History, Washington, D.C.; U.S. Army Military History Institute, Carlisle Barracks, Pennsylvania.

A special thanks is also due to William Kimball, author of *Vietnam: The Other Side of Glory*, for his editorial assistance and to my publisher, Dennis Bartow, for his confidence and support.

Introduction

0430 Hours (4:30 A.M.) July 18, 1967

To the west, towering black thunderheads had massed over the mountains of Cambodia before they began their march to the sea. High above our mist-shrouded ridge, they had given birth to a pre-dawn downpour. It was about thirty minutes before first light when I awoke to the steady drumming of water on my hammock. It had rained off and on most of the night, and drops were still filtering through the triple-canopied jungle. I was wet, but had managed to ward off the dank chill by wrapping myself in a piece of camouflaged parachute nylon.

Slowly unraveling from my nylon cocoon, I raised my head above the side of the hammock. Except for an occasional snore and nocturnal grunt, there was little indication that a hundred and fifty-eight Cambodian guerrillas and eight American Green Berets were camped within our small defensive perimeter astride a ridge line six klicks north of Quan-Loi, South Vietnam. Our mission had been code named "Blackjack 34," and our objective was to locate large enemy units operating in the area so that the 1st Infantry Division could engage and destroy them.

It was still too early to get up, so I lay in silence pondering the road that had brought me this far. My thoughts drifted back eighteen months, to the day I'd arrived at the coastal city of Nha-Trang in January 1966. Our twelve-member A-Team had flown from the 7th Special Forces Group at Fort Bragg, North Carolina.

When our C-130 rolled to a stop in front of the air terminal, we loaded our gear into waiting deuce-and-a-halfs and headed through Nha-Trang to the 5th Special Forces Group Headquarters. As we drove along the palm-lined streets, I was struck by the picturesque beauty of the city. Long strips of white, sandy beaches separated the azure blues of the South China Sea and the emerald-green mountains which overlooked this tropical paradise.

Breakers caressing the beach and the whitecaps glistening like sunlit crystals were a soothing sight to our flight-weary eyes.

The open-air restaurants, colorful storefronts, and white-plastered villas with their wrought-iron balconies lined the main boulevard, reminding us of its French Colonial history.

Smells of sandalwood, bougainvillea, spicy Oriental cooking, and the noxious belch of diesel fumes choked the stagnant street air. The narrow streets were congested with jeeps, cycalos, bicycles, Vespas, lambrettas, military trucks, and an occasional vintage Citroen, all jockeying for position as we negotiated the throng of pedestrians and vehicles. The raucous sounds of sputtering scooters, the cough of diesel engines, and the blaring of impatient horns heralded our attempts to inch our way through the crowded intersections. It appeared to me that the sole traffic law was that the biggest vehicle had the right of way.

Upon arrival at the Special Forces compound, we moved our foot-lockers and rucksacks into a squad tent, where we were greeted by a hobbled, gray-haired mama-san, her betel nut-stained teeth and gums as black as piano keys. She wore the traditional white blouse, black silk pants, and conical hat, and continued sweeping the concrete slab as we unpacked our clean fatigues, underwear, and toilet articles. When we were finished, she dutifully carried off our dirty laundry, and everyone took showers.

With sixty men and their equipment packed into a C-130, the flight from North Carolina had been long and cramped. We had left Fort Bragg in the cold early-morning darkness with a band playing John Philip Sousa and wives and girlfriends crying as they said, what would be to some, their last farewells. As our plane lifted off in the rain, most of the men quickly drifted off into a deep sleep. Some had partied heavily the night before, and the steel floor soon became slippery with vomit. After four days of flying with refueling stops in San Francisco, Guam, and the Philippines, we arrived, the relentless hum of the props still lingering in my ears.

The following morning Colonel William McKean, our group commander, welcomed us to Vietnam and assigned us the mission of constructing a new fighting camp near the small district capital of Duc-Phong in Phouc-Long Province about eighty miles northeast of Saigon. The camp would be located astride a major Viet-Cong supply and infiltration route forking off the infamous Ho Chi Minh Trail, which funneled men and materials south through Laos and Cambodia. From there we were to conduct counter-guerrilla operations against local Viet-Cong units and interdict the movement of enemy personnel and equipment through the area.

After making an aerial reconnaissance of the site, we decided to construct our camp on a hill about three klicks southwest of Duc-Phong. Half of the elevation was covered with bamboo and brush, while the rest consisted of rows of rubber trees. A few weeks later, we choppered into the area and began construction.

Our assault forces consisted of our twelve-member A-Team, a detachment of Vietnamese Special Forces, a Cambodian company that had been transferred to us from the A-342 Special Forces camp at Dong-Xoai, a small contingent of Navy Seabees to help clear the hill and build a runway, and two companies of Chinese Nungs from the Bien-Hoa Mike Force. The Nungs were descendants of Kuomintang forces who had retreated into Indochina at the end of the Second World War. They were professional mercenaries for whom the war had never ended. By aggressively patroling the surrounding area they kept the Viet-Cong on the defensive while we were engaged in the initial stages of construction. Once our concertina wire was strung, our trenches dug, and our runway cleared, they returned to their home base at Bien-Hoa.

Because enemy battalion- and regimental-sized units were suspected of operating in the Duc-Phong area, we concluded that we would need more than one Cambodian company to carry out our mission. In an effort to increase our manpower, we established contact with the chief of the local Stieng Montagnard tribe. The Stieng were one of the primitive hill tribes that inhabited the convoluted highlands of Vietnam.

There was no love lost between the "Yards" and the Vietnamese lowlanders. They had been victimized by the Vietnamese from both sides, so they mistrusted the South as well as the North. However, they reserved a special hatred for the North. Because their remote mountain villages often straddled North Vietnamese infiltration routes, they were repeatedly subjected to communist atrocities. Their women were raped, village chiefs beheaded, rice confiscated, and their young men forcibly conscripted. Many villages had packed up and fled, but some tribes refused to leave their ancestral homelands and embraced the help we offered.

Not only were the Vietnamese and Montagnards long-standing enemies, but they were ethnically different as well. Unlike the Vietnamese, who were slight of frame, delicate, thin-boned, and amber brown in color, the "Yards" bodies were hard and compressed, tough and wiry, with a reddish nut-brown tint to their skin. While the Vietnamese had almond-shaped eyes, the "Yards" were more rounded, without the extra Oriental fold of skin in the corners. The sound of their language also differed. While Vietnamese had an almost melodic, singsong sound, the Montagnards' language was a mixture of singsong and guttural tones which had a "clippity-clop" quality when they spoke.

My introduction to the local chief was like an introduction to primitive man. He was gnarled and ancient with leathery skin and shoulder-length black hair. Large pieces of elephant tusk pierced his earlobes, a beaded necklace hung around his neck, a dozen brass bracelets jangled on his wrists, and a loincloth was bound around his waist. He looked more Commanche than Asian. While we talked, he puffed on a homemade cigar that smelled like burning hemp. When our discussion ended, he tossed it on the ground and crushed its burning glow under his thick, callused heel.

With his assistance we were able to recruit, arm, and train a force of four hundred Montagnard light infantry. When the Montagnard recruits arrived at camp they wore nothing more than red and black loincloths and carried crude spears and crossbows.

At first they appeared to possess an innocence which would be no match for the Viet-Cong. However, as time and training progressed, we grew to admire the innate qualities that made them tenacious warriors. This, combined with their extensive knowledge of the surrounding terrain and people, enabled us to mold them into an effective fighting force.

In October 1966, we received a coded message that our new group commander, Colonel Francis "Blackjack" Kelley, needed volunteers to form and command a Mobile Guerrilla Force (M.G.F.). Kelley's plan to introduce American-led guerrillas into the conflict represented a significant shift in strategy. From the beginning of our involvement in the war, Special Forces had been primarily employed as advisers to the Vietnamese Special Forces, which in turn commanded Vietnamese, Montagnard, Cambodian, and Chinese Nung units in their conduct of counter-guerrilla operations.

I considered an American-commanded unit pressing guerrilla operations against the Viet-Cong and North Vietnamese forces a challenging concept. I had always thought that the policy of limiting Special Forces to static counter-guerrilla advisory roles was a tragic waste of combat skills and training. I was convinced that the best way to beat the enemy was to out-guerrilla him. By employing irregulars who were better equipped and better trained, we could beat Charlie at his own game.

Following a discussion with my A-Team commander, I decided to notify Nha-Trang that I would be willing to extend my tour in-country for another six months in return for reassignment to the M.G.F. It was a decision laced with mixed emotions. I wouldn't miss the endless steel-gray skies, torrential rains, and boot-sucking mud of the monsoon season, the daily stench of diesel fuel burning the contents of the camp's four-hole latrines, or our French-trained cook, who threw cinnamon on everything he dished up, but I would miss my friends and comrades. I suppose what I most regretted leaving was the holding of sick call in remote Montagnard villages. It gave me pleasure and a rewarding sense of accomplishment to aid people who wouldn't otherwise have been helped.

Within two weeks I boarded a C-123 on my way to Bien-Hoa with orders to report to Captain James Gritz.

When we landed, I picked up a couple of cheeseburgers and a chocolate milkshake at the P.X., then hitched a jeep ride the short distance through the town to the Special Forces compound. Bien-Hoa seemed especially hot, dry, and dusty that day—the air thick with the smell of exhaust fumes and human waste. Throngs of American and Vietnamese soldiers, peddlers, prostitutes, and money changers crowded the narrow sidewalks as we sped past the shantytown shacks of tin and ammo crates, sleazy bars, souvenir shops, and whorehouses. In our wake we left still another layer of powdered red dust, the consistency of fine flour. After arriving at the compound, I checked in with the Sergeant Major and was assigned to my billets.

Before reporting to Gritz, I got a fresh haircut at a Vietnamese barber shop, spit-shined my jump boots, took a hot shower, and slipped into a set of heavily starched jungle fatigues. I was nervous about the meetings, not knowing what to expect. As I waited to see the Captain, I found myself repeatedly wiping my sweaty palms on my trousers.

When I finally got to meet him, I was greeted by a

man who stood about five foot nine inches with sandy brown hair and piercing blue eyes. He welcomed me with a warm smile and handshake and told me he was glad to have me on board. For about thirty minutes we sat in a very relaxed atmosphere and discussed the M.G.F. and the role I would play.

As we spoke, I could see he was an original—a professional soldier, but an unconventional thinker; a leader, but not a pompous elitist. Probably the single thing that impressed me most was the fact that he was very open to ideas. When we finished our preliminary talk we passed into another room, where I met the other members of the M.G.F. team. All of them were career Special Forces soldiers who had come from A-Teams all over Three Corps. I hadn't known any of them before, but if my gut instincts were right, we had the makings of one hell of a team.

In order to gather our indigenous force, we relied on an underground Cambodian organization known as Khmer Serei. They had been selected from among the other ethnic groups because of their inherent discipline, physical strength, stamina, good-naturedness, tactical prowess, ability to execute silent operations, and intense hatred for the Vietnamese. They were a people without a country; the Vietnamese didn't want them in Vietnam, and the Cambodian government under Prince Sihanouk wouldn't allow them to live in Cambodia. For years many of them had lived as nomadic guerrillas in the jungle, fighting and killing both North and South Vietnamese. Through a chain of contact whose links extended throughout the Third and Fourth Corps regions, the Khmer Serei raised a force of two hundred of its best men.

On November 10, 1966, we completed our recruitment phase in Bien-Hoa and trucked everyone the short distance to the Special Forces camp at Ho-Ngoc-Tao. The camp was located on the Bien-Hoa-to-Saigon highway a few miles north of the capital. The flat, sandy terrain was in stark contrast to the verdant green jungles of Duc-Phong.

The morning following our arrival, the Bodes (Cambodians) were broken down into four platoon-sized units as a languid morning sun broke free from a mist-layered horizon. From their motley appearance they looked like anything but an effective fighting force that day. Some had gray beards while others weren't old enough to shave. Many wore black pajamas and tire-tread sandals. A few displayed red, green, black, or maroon berets with an odd assortment of medals on their chests from the United States, France, South Vietnam, and the Viet-Minh. Even though they appeared to be a rag-tag bunch, I could sense that they were something more. When the platoon sergeants barked orders calling them to attention, their lines snapped straight as rulers. Silence reigned, and no one budged. These were soldiers in every sense of the word. The Khmer Serei had done their job well.

From November 13 to December 15 we trained sixteen hours a day, seven days a week. Our typical working day began in the predawn darkness about two hours before breakfast with a long run, followed by calisthenics. After eating, we trained the Cambodians in such basic skills as marksmanship, hand-to-hand combat, and first aid. Since the unit was to be engaged in unconventional operations, mining, booby-trapping, sniping, special weapons, and use of other devices were also taught. After dinner we practiced such skills as night-firing techniques, movement at night, light and noise discipline, and setting up night ambushes. Whenever we had a few hours off, everyone enjoyed playing volleyball or a game similar to Italian bocce. The volleyball games were pretty even; the Americans were taller, but the Bodes were more agile.

While at Ho-Ngoc-Tao, we organized a Headquarters Unit, a Reconnaissance Platoon, and three Main Force platoons. The Headquarters Unit consisted of the M.G.F. commander, an American radio operator with a PRC-74 radio, which would be used to communicate with Bien-Hoa by Morse code, a Cambodian company medic with a major surgical kit, a Cambodian interpreter, and a ten-member Headquarters Security Section. The Reconnaissance and the three Main

Force platoons had American commanders and deputy commanders. Each of these consisted of approximately thirty Cambodians, including a Cambodian platoon sergeant and three Cambodian squad leaders. In addition to command responsibilities, each American was also assigned duties as specialists in one or more areas: operations and intelligence, communications, medical, light weapons, heavy weapons, or demolitions.

On December 15 we completed our initial training and flew to Duc-Phong to field test the guerrilla tactics developed at Ho-Ngoc-Tao. Our return was a pleasant change, since it afforded me the opportunity to see old friends. We spent the first two days in the rolling green hills south of camp practicing tactics and aerial-resupply methods. While at Ho-Ngoc-Tao we had initially planned to resupply our operations by parachute-dropped supplies and ammunition from Air Commando-flown C-123 or C-130 aircraft, but we soon concluded that large, slow-flying aircraft would compromise our location. As a solution to the problem, we tested a method in which A-1E fighter aircraft dropped supply-filled napalm containers pre-rigged with reserve parachutes. We saw that resupply methods resembling fighter bombing runs would alert no one to our presence.

Our first practice drop that day overshot the clearing by about fifty yards, and the chutes snagged in the congested canopy. On the second flyby we developed a system where the pilot released his load over an orange ground panel on command from the M.G.F. commander. The olive drab parachutes opened at about one hundred feet and the chutes, with their silver napalm containers attached to shroud lines, drifted like silver seed pods into the center of the clearing, landing with a dull thud. Once on the ground, the napalm containers—tied shut with nylon lines—were cut open and their supplies distributed to the troops.

On our third day after relocating to Duc-Phong our Mobile Guerrilla Force was volunteered for a top-secret mission to recover a super-secret Black Box from a U-2 spy plane which had exploded at an altitude of 26,000 feet, strewing wreckage over a vast area. Because it had been calculated that the Black Box could have landed anywhere within a 440-square-mile cone-shaped area of congested jungle, our mission could be compared to finding the proverbial needle in a titanic haystack. After four days and numerous skirmishes with V.C. units, a patrol that was forced to search on its hands and knees through a snake-infested mangrove swamp hit pay dirt when it located the missing footlocker-sized instrument intact and uncompromised.

On January 4, 1967, Colonel Kelly assigned us our first guerrilla mission, codenamed "Blackjack 31." The operation would be mounted in War Zone "D," a Viet-Cong stronghold. During this mission our Mobile Guerrilla Force was whipped into fighting shape by fifty-one separate engagements with V.C. units.

One of the lessons learned from Blackjack 31 was that American-led guerrilla units were capable of conducting unconventional operations in V.C. controlled territory for extended periods of time. Our Mobile Guerrilla Force was proving that we could use the jungle to our advantage, using Charlie's sanctuary to beat him at his own game.

On February 7, we were extracted by choppers from War Zone "D" and ferried back to Duc-Phong, and later that day to Bien-Hoa, where all of the Americans were decorated by Colonel Kelly and the Bodes given a welcomed R & R. The company was then trucked west to our new camp at Trang-Sup.

After a thirty-day leave back in Buffalo, I returned to Bien-Hoa where I talked a chopper pilot into giving me a hop to Trang-Sup. Arriving there, I found that the company had established itself in an abandoned French-built compound next to the Special Forces camp. Its crumbling stucco walls pockmarked by bullets and time and the rusted coils of concertina wire were haunting reminders of another war. Our new home was situated about six klicks northwest of Tay-Ninh City, not far from the foot of Nui-Ba-Den Mountain, or "Black Virgin Mountain" as it was known to many Americans.

The camp was surrounded by jade-colored rice paddies, a few scattered palm clusters, and dusty red roads rising a couple feet above the mustard paddy waters. The lone mountain, which I assumed to be an extinct volcano, seemed perpetually brushed by clouds.

Over the next few months, the camp at Trang-Sup served as a base to launch a number of major operations. On May 2, we were inserted by choppers into a V.C. stronghold near Chi-Linh, where part of our unit was immediately surrounded by elements of the 271st and 273rd Viet-Cong Main Force regiments. During the day-long battle we were nearly overrun by repeated human-wave attacks from fully uniformed V.C. as well as khaki-clad Chinese mercenaries. For some unexplicable reason, the enemy broke off the attack and melted back into the jungle just when we had nearly run out of ammunition.

As I lay in the morning stillness listening to the muffled patter of droplets splashing against broad leaves and my hammock, it felt good to be alive. Vietnam had been a mental scrapbook of mingled joys and tragedies. Indeed, there had been times of brain-numbing monotony and gut-wrenching carnage, but there were also special times when it seemed that everything within you simply savored the essence of life just because you had lived so close to death.

My last trip to Nha-Trang had been that way. It had all seemed so out of place. I had bought a six pack of Coca-Cola, a pair of swimming trunks, and a bottle of Coppertone at the P.X. and caught a ride down to the beach.

The scent of salt air blowing off the bay, the sound of palms ruffling in the wind, and the pleasant sensation of warm sand squeezing between my toes were a refreshing contrast to grueling weeks in the bush. I spread my camouflaged poncho liner a few yards from the pounding surf, then ran into the backwash, diving headfirst into a large wave. The warm saltwater cleansed my jungle scrapes and cuts, and for about thirty minutes I lost all track of the war as I body-surfed the rolling breakers. Finally, after one too many mouthfuls of saltwater, I retired to my liner where I sat rubbing tanning lotion over my body and soaking up the sun.

From a restaurant down the beach, I could hear the Beach Boys blaring from a loudspeaker. A torrent of nostalgic memories played upon my emotions as I listened to the lyrics, "I wish they all could be California girls . . ." drift across the sands. It seemed strange how certain songs conjured up different times and places. It was also odd that war could have so many moods—so many haunting realities. One day you were knee-deep in leech-infested slime or brooding over the bloodied bodies of your friends, and the next day you were relaxing on a tropical beach, sipping Coke and fantasizing with the Beach Boys. Vietnam was like that. It could be so brutally real, and yet so very unreal at the same time—like one of those recurring dreams which never seem to end.

The here and now reasserted itself as the annoying whine of a hungry mosquito about my ear snapped me back to the present. I squinted and yawned, then took a measured look at my watch. It was about that time . . .

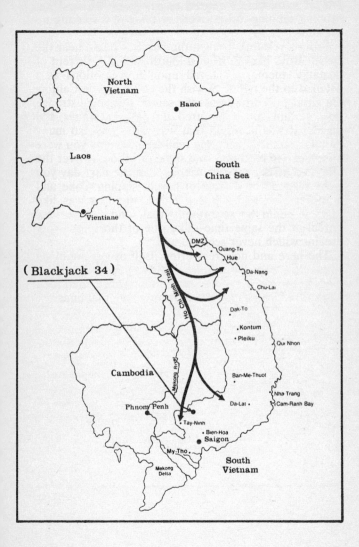

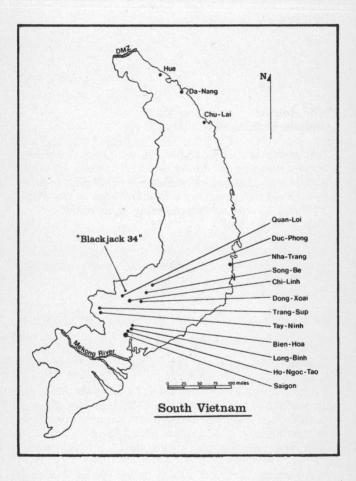

DMZ

Hue

Da-Nang

Chu-Lai

N

Quan-Loi

Duc-Phong

Nha-Trang

"Blackjack 34"

Song-Be

Chi-Linh

Dong-Xoai

Trang-Sup

Mekong River

Tay-Ninh

Bien-Hoa

Long-Binh

Ho-Ngoc-Tao

0   25   50   75   100 miles

Saigon

South Vietnam

NEWS CLIPPINGS

The American forces total 466,000 men
Buffalo Evening News, July 18, 1967

The polls had given Lyndon Johnson a long cold winter and a dampening spring, but with summer his popularity burgeoned and his sudden rise in the polls induced such a state of ebullience and playfulness in the President that he took up bicycle-riding at his ranch.
Life, July 21, 1967

The nationwide rail strike disrupted the country's economy yesterday, crippling the movement of people, mail and food supplies.
The New York Times, July 18, 1967

In the first five months of 1967, the South Vietnamese suffered 3681 battlefield deaths. The Americans lost 2853.
Buffalo Evening News, July 18, 1967

Three war protesters were carried out of the Pentagon in wheelchairs today as defense officials laid down a policy of prohibiting announced demonstrators from expressing their dissent inside the building
The New York Times, July 18, 1967

Joe Namath, the New York Jets star quarterback, headed the 51 holdovers who reported to training camps today at Peekskill Military Academy.
The New York Times, July 18, 1967

James Lee Barrett is a script writer from Hollywood who likes realism. In order to gather material for the John Wayne movie, "The Green Berets," he went on a tour of Special Forces camps throughout Vietnam.
Army Digest, July 1967

The all night curfew in Newark was eliminated as New Jersey's Gov. Hughes said that "the rioting and looting are apparently over and the violence has ceased."
The Wall Street Journal, July 18, 1967

Gemini: Your ability to cooperate will be tested, and collaboration will succeed where independent action would be of no avail.
Buffalo Evening News, July 17, 1967

1

0500 Hours (5:00 A.M.)

The predawn smells of wet foliage, rotting humus, and moist earth hung heavily in the air. The sky above the trees was beginning to glow with the first hints of dawn as the jungle stirred to life.

I sat up tentatively in my hammock and dangled my bare feet over the side only to be shocked by the sensation of cold mud beneath my soles. Balancing in my suspended perch, I reached into my rucksack to remove an army-issue can of foot powder. A little powder between the toes was one of the rare pleasures the jungle permitted. I picked up my boots, turned them upside down, and gave them a vigorous shake to dislodge any creatures that may have sought shelter from the downpour. I didn't need any surprises this early in the morning.

After lacing up my boots, I stood and stretched, listening for any unusual sounds. Except for the exotic sounds of insects, birds, and the faint rustling of monkeys, everything seemed normal. I did a few toe touches to loosen my cramped back muscles and get my juices flowing. Sleeping in a hammock had one disadvantage— you couldn't roll over, and fought a constant battle to get comfortable. There was only one position and that was flat on your back.

Though my morning stretch had brought my system to life, I was in no mood for a breakfast of cold ham and lima beans, so I dug out a package of lightweight, dehydrated Vietnamese rations. A universal loathing of prepackaged food in olive-drab cans was shared by

all. In spite of ingenious recipes and in-the-field con-
coctions, it was a rare troop who savored the taste of
C rats. Still, most of my team members didn't relish
the taste of dehydrated rice rations either. I was an
exception. They had the advantage of being a lot
lighter than C rations, and after more than a year of
bush experience, I had come up with a number of
variations, which included such gourmet delights as
rice with instant cream and sugar, rice with cocoa mix,
rice with dried carrots, rice with hot peppers, rice with
instant soup, rice with dried minnows, rice with dried
shrimp, rice with dried spinach, and rice with Tabasco
sauce. This morning I selected rice à la dried minnows. After adding a half-canteen of water and a few
dried minnows to the plastic bag the meal came in, I
tied off the top with a rubber band and set it on a
nearby stump. In about fifteen minutes, the water
would be fully absorbed by the rice.

I glanced to my left and recognized the silhouette of
SFC Bob Cole rolling out of his hammock. Well over
six feet tall, Bob was a huge black man who reminded
me of James Earl Jones. I could never quite figure out
how someone his size could sleep in a small Vietnamese
hammock. To the Bodes he was affectionately known
as Trung-si Camau (Sergeant Black). They were awed
by the fact that the chocolate-brown color of his skin
was as dark as their own, yet he was so large in
comparison to their slight frames. Bob was an Operations sergeant who came to the M.G.F. from one of
the Special Forces camps in Tay-Ninh Province. He
had been assigned to the Third Platoon after George
Ovsak was killed at Trang-Sup.

"Hey, Bob, you sleep okay?" I asked in a hushed
voice.

"Yeah, not so bad. I got up around two-thirty." He
yawned. "Checked the guard and went right back to
sleep. I guess when you hump all day you sleep all
night," he added as he sat in his hammock lacing up
his boots.

"Well, if the rains let up we should get a chance to
dry out."

"Looks like it's breaking up," he said while staring up at the sky. Through patches in the cloud cover you could see a few stars in the early morning sky.

"I hope so; my feet have been wet for so long they look like a couple of bleached prunes." Having soaked for hours on end, the skin crinkled in opaque wrinkles, looking like the last vestiges of life had been squeezed out of them.

His boots laced, Bob took a couple of steps to where I was untying my hammock.

"You hear those explosions last night?" he whispered.

"Yeah, around three-thirty. Sounded like a Sky Spot going in a few klicks north of here."

"You think the Lieutenant called in a Sky Spot?"

"May have," I answered.

"It's amazing how they can bomb a target in the middle of the night."

"I think it's all done with computers. We call the coordinates of the target back to the ALO in Bien-Hoa. He phones them down to the III Corps DASC and thirty minutes later—goodnight Charlie! From thirty thousand feet you can't even hear the planes come in."

"You say it's all computerized?" he asked. I guess we were all amazed by some of the state-of-the-art wizardry and sophisticated electronics being tested.

"Think so. I'm not sure exactly how it works; but from what I've heard the coordinates are fed into a computer, the aircraft locks onto a radar beam, and the computer calculates the exact bomb-release point so they can land right on target."

"How accurate are they?"

"All I know is that the Air Force doesn't like us calling them in any closer than six hundred meters, but when it's gotten tight, we've brought 'em in a lot closer than that."

"I guess the key is being real sure of your position," Bob chuckled. "If you're off a few hundred meters you're history."

"You got it. When we used it on Blackjack 31 I almost shit my pants," I said. "That was too close for comfort."

"What happened?"

I explained that about two in the morning one night we spotted six big cooking fires—probably a V.C. company—on the next ridge. We contacted Bien-Hoa and requested heavy ordinance be brought in on the target. About thirty minutes later the air was filled with the soft whistle of bombs tumbling out of the blackness. As the whistle grew louder we all hit the ground. I could feel my heart pounding faster and faster. Then the jungle lit up as if an enormous flash bulb had gone off, and the ground buckled and heaved from the concussions with such force that it seemed as if someone were literally shaking the jungle floor beneath us.

"I betcha a lot of prayers were going up to Buddha," Bob grinned.

"You'd better believe it. Every last Bode had his Buddha crammed in his mouth. The problem in the Dong-Nai Valley was that the terrain looked like a thousand golf balls on a pool table. It all looks pretty much the same whether you're humping through it or flying over it."

"Gotta make damned sure of your coordinates," Bob concluded.

As we talked, Thach, the Cambodian platoon sergeant, could be heard stirring the Bodes. Since the Viet-Cong usually attacked at first light, he made it a practice to have everyone saddled up and ready to move before dawn. Bending over beside my rucksack, I opened the side pocket and removed a toothbrush and toothpaste. A splash of water on my face and the sweet smell of Colgate was a real treat. Even though my body was covered with layers of dried sweat, mosquito repellent, and jungle grime from the previous day, this morning ritual somehow made me feel clean.

I slipped into my still-damp camouflaged fatigue jacket as Bob squatted beside me and switched on our PRC-25 radio.

"I'd better check in," he said matter-of-factly. "Is our primary frequency still 42.70?"

"Yeah, 42.70," I told him after checking my commo

pad with a small pen flashlight. The jungle was still dominated by slate grays when Bob picked up the handset and whispered into the mouthpiece.

"Fox Control, this is Fox Three, over. Fox Control, this is Fox Three, over." It rasped to life.

"Fox Three, this is Fox Control, over," Lieutenant Condon responded from his position inside our perimeter.

"Fox Control, this is Fox Three. This is a commo check. How do you read me? Over."

"Fox Three, I read you five by five. How me? Over."

"Roger, Fox Control. I read you same. Out."

When Bob completed his morning radio check we finished packing our rucksacks.

"We'd better change that battery," I said.

"Yeah, it's about that time. I'll rig it with a grenade," Bob said.

"If Charlie's on our trail he'll pick it up for sure. I think they've got a way of recharging 'em."

"I'll fix it for instant detonation," Bob smiled.

We found that if we didn't rig hand-grenade booby traps for instant detonation, the normal four-second delay gave the enemy plenty of time to jump clear of the explosion.

Looking up through isolated holes in the blanket of vegetation, we saw welcome patches of blue begin to appear. It was going to be a clear day. As I listened to the radio I heard Recon and the First and Second Platoons making their commo checks with Lieutenant Condon. The familiar sound of their voices was reassuring.

"Bac-si (Doctor), come quick," a hushed voice called to me from about ten meters away. Groping my way through a thick stand of bamboo, I moved slowly toward the sound of the voice. Anticipating a serious medical problem, I felt my heart rate accelerate. When I neared the source, I could see that it was the voice of Danh, our Silent Weapons Specialist.

"What's wrong, Danh?"

"Bac-si, Kimh have thing on mouth."

"What type of thing?"

"Come look."

Kimh was sitting on his hammock gagging, his mouth wide open and his tongue extended with a blood-bloated brown leech feeding on the end of it.

"I told you not to sleep with your mouth open," I said with a sense of relief.

Although smoking was not permitted, I told Danh to light up a cigarette. He threw a poncho over his head to hide the flash of his lighter. This was risky because you could also smell the telltale scent of tobacco far downwind. When Danh handed me the cigarette, I carefully touched the sluglike sucker with the glowing tip of the cigarette. In a few seconds it released its hold and dropped off, enabling me to crush it into the mud with the heel of my boot. Kimh stood there, spitting.

"Number ten, number ten," he grunted in disgust.

Kimh sat down in his hammock as I removed the canteen from his rucksack and crushed a few salt tablets in a cup of water.

"Here, Kimh, wash your mouth out with this."

After gargling and spitting for a few more minutes, he flashed me a toothy grin.

"Feel better?" I asked.

"Much better, Bac-si. Thank you."

I gave him a pat on the back and headed back to where Bob and Thach were sitting on a large fallen tree eating breakfast. Thach was the oldest man in the platoon, somewhere around forty. He had the typical Cambodian build—lean and sinewy; a compressed little man with a yellow-brown tint who stood about chest-high. Thach had a friendly face with a disarming smile which concealed a fierce hatred for the Vietnamese and intense loyalty to us and his men. He had served as a squad leader but took over as the platoon sergeant when his predecessor was shot in the stomach near Phuoc-Vinh. The wound was very serious and he was still recovering at the 24th Evac Hospital in Long-Binh. Thach had survived more firefights than anyone could count and was one of the best soldiers I'd known. His jungle savvy was an indispensable asset to our team. He was a man of contrasting personalities. During off-duty hours he was a very easygoing person who had a fatherly relationship with the younger Bodes in the platoon, but during an operation he became a hardened warrior who tolerated nothing less than instant, willing obedience from his men. He knew that discipline was one of the keys to survival. A unit that fought as a group of individuals wouldn't last long, but a unit that fought as one could slug it out with anyone. On more than one occasion I had seen him sink his boot in someone's butt. But he never really hurt any of his men—just scared the hell out of them, so that his troops feared him more than the V.C.

The morning was calm and cool as the light pushed back the curtain of grays which dulled the jungle colors. Overhead, a few patchy clouds scudded away harmlessly to the east. It was one of those Vietnam mornings you both loved and hated. You loved it because the air was refreshing and the sky resplendent with color, yet you hated it because the rising sun would soon be baking the jungle with an oppressive heat.

As the jungle colored in, I was overwhelmed by its beauty and variety. Towering brown-black trees supported a canopy of green foliage like the four-story pillars of an ancient temple. In the lower levels of the canopy, gnarled vines twisted off in all directions or dangled like limp tentacles from branches overhead. Occasionally, vines ensnared the trunks of trees as if struggling to strangle them in some quiet death grip. At lower levels, the jungle was clotted with lush foliage. Here and there stood stands of bamboo clumped together like bundles of lime-green poles and enormous broad leaves and palm fronds. The smell of mold, mildew, and decaying vegetation accented the air. Tangled vines, vegetation, ferns, and moss were wet and dripping from the perpetual humidity. Everything seemed to sweat in the dawn.

"Everything squared away?" Bob asked.

"Yeah," I said, as I removed a can of peaches from my rucksack and sat down between them. "Kimh had a leech on the end of his tongue."

"Come on—you're kidding," Bob said. "Well, I guess I've seen them in worse places."

"You know Kimh long time?" Thach inquired as he ate his rice with a plastic C-ration spoon.

"Well, we've spent over a year together," I answered, thinking how long a year really was to know someone in Vietnam. With troops constantly coming and going, relationships didn't last long in the field, even though they were often some of the most intimate of friendships—friendships forged in the crucible of war. He was just one of the survivors: someone who, through luck, skill, or something, had managed to stay alive.

"He's a good man," Bob said as he used his metal canteen cup to mix up a batch of cocoa.

"I know," I said, working open the lid of my peaches.

About a week after reporting to the M.G.F., I'd gone back to Duc-Phong and smuggled him and a few others out on an Air America plane that was ferrying up a load of pigs from Saigon. I had to sneak them out because the Vietnamese had turned down their request to go with me. The L.L.D.B. (Vietnamese Special Forces) were madder than hell when they found out and were still looking for them.

"Yeah," Bob said, taking a sip of his cocoa with a grimace. "The Bodes are number one, but this cold cocoa is number ten."

"He still hasn't recovered from those grenade wounds he got when we hit that P.O.W. camp near Chi-Linh. When he was med-evaced to the Vietnamese hospital in Tay-Ninh, they didn't even treat him."

"How come?" Bob asked.

"The Viets don't like the Bodes, I guess."

"Vietnamese want to kill all Cambodians," Thach added with contempt.

"Didn't you take him over to that inflatable hospital at the 196th?" Bob asked.

"Yeah, as soon as we got back."

When I'd returned to Tay-Ninh, about three days after Kimh got hit, I drove immediately to the hospital to see how he was doing. I found him lying on the floor, still covered with dirt and dried blood. After telling the hospital administrator what I thought of his place, I put Kimh in my jeep and drove him to the 196th Light Infantry Brigade's M.A.S.H. hospital.

"They took good care of him, didn't they?"

"Are you kidding? He was the only patient on the ward—an air-conditioned one at that. He even had three or four American nurses taking care of him."

"Think he was getting any?" Bob laughed.

"I'll tell you this, he didn't want to leave when I went out to pick him up. You guys want some peaches?" I passed the half-full can to Thach.

"Hey, Bac-si, you and Trung-si Cole come Kampuchea when we go?" Thach asked.

"Cambodia? What for?" Bob wanted to know.

"In Vietnam, government and V.C. want kill all Cambodians because they no like. In Kampuchea, Sihanouk sau lam (not good), so we go Kampuchea, kick out number ten Sihanouk, and all Khmer (Cambodian) people live in peace."

"We'll have to check that one out with Colonel Kelley," Bob said, trying to act serious.

"Sounds like something Blackjack would go for," I added.

"Hey, Jim, looks like your rice is ready."

I grabbed the now-bulging bag of rice from the stump, and as we ate Bob broke out his acetate-covered map and spread it on the ground in front of us.

"Gimme a little of your hot sauce, will you, Bob? This rice really tastes flat." He reached into his ruck-sack and handed me a small bottle of Tabasco sauce.

"You lift this from that French restaurant in Nha-Trang?"

"You know I wouldn't do anything like that!" Laughing with a feigned innocence as I sprinkled some on my rice.

"How can you eat those cold C's this early in the morning?" I asked.

"They're not so bad," he answered as he sank his fork into a can of ham and eggs.

"I'll tell you what. When we make camp tonight I'll trade you a can of ham and lima beans for a bag of rice," I said.

"Sounds good to me."

"Speaking of food, what d'ya say you, Thach, and I head down to Saigon for a couple of days when we get back?" I asked.

"Great. We could stay at the Villa on Pasteur."

I always looked forward to staying at the Villa for a night or two. It was a stately old French house on a palm tree-lined avenue. I especially liked the smell of the clean white sheets on the beds and bacon and eggs for breakfast.

"How about stopping at that U.S.O. near Tu-Do Street? They've got great cheeseburgers and milk-shakes," I added.

Whenever I got down to Saigon I always found time to stop at the U.S.O. While filling up on cheeseburgers and chocolate milkshakes, I always caught up on what was going on in the rest of the world by browsing through their large collection of current newspapers and magazines.

"What about it, Thach?" Bob asked. "How'd you like a few burgers?"

Thach shrugged. "What burgers? If we go Saigon, you and Bac-si come stay my family in Cholon."

"It's a deal," I said. "When we get back to Trang-Sup we'll head out as soon as we get the troops squared away."

Thach removed a wallet from his pocket, carefully took out a waterproof plastic bag, and proudly dis-played a picture of his wife.

"She good cook. You show her how make burgers. O.K., Bac-si?"

"We'll pick up some hamburger and rolls at the Cholon P.X.," Bob said. "And we'll have ourselves a real American barbecue."

"What's our route of march today?" I asked as I chewed on a few minnows.

"Well, let's see." Bob used his finger to point to the terrain features on his map. "We're on this ridge line with the creek off to our east, and, ah, we're going to continue moving north up toward the Loc-Ninh/An-Loc border."

"Doesn't look too bad," I acknowledged. "We shouldn't have any trouble making fifteen or sixteen klicks."

"This good area for operation," Thach added. "Mountain not big and have much water."

Thach was right. The area had many features that made it ideal for Mobile Guerrilla operations. Being Light Infantry and highly mobile, we could cross country much quicker than larger, more heavily armed units. In the low area we could navigate around the swamps and mangroves and move speedily through bamboo. Except for the ridge lines, growth was usually thicker at the higher elevations. If we had to move over high ground and couldn't travel the ridge lines, our movement could be slowed to two hundred to three hundred meters per hour. If there were elephants in the area we could also use their zigzag trails if they coincided with our route of march.

Because of the area's favorable conditions it was also ideal for large enemy base camps. Usually whatever was advantageous to us was also advantageous to Charlie. Its high-speed trails and abundant water supply were, for the most part, not visible from the air. Experience had taught me that if an area had all of this going for it, there was a very real possibility it also concealed large enemy base camps.

"Let's hope we keep well to the west of those open swampy areas," I said, pointing to the corresponding areas on the grid map. "They can be bad news."

"Got a lot of rubber up in that area, too," Bob said. "Probably owned by that asshole we ran into back at Quan-Loi."

When we had arrived in Quan-Loi, a Frenchman driving a new black Citroen and dressed in a white suit and pith helmet screeched to a halt in front of our formation. He was upset because we were standing on his grass. With a heavy French accent, he threatened to sue the United States Government if we damaged any of his rubber trees.

"From what I've been able to figure he must be playing both sides of the fence," I said. "Must be paying off the V.C. and selling the rubber to the States."

"One of the Bodes wanted to booby-trap the Citroen." Bob laughed. "But you're right. Here he is living in a big house with hundreds of plantation workers and servants and the Cong haven't greased his ass. Something ain't right."

"You don't think he knows anything about our mission, do you?"

"Hope not. You know damn well he'd sell us out in no time flat."

"Well, if we make contact we'll call in a B-52 strike on his rubber."

Bob looked at the map with a mischievous smile. "I figure three strikes will take out the whole plantation. What d'you think?"

About that time SFC Ernie Snider, known as Duke to his friends, walked up to us.

"We'll be moving out in two columns in about thirty minutes," he told us. "The Lieutenant wants the Third Platoon to take point on the left and Recon to take point on the right."

"Can do," Bob said as he folded his map and slipped it back into his fatigues.

"Hey, Duke, you'd better do something about that bald head. You can spot it a mile away—it looks like a polished cue ball," I said as he laughed and walked off toward the Second Platoon's position.

"Trung-si Cole and I not need camouflage," Thach said. "You and Trung-si Snider too white to hide in jungle."

"Won't argue with that one," I said.

"Duke's something else. Probably the best demo man in the country," Bob said. "On the Phuoc-Vinh and Dong-Xoia missions his toe poppers and booby traps saved our ass more than once."

"Yeah, Charlie's trackers were hot after us on that one."

"They were madder than hell about us hitting that training camp. Remember all those V.C. sitting in bleachers for a map-and-compass class?" Bob said. "Reminded me of one of our training classes back at Bragg."

How could I forget? One of the Bodes told me that when the instructor saw us standing there in the tree line, about ten feet from his podium, his face turned white and his jaw dropped. He just stood there for a moment with his mouth agape before one of our guys stitched him across his chest with a burst. He never said a word.

"Yeah, we really caught 'em with their pants down on that one," Bob added.

"V.C., he think he safe in his area, not have guard," Thach said.

"You know my hair still hasn't grown back where that bullet gave me a new part," Bob said as he rubbed his head. "I won't forget that day for a long time."

Bob was lucky that day. After overrunning the bleachers and the kitchen areas, he and I and part of the second squad were chasing about a dozen V.C. deep into the camp. Both of us were moving across a small clearing when a burst of machine-gun fire from a wood line about twenty feet in front of us shot off his bush hat and put two rounds into one of my canteens. Both of us instinctively hit the ground behind a large anthill—the only cover in the clearing. I quickly checked his head and found that the bullet had only creased his scalp—nothing serious. But if it had been a hair lower it would have cracked his skull like an egg. We both tried to return fire, but every time we raised our heads the enemy machine gunner opened up with a burst that knocked off the top few inches of the hill, pelting us with dirt. Suddenly, over the crackle of gunfire explosions we heard three long blasts on a whistle echoing through the jungle. It was the signal to break off contact, but we couldn't move an inch. If we didn't do something quick the V.C. would outflank our position and catch us in a cross fire. Lying out in the open with only the silhouette of an anthill for protection gave me a naked feeling. We were dangerously exposed and had to act. As a last resort we both lobbed fragmentation and C.S. gas grenades in the direction of the machine gun. As soon as they blew we leaped to our feet, fired a quick magazine into the wood line, and sprinted for the tree line.

A couple of minutes later we ran into a squad of Bodes who had come back to look for us. When I asked Bob if he was going back to look for his hat he gave me a dirty look, as if to say "Give me some slack." Since then I've taken a perverted pleasure in reminding him that he has no sense of humor.

I scooped a small hole in the jungle floor with my entrenching tool and buried our meager scraps of garbage—a couple of plastic rice bags and a few crushed C rat cans.

"Thach, make sure the platoon area is completely policed before we move out," Bob said. "Yesterday I saw some toilet paper someone didn't bury."

"Will do," Thach said as he stood up to leave.

"Thach, before you go I'd like to cover a few things with you," I added.

"Sure, Bac-si," he said as he settled back on his haunches.

"First—yesterday Lieu and Tang had their M-16 selector switches on full automatic. Make sure the three squad leaders check every weapon every morning. That means a round in the chamber and the selector switch on safe," I said, while removing my rifle-cleaning kit from my rucksack.

"If squad leaders not do their job they be punished," he promised as I passed him my silicone cloth.

"With enemy units in the area, we don't need an accidental discharge," Bob commented. "Jim, hand me your chamber brush." I passed it to him, still reflecting on his last words.

Bob was right. As a light infantry guerrilla force we wanted to select the time, place, and circumstances of all contact with the enemy. As guerrillas we initiated contact, ideally, only when we had thoroughly calculated the odds and were fairly certain we could win.

"Another thing," I added. "Last night I noticed some of the guys didn't clean their weapons. Every night, every weapon in the platoon has to be broken down, scrubbed with solvent, and oiled. As soon as our night perimeter's in place, break 'em down into twos—as one man cleans his weapon the other stands guard. Then they switch."

"Just make sure they don't all break 'em down at the same time," Bob added.

"Okay, Trung-si."

I was concerned about the weapons. Every time we got into heavy contact some of our M-16's jammed. I suspected that it was due to high carbon content ammunition and poor workmanship on the M-16's.

We also had problems with our Japanese-made indigenous rucksacks and B.A.R. belts. The rucksack required constant maintenance and often tore out at the strap connectors. When the B.A.R. belts were fully loaded with ammunition they usually tore out at the eyelets. Our camouflaged fatigues weren't much better. After a couple of weeks in the jungle, the crotch had a tendency to tear. The Bodes wore Japanese-made boots also of questionable quality. They often came apart at their soles.

"You still have that roll of green tape I gave you back at Trang-Sup?" I asked as Thach finished applying a smooth coat of oil to his rifle.

"It in pack," he said, pointing to his rucksack.

"Good. Make sure everyone's grenade pins are taped down tight; that means H.E., gas, and smoke."

"We don't want 'em catching on branches and going off," Bob said. "Use that green tape to secure anything that makes noise—and remember, no slings on the weapons. Tape down the swivels so they don't get caught on brush."

Voicing my own concern with a practical sense of seriousness, I said, "Thach, you've got to keep on the squad leaders' asses. You can't do it all yourself."

"I know, Bac-si. I am old and have fought for many years; they are young and sometime I try to do all. You know I was at Dien-Bien Phu," he said. His leathery, weathered face proudly portrayed the scars of countless battles.

"I understand, Thach," I conceded, "but if you want 'em to live you'd better tighten up on the squad leaders." I looked into his brown, bloodshot eyes and put my hand on his shoulder. He smiled, revealing a set of gold-capped teeth covered with rice.

"I know, Bac-si."

"One other thing," Bob added as he pinned a wet pair of socks to the outside of his rucksack. "Yesterday a few of the guys looked like they were taking a stroll at the Saigon Zoo. They can't be daydreaming; they've gotta keep alert at all times. That means their thumb on the selector switch, finger on the trigger, and eyes open."

Thach nodded his agreement. "Today I keep Son and his machine gun behind me," he said.

"Good," Bob said as he adjusted the canvas webbing of his ammunition harness. "Make sure he understands he's to maintain visual contact with you at all times. No falling behind."

Our M-60 was the most effective weapon in the platoon. Its rate of fire and killing power was coveted by all line troops. In the event of enemy contact, it was critical that we be able to deploy it to the point of contact. If this proved possible we could often gain fire superiority and overrun the enemy's position before he could deploy on line. It was similar to capping the "T" in naval warfare.

"Yeah, and tell Danh we put that silencer on his Sten so he can take prisoners. That means arm and shoulder shots only, nothing to the head or chest," I added as I checked the twenty-five ammunition-filled magazines in my B.A.R. belt.

"No leg shots either," Bob said. "We don't want to have to lug some wounded Cong through this terrain."

It took six to eight men to carry a wounded man any distance. The Bodes would carry an American or fellow Bode until they dropped from heat exhaustion or sun stroke, but weren't all that enthusiastic about carrying a wounded V.C.

"Okay, Trung-si," Thach said. "I go now. Talk to squad leaders."

"Keep a close eye on Lieu," I said. "This is his first operation and I'm a little worried about him." Thach nodded and then headed for the perimeter. After Thach left I told Bob that I was concerned about Lieu because I had a feeling he didn't have what it took to be a member of the M.G.F. As a possible weak link he could jeopardize the lives of others.

A couple of weeks earlier he had been assigned to go down to Saigon with me to pick up a load of Budweiser and Coke. After hitchhiking from Trang-Sup to Saigon, we found that there weren't any large trucks available at the Special Forces Compound on Cong-Ly or at the Villa on Pasteur.

As a last resort we caught a cycalo ride out to the Cholon P.X. Once there, we stood near the front entrance, waiting for someone to park a truck. After about fifteen minutes a PFC from the 1st Logistical Command drove up in a new two-and-a-half-ton truck and parked about fifty meters down the street. As soon as he entered the P.X. we jumped into the cab. Lieu was too nervous to drive, so I drove it to a nearby body shop that was owned by a Nung who I knew from Bien-Hoa. He quickly painted out the 1st Logistical Command's numerals and replaced them with A-303 and U.S.S.F.

From there we drove to the Saigon Beer and Soft Drink Distribution Center to requisition a truckload. It was as large as a city block and stacked inside its barbed-wire fence were what looked like thousands of cases of every conceivable brand of beer and soft drink warming in the open. It was a beehive of activity that day as trucks from all over Three Corps were being loaded by fork lifts.

After a fork-lift driver loaded pallets of beer and Coke onto our truck we drove to the front gate, where we were stopped by a Vietnamese guard. I pulled a receipt out of my briefcase and showed it to him. After comparing it with our cargo he returned the receipt and waved us through the gate.

About a block away I pulled the truck over to the shoulder and showed Lieu the receipt. The date on it was almost a year old and I had managed to keep it in mint condition by storing it in my briefcase. After I explained that we've been using the same bogus receipt over and over without paying for anything in almost a year, he turned white. He was convinced that the White Mice were going to arrest us.

On our drive back to Trang-Sup we hoped to pick up a convoy at Cu-Chi, but no one else was on the road that day. The road from Cu-Chi to Trang-Sup was especially dangerous because the enemy often mined it or set up ambushes. Rather than return to Saigon we decided to go it alone. With Lieu riding shotgun armed with my Swedish "K" submachine gun I put the truck into high gear and drove down the center of the road as fast as it could go.

When we finally pulled in the front gate at Trang-Sup, Lieu and I parked in front of the team house and downed the first two cans of beer. It was warm and nasty, but we thoroughly enjoyed the spoils of war.

Nothing was simple in Vietnam. Even something as seemingly easy as picking up some beer and soft drinks could become complicated. Every time you assumed that everyone knew everything they were supposed to know, or would do everything they were supposed to do, it could cost you lives. Nothing was routine. Because we had suffered so many dead and seriously wounded in recent months, this problem became more acute than ever. It was further complicated by the fact that our early departure from Trang-Sup reduced the amount of time we could devote to training replacements.

We had to move out more than a week earlier than planned because a few Bodes had beaten the hell out of a high-ranking South Vietnamese officer in a Tay-Ninh barbershop and stolen his silver-plated pistol. When we refused to conduct a search for the guilty Bodes, the White Mice and a Vietnamese armored unit threatened an all-out attack on our camp. In order to avoid a potentially explosive situation we flew out as soon as we could issue food and ammunition.

"I'm gonna take a quick crap. Back in a couple of minutes," I said to Bob as I grabbed an entrenching shovel and headed into the dense brush. I walked to a spot about ten meters outside the perimeter, where I encountered a solid wall of thorn brush, dug a small hole, and squatted.

No sooner had I dropped my trousers when a malevolent cloud of hungry mosquitos swarmed over my exposed buttocks. I tried batting them away with my hand as they dove and darted, trying at the same time to maintain my balance. Squatting over my makeshift latrine I was pleased that we had something as basic as toilet paper. I thought back to Blackjack 31, where I ran out of paper and had to use green leaves instead —I'd never forget the day I used poison-ivy leaves by mistake.

My thoughts and the silence were interrupted by the "whack, whack, whack . . ." of M-16 fire, followed by the distinctive, methodic sounds of AK-47's. Damn! Of all the things to be doing during an attack, I thought as I yanked up my pants, grabbed my M-16, and ran in a low crouch back toward the perimeter. As I approached the Third Platoon sector, I could see that the Bodes were already in defensive positions with their weapons pointed in my direction. In order to avoid a haphazard firing by a surprised Bode, I let out a loud "Wetsu." Wetsu was used as our running password when quick identification was required. Reentering the perimeter, I felt a great sense of relief that I wasn't shot by my own men: you definitely didn't want to get caught outside the perimeter during a firefight. As I approached Bob I could see that he was down on one knee talking on the radio.

"What's going on?" I asked.

"Second Platoon spotted a couple of Charlies approaching their sector."

"What were they wearing?" I asked.

"Black uniforms and carrying AKs."

"They wearing rucks?" I asked, trying to determine whom we were up against.

"No."

"Everyone okay?"

"Yeah, no casualties," he said, rising. "Let's get the troops ready to move. Charlie could be back with a regiment."

Running into a few Viet-Cong in the middle of the jungle was significant because the enemy did not normally move cross-country. When possible he traveled on established trails, roads, or animal tracks. They might have been trackers, but if that were the case they surely would have set off one of the many booby traps Snider had left along our route of march.

In this area the local V.C. were organized into six-to-twelve-man cells. They were usually responsible for maintaining the base camps serving as guides for Viet-Cong and North Vietnamese Army (N.V.A.) main-force units infiltrating through the area, and providing security when their camps were occupied. Since they were not carrying rucksacks and wore black uniforms, I had to assume that they were part of a local security unit. They were either on a patrol from a nearby base camp or were part of an outpost, or listening post, that had been set up to guard the most likely avenues of approach to their camps.

That they got away was bad news. Our contact probably meant that we had forfeited the crucial element of surprise. They now knew we had penetrated their area and were probably on their way to inform their superiors.

If the three were from a base camp that was occupied by a V.C. or N.V.A. battalion or regimental-sized unit, their next move would probably be to deploy against us. If large units were present in the area there was a good chance that they would comprise regiments from the 9th Viet-Cong Division—the same regiments we had tangled with a few weeks earlier on the Chi-Linh and Dong-Xoai operations. If they were N.V.A. main-force units they could be the crack 101st, 141st, or 250th regiment. There was also a possibility that regiments from the Viet-Cong's 7th Division had moved into the area.

We also knew that the enemy could mobilize and field a number of platoon- and company-sized units against us. These were under the command of the Viet-Cong Province Committee and were usually difficult to deal with because of their extensive knowledge of the local terrain.

Our early-morning contact was ominous and predicted a long, hot day.

As I surveyed the platoon area I could see that just about everyone was ready to move. Some of the Bodes were fidgeting nervously with their weapons while others kept a watchful eye on the surroundings—eyes darting purposefully in nervous anticipation. All the men were on their feet with rucksacks on their backs and their weapons cradled in their hands. Bob helped Ly, the Third Platoon Radio Operator, get his PRC-25 radio and the rest of his gear secured on his back. It was heavy and cumbersome, but Ly was strong and resilient and never complained. Once he got the rucksack on he bounced a few times to settle the load. He was a lot like Bob, a quiet person who exuded an inner strength that engendered confidence.

"I okay," he said as he adjusted two pieces of foam rubber he had attached to the inside of his shoulder straps to keep them from tearing the skin off his protruding clavicles.

"You stay close to Trung-si Cole," I advised in return as I put on my harness and buckled the ends of my B.A.R. belt.

"Like stink on shit," Bob quipped.

Our PRC-25 radio was our only voice contact with the Forward Air Control (F.A.C.) aircraft that proved to be our great equalizer. We used the small single-engine Cessnas on a daily basis to give us six-digit fixes on our location, call in air strikes, direct resupply aircraft to our drop zones every four days, and at times to serve as a communications relay back to the Forward Operations Base (F.O.B.).

Early every morning the F.A.C. usually made a fly-over of our area to see if he could detect any enemy movement or activity. If we made heavy contact during the day he would assist us in directing fighter, bomber, and chopper gunship air strikes against the enemy. When we set up our night defensive perimeter at twilight, he often supplied us with critical six-digit fixes that enable us to compute our location within a hundred meters in case we had to call in a Sky Spot or artillery support during the night.

Normally we made contact with the F.A.C. by PRC-25 radio when we first heard the faint drone of his engine. After we established radio contact we gave him a compass heading to our position and once there we used an air force "White Dot" signal mirror or orange ground panel to give him our exact location. If we were under a thick canopy and not visible from the air, we gave him a heading and then a "now" when he was directly over our position. When we were locked in a firefight and weren't concerned about giving ourselves away, we marked our position with colored smoke.

I lifted my rucksack by the straps, swung it around to my backside, and got the straps up as far as my elbows, struggling with its awkward weight.

"Damn, this thing's heavy," I said as I bounced a few times to work the straps up to my shoulders. Once secured it didn't feel bad at all. In fact, I'd reached the point where I felt out of place without it.

"Look, Ly," Bob said, pointing to his breast pocket. "My commo pad's right here. If I'm hit, get it and the radio to someone who speaks good English. Those F.A.C. pilots don't speak broken Bode." Ly nodded that he understood.

"Bac-si, if you or Trung-si Cole die I eat your heart," he said.

I turned to see if he was joking, but one look into his face and I knew that he wasn't. He was dead serious.

"What?" I asked.

"If soldier die, his friend eat heart—by this they take his spirit. Is great honor."

I'd heard of the practice but didn't quite know what to say. Not wanting to offend him, but at the same time wanting to discourage the idea, I fought for an answer.

"Ly, it's an old American custom that a soldier must be buried with his heart if he is to be with his ancestors."

"Oh," he said with a disappointed look. I stood there adjusting my scarf and compass that hung around my neck, hoping that he got the message. Bob smiled, half winking, and gave me a nudge in the ribs.

As we waited for word to move out, Bob rigged a grenade for instant detonation. He first disassembled it and removed the four-second timing device. Then he reassembled it, removed the pin, and placed it in a small hole he had dug with his survival knife. Finally, he gently placed the used PRC-25 radio battery on top of the grenade. The next person to touch the battery would be a dead man. As I waited, I felt a tug on my rucksack and turned to see who it was.

"Kimh, my friend, sak sa bai?" I asked.

"I am fine," he said as he grabbed my arm and shook my hand. He smelled as though he had just put on a lot of mosquito repellent. Evidently he was determined not to have any more problems with leeches.

Kimh was our platoon medic, spoke excellent English, and was a very good friend. With his well-combed, jet-black hair, steel-rimmed glasses, and spare frame he appeared more like a schoolteacher than a guerrilla. No matter how long we stayed in the jungle he always looked clean, which might have something to do with the fact that the Bodes didn't generally have facial hair. Most of them retained a boyish look well into their thirties.

I first met him at Duc-Phong when we were building our hospital. At first, progress was slow because none of the Montagnards or Cambodians assigned spoke a word of English or knew anything about medicine. My assistant at the time was a young Montagnard named Yen. After three days of first-aid training he changed it to Dr. Yen. When a Vietnamese woman came to the hospital with a headache, he took two aspirins out of a bottle and, using surgical tape, attached one to each temple. One of the Americans complained that Dr. Yen had tried to put an Ace bandage around his neck when he complained of a sore throat. Needless to say, I had to keep a close eye on "the Doc."

A couple of weeks after we had opened the hospital Kimh entered and in perfect English stated that he was a medic, and wanted to work with me. Without hesitation I agreed and put him to work. That same day Kimh came in with one of the local Montagnard village chiefs. The old bandy-legged chief said he was in much pain and kept pointing to his loin-cloth-clad rear end. When I asked Kimh what the chief's problem was, he told me that he wanted an injection, preferably something in red if we had it. Rather than waste any valuable medicine, Kimh suggested we give him a shot of sterile water. Well, we gave him the injection, he recovered almost immediately, and in deep gratitude invited me to his longhouse for dinner. I'll never forget his gaping pomegranate grin of betel-nut gums, lips, and toothy snags.

That night at a tribal ceremony I was made a member of the Stieng tribe and was presented with a red and black loin cloth and the traditional brass bracelet of brotherhood. During the rituals everyone took turns drinking homemade rice wine from a thirty-gallon earthenware vat. We drank through a three-foot bamboo straw which, after a few rounds, became covered with betel nut and drool. When my head began to spin from the potent brew, I tried to fake drinking, but failed to do so because the straw was notched. Every time it was my turn I had to drink the wine down to the next lower notch. I guess it was a Montagnard version of "Chugalug."

The following morning I woke up with the dry heaves and the world's worst hangover. I felt like a construction crew was working the inside of my head over with jack hammers. I had nothing on but my loin cloth and couldn't remember how I got back to camp. From that day on, Kimh and I worked together and we grew to be close friends.

"Any problems today?" I asked him.

"Just two," he said. "We have a bad cough in the first squad and a possible case of malaria in the second."

The cough worried me. On a still day, the sound of a cough could carry for quite a distance.

"What did you give him?" I asked.

"Some Terpin Hydrate and Cepacol Lozenges."

"Well, if that doesn't work, give him some codeine. If all else fails that always does the trick. On that possible case of malaria, keep an eye on his temperature and ask Thach to have someone carry his gear."

"I'll keep a close eye on him, Bac-si."

"Are all the troops taking their malaria pills?"

"Oh, yes, every morning they take them in front of me."

"Good. What about water-purification tablets? I know they don't like the taste."

"I can't be sure," Kimh answered.

"The medics straight on using morphine?" Bob inquired.

"When they use it they will pin the empty syrette to the patient's collar," Kimh said.

"Okay," I said.

On the Blackjack 31 operation one of the Bodes had been shot in the arm and was given morphine by three different medics. A short time later he died of an overdose.

As Kimh and I talked, I turned and saw Kien, a rifleman in the second squad, limping toward us. He didn't speak much English, so Kimh asked him a few questions in Cambodian.

"What's his problem?" I asked.

"He says his foot is bleeding and he needs mole-skin," Kimh answered.

"You'd better fix it quick, Kimh. We're getting ready to move out," Bob said.

"I go now," Kimh said as he grabbed Kien by the arm and escorted him back to his position.

Kien was a short, stocky Bode who was a great soldier but had a tendency to steal anything he could get his hands on. He always started an operation with the lightest rucksack in the platoon and finished with one weighing over a hundred pounds. With everything under the sun tied to the outside of his rucksack, he often resembled a traveling junkman.

On Blackjack 31 he lost three toes of one foot when he stepped on one of our own booby traps. The day before the accident we had captured a couple of ruck-sacks and one contained what looked like a large bearskin. Before moving out that morning, we placed the rucksacks along the edge of a well-used trail and booby trapped them with a claymore mine attached to a pull device. We also buried two M-14 toe-popper mines in the dirt next to the rucksacks. When we lined up to move out we passed the word down the line that they were booby trapped. But Kien just had to have that bearskin. A couple of minutes later there was a loud explosion. When I got to him I found that one of the M-14 mines had blown off a few of his toes, broken his leg, and sent some pieces of shrapnel into his testicles. As we bandaged his wounds he seemed more embarrassed than concerned about his wounds. I guess it was a major loss of face for him. Later that morning we evacuated him to Bien-Hoa. But when the chopper lifted off I could see what looked like the bearskin clutched under his arm.

As the Third Platoon lined up to move out, Danh was on point, followed by me with a map and compass. Bob was third, followed by Ly with the PRC-25 radio. Thach was the fifth man in the column, then Son with the M-60 and the rest of the "Third Herd" in tow.

Danh was a sixteen-year-old who had been with the unit since it was formed at Ho-Ngoc-Tao. He stood about five foot three, was well built, had black wavy hair, and possessed a great sense of humor. He was also very intelligent and agile—two qualities that made him the best volleyball player and the best point man in the platoon.

"You about ready, partner?" I asked.

"I ready, Bac-si." He smiled.

Danh stood with his rucksack slung on his back, machete in his right hand, and silencer-equipped MK-II British Sten gun resting on the left side of his ammunition belt.

"Better put that machete away," I said.

"Not use today?"

"No, don't use it unless you really have to. It leaves a trail a blind man could follow. Use your hands and arms to push aside the brush."

"Yeah," Bob added. "The machete makes too much noise. You can hear the chopping a mile away."

Danh slid the razor-edged machete back into its sheath while Bob handed him a pair of leather work gloves that would protect his hands from the thorns.

"Bac-si, you have?" Danh asked, pointing to the Buddha cloth he had tied around his neck.

"You'd better believe it," I said as I took a small plastic bag out of my jacket pocket and removed a white cloth the size of a handkerchief.

As I uncovered the cloth, you could see that it was covered with skillfully drawn Buddhist designs and symbols. When we were at Ho-Ngoc-Tao, Danh spent many days preparing the cloth and presented it to me just before the Black Box mission. Although I wasn't a Buddhist it was one of my most valued possessions and I carried it everywhere.

"I've got mine, too," Bob said. "When you operate in Buddha's territory you treat the guy right."

Bob turned to Thach.

"Pass the word down the line not to touch that booby-trapped battery," pointing to a small clearing about five meters from where he was standing. Thach turned to Son and passed the word down the line.

"Fox Three, this is Fox Control. Over." Lieutenant Condon radioed.

Ly gave the handset to Bob.

"Fox Control, this is Fox Three," he answered as he depressed the squelch button.

"Fox Three, this is Fox Control. Let's get this show on the road. We're burning daylight. Over."

"Roger, Fox Control. We're moving out."

Bob handed the handset back to Ly as the order to move out was given and the column lurched forward.

NEWS CLIPPINGS

Adm. U.S. Grant Sharp, commander of the American forces in the Pacific, said yesterday the North Vietnamese underestimate the determination of the United States to win the war in Vietnam.
Honolulu Star Bulletin, July 18, 1967

Brand New '67 Mustang—$2249
Courier Express (Buffalo), July 18, 1967

Mr. Ellsworth Bunker, the American Ambassador, told Vietnamese newsmen Saturday that successful elections in September will not by any means mark the completion of the progression toward representative government and full participation of the citizenry in the politics of the nation.
Saigon Daily News, July 18, 1967

Tel Aviv—After an unexplained delay of 30 hours, U.N. ceasefire observers formally began their operations along the quiet banks of the Suez Canal at 6 p.m. Monday.
Los Angeles Times, July 18, 1967

Yaz, "Old" at 27, heads Boston's Kids.
The Atlanta Journal, July 18, 1967

Mrs. Minh appealed to the National Assembly to allow her husband to return to campaign. Gen. Minh, better known as "Big Minh," has been in exile in Thailand for several years as ambassador-at-large and is trying to return to Vietnam to run for President in the Sept. 3

elections. The nation's ruling generals, however, have declared that he cannot return for "security reasons."
The Saigon Post, July 18, 1967

The effects of the strike on the Vietnam war effort were also noted, company officials said. Norris Industries Inc., Los Angeles, said five rail carloads of "various types of ordnance" failed to meet a delivery schedule yesterday.
The Wall Street Journal, July 18, 1967

There is a catch, too, in the polls on Richard Nixon. Long the favorite of the Republicans high and low, he has consistently led the other Republicans in the polls and gets up to 46% of all the votes.
Life, July 21, 1967

Rock'n'roll radio stations are programming more and more albums. Not just the Beatles, the Rolling Stones, but groups including the Jefferson Airplane, Grateful Dead, the Moby Grape, the Fifth Dimension, Country Joe and the Fish, The Grass Roots, Bob Dylan, the Doors, the Who, the Cream, the Hearts and Flowers, Donovan.
Billboard, July 22, 1967

2

0610 Hours (6:10 A.M.)

Only rarely did splinters of sunlight pierce the world
of shadows beneath the jungle canopy. The few that
did glowed a translucent white when they touched the
ground mist on the jungle floor.

As our column threaded its way through the thick
tangle it resembled two long snakes slithering through
the scattered undergrowth. With a catlike grace, Danh
crept forward on point, pausing every few paces to
scrutinize every color, every contour, for any irregu-
larity before resuming his quiet footfalls, his eyes cautiously surveying the jungle for trip wires suspended
tautly a few inches above the jungle floor, a section of
black Claymore wire trailing off through the rotting
leaves, or punji pits. His senses were tuned to near
perfection as his brain sorted every shred of stimuli for
possible danger—the gentle rustling of palm fronds,
the subtle crack of a twig, the smell of Vietnamese
cooking. On point, primal instincts are electrified. It's
a raw game whose outcome depends upon every
thought, every reflex, every nerve being alert and
poised for fight or flight. All the skills acquired in the
jungle were brought to bear. As we proceeded, the
column followed the pace set by the point man, tentatively moving forward when he moved, halting when
he halted, then releasing itself once more in harmony
with Danh's signals.

I followed about five meters behind him, helping
him navigate with my map and compass. To keep him
on a northerly azimuth, I adjusted his heading about

every fifty meters. When necessary, I used hand and arm signals to adjust our course to the right or left. We had played these parts often and worked well together.

For at least the first hour of march, we skirted a ridge line to the west. A small stream ran parallel and a couple of hundred meters to our east. Navigation would be no problem. A seasoned point man, Danh moved slowly and deliberately. He knew that if he moved too fast the column would expand and contract like a giant rubberband. Those near the front would have no trouble keeping up, but those near the tail end would be run into the ground. If the column got too strung out it would be impossible for everyone to maintain visual contact with the person in front and behind him as the column zigged and zagged through the thick undergrowth. This breakdown would affect our ability to react quickly if we made contact with Charlie.

Duty in Vietnam usually consisted of extended periods of peaceful silence or intense boredom occasionally interrupted by violent convulsions of high intensity. The unit able to move the quickest and shoot the straightest in a firefight normally came out on top. Back at Trang-Sup, we had spent days practicing immediate-action drills based on enemy contact from every possible direction. We grew expert at it, and I felt confident that we could slug it out with the best of them.

As the sun inched higher into the sky, its brilliance began to penetrate below. As we pressed forward through the lush foliage, I hoped that I would dry out, but knew that the jungle would soon become a sweltering steam bath. Except for the soft rustling of broad leaves or the brittle "clackety-clack" of bamboo from an occasional breeze, everything was still. In the canopy above, leaves fluttered in the sighing breezes reflecting light like a million tiny mirrors. Every now and then, you could hear the screech of a bird or glimpse a few monkeys scampering from tree to tree. But so far, there were no signs of any enemy units.

The jungle terrain began to thin out as we moved further north. I could see for ten to twenty meters in all directions, and except for random clumps of secondary growth, movement was fairly easy. The only things slowing us down were the large trunks of moss-encrusted trees which crisscrossed the jungle floor and the hanging "wait-a-minute" vines whose sharp, needlelike thorns stabbed and slashed the exposed flesh of your hands, face, and ears, causing the wounds to fester quickly in the moist heat. Whenever you got hooked, you had to stop to remove the thorns from your skin or fatigues.

After about thirty minutes, Danh stopped and motioned me forward.

"What's up?" I whispered. He smiled and pointed to what appeared to be a fresh trail trampled into the brush. Judging by its size, I figured it must have been made by a fairly large enemy force.

"Looks like beaucoup V.C. came through here," I said.

"No V.C.," he hissed.

"What d'ya mean?"

Bob, Thach, and Ly came up to where we were standing.

"Looks like a fresh V.C. trail," I said.

"Not V.C." Thach chuckled. "Phants."

"What the hell is a phant?" Bob wanted to know.

"Big phants," Danh said, making exaggerated stomping motions with his feet.

"Big phants, big nose," Thach added, dangling his arm in a clumsy imitation.

"You mean elephants," I offered.

"El'phants, el'phants, Bac-si," Thach said. "This morning el'phants come here."

"Think the V.C. were using them to carry equipment?" Bob asked. Danh squatted and closely examined one of the impressions in the spongy floor.

"No," he said. "El'phants live in jungle."

"You're right, if they were using them for transport they'd probably stick to the main trails," I said.

"Why should they bust brush," Bob mused. "Let's keep moving."

Resuming our march, I felt a bit embarrassed that I hadn't recognized it as an elephant trail. I had seen them before, particularly north of Saigon in War Zone "D." The animals always seemed to be afraid of us and fled whenever we got near. A couple of times the terrifying sound of them crushing through dried bamboo thickets in the middle of the night scared the hell out of me. With a little imagination, they sounded like a thousand V.C. surrounding our position.

As we continued, my eyes darted back and forth, scanning for signs of the enemy. It was amazing how much my physical perceptions had improved since I'd arrived in Vietnam. My sensitivity to smells had developed to a point where I could detect enemy troops and base camps long before contact was made. More than anything else it was the distinctive smell of Vietnamese cigarettes that gave them away. When I thought about it, I realized that the only thing that got me through my first few months was a lot of luck. I had made some stupid mistakes, but was still living to talk about them. Five years of Marine Corps and Special Forces training had taught me the mechanics of soldiering, but time proved there was no substitute for experience. It was a combination of training and experience that enabled me to develop a skin feeling for things. It was kind of a sixth sense one acquires in combat—a sense which often meant the difference between life and death.

I also noticed that the longer an operation lasted the closer I grew to nature. During the first few days my back ached from the rucksack, I drank a lot of water, our rations tasted terrible, and I was comparatively insensitive to my physical environment. But as time passed the pains disappeared, I drank less water, the food seemed to improve, and my senses grew keen. I became more and more animallike—bred to survive in the jungle. On a few of the longer operations, I actually felt disappointed when they ended.

We had been humping for about an hour when we arrived at the bank of a clear stream that ran from the northwest to the southeast. Looking at my map, I could see that it was part of the same stream that we had been moving parallel to. My face was flushed from the steady hump. Having worked up a good sweat, I was longing for a drink. The bitter taste of salt on my lips only added to my thirst.

Bob called Headquarters, and Lieutenant Condon told him to take a break after we forded the stream. As I stood on the ten-foot bank looking at the slow-moving water, I daydreamed of big fish swimming just below the surface; a pan-fried trout would really hit the spot.

"Okay, Jim, let's get across," Bob said.

"Right." First Danh, then I slid down the slick mud bank into the water. As we sank ankle-deep, I could feel the cool water squish in and out of the meshed vents in my jungle boots. Our feet stirred up clouds of silt, sending a light brown current of muddy water downstream.

"Better fill up," I advised Danh. "No telling how long it'll be before we hit water again."

The surface gulped and bubbled as we submerged our canteens. When we finished, Bob, Thach, and Ly slid down the muddy bank.

"Man, I wish we had time to take a bath," Bob said as Thach helped him remove canteens from the pockets of his rucksack.

"We wish you had time to take a bath too," I laughed.

"You turkeys ain't smellin' too great either," he said, playfully splashing me with a handful of water. Thach removed his hat and buried his head in the stream.

"Water feel good." He cupped his hand to drink.

"You'd better use your Halazone tablets," I said.

"No sweat, Bac-si. This good water. It not have shit in it."

Convincing the Bodes to use Halazone tablets was a constant contest of wills. They realized that a canteen of contaminated water could disable a man for days, but at the same time they really hated the taste of the tablets. Maybe in our After Action Report I'd recommend that they start making them in Kool-Aid flavors.

After helping Danh replace his canteens in his rucksack, we dug the toes of our boots into the soft mud on the opposite bank, grabbed a few small trees, and pulled our way up the slope. I was just joking about taking a bath, but when I thought about it, I realized that after a few days in the field our bodies didn't seem to smell. Did we all smell so bad we couldn't smell each other, or did the fresh air, sweat, and rain have a cleansing effect on our bodies?

We waited for Bob, Thach, and Ly to finish filling up, then moved to a position about seventy-five meters from the stream, where we removed our rucksacks and stretched out on the ground.

Since the ground was damp and yielding, we left a clear trail. The rest of the company would have no trouble following to close the gap.

"That mosquito repellent you brewed is really holding up," Bob said.

"Yeah, I mixed it with some lanolin to give it body. When it's mixed with oil it doesn't wash off when you go through water," I said. "I've got a couple of extra bottles if you need any."

"I'm in good shape," he said.

"If you keep it on heavy around the tops of your boots and around your waistline it keeps the leeches off."

I added Halazone tablets to the three canteens I had just filled up and drank from one that remained from Trang-Sup. After downing a few gulps and taking two salt tablets I felt refreshed, even though the day promised to be a scorcher. Although it was still early morning, the temperature had already risen about twenty degrees, soaring into the nineties, trying to keep pace with the humidity.

"We'll probably be here for about fifteen minutes," Bob said. "Thach and I are gonna take a walk down the line to see how everyone's doing."

"Okay, I'll stay here with Danh."

As I sat reclining against my rucksack, I could feel a bubble rising on my gum just above my front teeth. One of my front teeth had been shot out a few months earlier and was abscessing again. While Danh finished what rice remained from his morning meal, I punctured the bubble with a twenty-gauge needle and pushed the pus out onto the ground. With the pressure relieved I felt much better.

"You get fixed, Bac-si. It make sick," Danh said with obvious concern on his face.

"I tried," I said. "The dentist at Nha-Trang said I had to wait till I get back to the States. I probably should have had it fixed at the V.A. hospital when I was back home on leave."

Looking at Danh, I found myself wondering what would become of him when I was gone.

"What are you gonna do when the war's over?" I asked.

"War always here, Bac-si. It not end. No matter who win, Cambodian lose," he said. "I fight till I die."

"That's no way to look at it," I said, trying to seem as convincing as possible. Still, in my heart I knew that Indochina had been ravaged by war for centuries. The Chinese, Burmese, Cambodians, Japanese, Vietnamese, French, and Americans had all taken their turns, and there was no reason to expect anything would change in the foreseeable future.

"Maybe I go America with you. I be engineer," he said.

"We'll go to the University of Buffalo together. You'd probably freeze your balls off." I laughed. But it would be great if I could figure out a way to take Danh and Kimh with me back to the States. Danh had the ability to become an engineer, and I felt if he applied himself Kimh could become a doctor. If they remained here, the war would catch up with them sooner or later. No matter how good you were, the fortunes of war dictated that your head and a bullet would eventually meet at the same place and the same time.

"Looks like everyone is across," Bob said as he and Thach returned to sit on the ground beside their rucksacks.

"How are the Bodes holding up?" I asked.

"Everyone seems okay." He took a long swig of water and wiped the sweat off his face with his scarf.

"I was telling Danh we'll get him into the States. What do you think?" I asked.

"Sounds like a good idea," Bob answered.

"With his dark skin we'd better send him north," I added. "He may have a problem down south."

"You same me," Thach said to Bob. "South Vietnam not like me and South America not like you."

"How'd anyone who never went to school get so smart?" Bob smiled, shaking his head.

"You still thinking about retiring?" I asked Bob.

"Naw, I'm good for another five."

"Got any plans for when you get back?"

"Maybe I'll go back to Bragg and find me a nice quiet job in a warehouse somewhere." He laughed.

"Who you trying to kid? I know you eat this stuff up. You thrive on it—you've been living on the edge too long to just let go," I said as I got up and extended my hand to help Danh to his feet. He held out his four-fingered right hand. His thumb had been shot off and only a short red stump remained. I clasped him by his wrist and pulled him up. As soon as we got our rucksacks back on, we were ready to move out on the same northerly azimuth. "Let's keep it slow for a few minutes," I said. "Give 'em a chance to close up." Thinking about his thumb, I wondered how Danh managed to fire his Sten with any accuracy.

I still remembered the day he lost it near Dong-Xoia.

On that particular morning the Third Platoon had been assigned the mission of conducting a day-long search for the enemy in an area measuring about twenty-five square kilometers.

During the mid-morning hours we moved through stretches of scrub brush and six-foot elephant grass without detecting a sign of the enemy. Early that afternoon we hit a large stream, backed off about one hundred meters, and began moving parallel to it. Later in the afternoon we were cutting and crawling through thick vines and vigorous jungle, about two hundred meters south of the creek, when we found a well-used north-south trail.

It had been one of those long, hot days. We needed water for our evening meal, so we left a two-man ambush on the trail and followed the trail north to the stream. The water was clear and slow-moving, with five-foot-high mud banks and measuring about ten meters across. Sliding down the bank and into the cool, knee-deep water was a welcome relief from the heat.

I had just finished filling my empty canteens when the two Bodes who had been left on the ambush ran up to the edge of the stream and told us that an undetermined number of V.C. were coming down the trail in our direction.

Bob hurriedly got the platoon across the creek and set up an ambush along its bank while I radioed our coordinates to Gritz, requesting a F.A.C. By the time I finished relaying the information, Bob had the platoon deployed. He, Danh, the radio operator, and I took up a position behind a large fallen tree. As we waited, I ran a Claymore mine out to the bank in front of our position while Bob passed the word not to fire until we blew the Claymore. A premature shot would give away the ambush.

A few seconds later I began hearing what sounded like laughter and the telltale singsong chatter of Vietnamese voices approaching. The voices grew louder as they moved down the trail. When they reached the creek, I could see that there were about six of them, carrying their weapons almost nonchalantly on their shoulders. I assumed they had no idea we were in the area. I was surprised that they hadn't picked up the distinct footprints of our American-made jungle boots. When the V.C. hit the bank, the first two slid down into the water. At first I was concerned when I noticed that they were wearing the same uniforms as ours: camouflaged indigenous fatigues and soft hats. If they'd been carrying M-16's instead of AK's we might have made the fatal error of mistaking them for one of our other platoons.

The third V.C. stopped at the edge of the bank and stared at the water. His facial muscles suddenly tensed—something was wrong and he knew it. He must have noticed that the water upstream was crystal clear while the water downstream was clouded with mud. It looked as though he was about to say something to his comrades when Bob blew the Claymore and the rest of the platoon opened up. For five seconds a hailstorm of automatic rifle fire filled the air, followed by silence. Several of the V.C. were sprawled in the shallow water and ribbons of blood faded as they trailed lazily downstream.

I put a fresh magazine in my M-16 and picked up the radio handset to relay the news of the ambush to headquarters. Bob and Danh were about to reenter the water to pick up the enemy weapons when a tremendous volley of fire erupted on the far side of the creek. The first shot pierced the heart of our radio operator, dropping him at my feet.

Bob, Danh, and I hit the ground behind the same tree. Looking to my left and right, I could see enemy troops firing and moving into position along the reverse bank. As Bob and Danh returned fire, I made contact with the F.A.C. which was now circling overhead. I told him that we had ambushed the point element of a company-sized or larger force and that we were now in heavy contact. He said that fast movers were in flight, so I popped a yellow-smoke grenade to give him an exact fix on our location. I requested a twenty-millimeter strike be delivered along the reverse side of the creek.

My conversation with the F.A.C. was interrupted by a tap on the shoulder. I turned and saw that it was Danh pointing to his hand. His thumb had been shot off. I gave the radio handset to Bob and applied a battle dressing over the stump. He didn't have any signs of shock or pain, so I withheld the morphine. The body has a built-in defense mechanism that sometimes reduces bleeding and pain when a person is first wounded. I'd seen it many times and also knew that he would be in a lot of pain when it wore off.

As soon as I finished covering his battle dressing with an Ace bandage, we both resumed firing. The F.A.C. was now in contact with fast burners screaming in from the east, directing their passes along the opposite bank. With engines howling, the phantoms swooped down in strafing runs, opening up with the buzzsaw "burrr!" of their twenty-millimeter cannons. Their firing kicked up a string of explosions as they worked their deadly swaths closer and closer to our position. After a few minutes of murderous pounding from the air, I felt a second tap on my shoulder. It was Danh. This time he was pointing to his shoulder. He'd been hit again. I checked his wound and was relieved to see that even though it was a deep flesh wound there was no bone involvement. While working on his second wound, we received word that large numbers of V.C. were crossing the creek up- and down-stream from our position. Since they couldn't launch a frontal assault across the creek, they had decided to try a flanking move to sandwich us in a crossfire with our backs pinned against the stream, then cut us to pieces.

Rather than risk encirclement, we decided to break contact. In an attempt to slow their advance, I called in napalm and bombing runs on the V.C. who were crossing the creek. While the air strikes dropped molten balls of jellied gas and five-hundred pound bombs, two fire teams lay down suppressing fire. We, in turn, filled the creek bed with a noxious cloud of C.S. gas and made a hasty retreat out of the pocket. Moving down the trail at a fast clip, we continued to call in air strikes to cover our rear. We had to move as quickly as possible because we didn't want to give the enemy on our flanks the opportunity to move ahead and block our pullback with an ambush. At the same time we prevented the enemy directly to our rear from catching up with us by popping smoke canisters every fifty meters. When the F.A.C. saw the smoke wafting up through the jungle, he knew that we were moving north and it was safe to direct air strikes anywhere south of the last smoke grenade.

After traveling about three hundred meters down

the trail, we cut back into denser undergrowth and pushed northeast. The last rays of daylight were fading fast as the rumble of an approaching thunderstorm preceded a curtain of darkness that spread over the jungle. About fifty meters into the clotted vegetation, we paused to set up a Claymore mine attached to a trip wire. If the enemy was still pursuing us, it would not only slow him down, but also give us a fix on his location. The slate-gray cloudburst finally broke with a clap of thunder, releasing torrential sheets of rain that came down so hard you couldn't see the man in front of you.

By holding on to the back of the next man's ruck-sack, we were able to keep everyone together as we felt our way through the bush. It was slow going as we slopped our way through the pelting downpour, pausing every few seconds for a flash of lightning to illuminate the jungle before groping a few feet further. The whole experience was nerve-wracking as we stumbled forward through the inky blackness, nearly blinded by the elements.

In three hours we managed to stumble on for another two hundred meters before setting up in a bamboo thicket. It was a cold, wet, miserable night, leaving us chilled to the bone. To conserve body heat, we slept back to back in a small circle. As soon as our Claymores were set up and everyone was settled in, I contacted Gritz and, using him as a relay, began calling in 175-millimeter artillery strikes on suspected V.C. locations in the area. We spent a near sleepless night shivering while the locomotive sound of projectiles passing overhead rent the air with their deafening concussions.

At first light, I changed all of the battle dressings and loaded the wounded up with penicillin and streptomycin. Bob sent out a few small patrols around our perimeter to see if there was any sign of the enemy. When they returned with the news that everything was quiet, we broke camp and headed north. A couple of hours later we linked up with Gritz and the rest of the company at a clearing and were able to call in a dust-off to evacuate the dead and wounded.

As Danh lifted off in the chopper that morning, he waved to me with a big smile on his face. He was flown to the hospital for medical treatment while we pressed on with the mission. When we returned to Trang-Sup after the operation, we found him standing on the airstrip waiting for us with that same warm smile on his face.

"Hey, Jimmy, wait one," a voice called. It was SFC Frank Hagey. He and SFC Bill "Fergy" Ferguson were the two Americans assigned to the Second Platoon. At thirty-seven, Frank was the oldest American in the unit, something like gramps to some of us. He had a wife and eight kids back at Fort Bragg and had joined us in March. He had previously been assigned to Trai-Bi, a small Special Forces camp in Tay-Ninh Province—just a few klicks from the Cambodian border. I was worried about Frank's health. He looked a lot thinner than he had when I'd first met him. His face had a slightly gaunt look and he had trouble hiding a slight limp; I could tell that his back was bothering him. Although he wouldn't admit it, I knew that he was in a lot of pain. A couple of months earlier he was driving a load of supplies from Saigon to Trang-Sup when his truck hit an anti-tank mine near Cu-Chi. The explosion blew him over thirty feet through the air and dropped him on his head.

Med-evaced to Saigon where the doctors sewed him up, he discovered he was paralyzed from the waist down. But within weeks he had regained movement and somehow managed to convince our headquarters in Bien-Hoa to allow him to return to full duty.

"You got a couple of them Meprobamate tablets," he whispered in my ear. I think he knew what I knew.

"You sure you're okay?"

"I'm in great shape." He beamed unconvincingly. "My lower back gets a little tight every now and then. But other than that I'm a hundred percent."

"Bull, Frank, I know you're lying like a rug."

"I'll be all right. Just need a little something to loosen up my muscles."

"Okay, tell Kimh to give you a couple of tablets," I

said. "Get back to me if it doesn't help." He gave me the thumbs up.

"God and country." He turned and moved back down the line.

"On our next break tell Fergy to keep a close eye on him," Bob said as we moved out on our northerly azimuth.

"Will do," I answered. "May have to have the Bodes carry his gear."

After we'd moved on for about ten minutes a distant explosion broke the silence. I wheeled toward the direction of the sound and took an azimuth, using my compass.

"Two hundred degrees," I said to Bob. "A perfect back azimuth."

"Probably that booby trap we left in camp this morning," he said.

"Mister Charles must be trying to track us again."

"He's tried that before," Bob said. "We better keep moving."

As we set out, I thought about the trackers. If we were lucky, booby traps and stay-behind ambushes would keep them off our backs. However, things could get rough if they were able to get a fix on our location and had time to deploy battalion- or regimental-sized units against us.

Looking at my map as I walked, I could see that we were passing within a couple hundred meters of a large open area that we'd like to keep well to the west of. A klick to the east of the clearing I noticed the evenly spaced dots of another rubber plantation. If the war ever ended, this country could realize its potential: rubber, minerals, lumber, oil, not to mention tourism. Places like Nha-Trang and Vung-Tau had some of the best beaches in the world. Maybe after the war I'd come back and get involved in its reconstruction.

Without warning, Danh suddenly stopped and sank to one knee, raising his left arm to halt the column. I relayed the signal to Bob as Danh slipped out of his rucksack and began crawling forward. As I waited, my eyes scanned our left flank. Although I was drained from the hump, I now felt full of energy as a sudden dose of adrenaline surged into my system. After what seemed like a long minute, Danh came trotting back to my position.

"Bac-si, big V.C. trail. Much use," he said. I turned and motioned Bob forward.

"What's up?" he whispered.

"Looks like a well-used trail up ahead," I told him as I double-checked my map.

"Let's have a look-see," he said as we removed our rucksacks. Bob, Danh, and I moved ahead for about ten meters until we hit a wall of densely compacted brush. Using our hands to separate the leaves and vines, we quietly inched our way forward. As we parted the leaves, we were surprised to find the jungle suddenly dissected by a trail which measured about five meters across. With my head perched out through the wall of vegetation at the trail's edge, I could see that vehicles had worn two parallel strips of muddy, water-filled ruts. They extended for about fifty meters in both directions until they disappeared into the surroundings.

"Look at this," Bob said. "Looks like the Lincoln Tunnel."

The V.C. had cut away the brush and small trees and left the branches and leaves of the big trees to form a trellised tunnel, overhung with tangled vines, interwoven branches, and thick foliage.

"Tell you one thing. You'd never spot it from the air and it ain't even on the map," I said. "The closest trail is supposed to be northwest of here."

"Many V.C. use," Danh whispered, shaking his head with obvious concern.

"That's no lie. They probably run convoys down it," Bob hissed.

"Must be part of the Ho Chi Minh Trail," I said.

"Look," Danh said pointing to our left. Down the trail I saw what appeared to be a deuce-and-a-half. It was parked off to the side of the trail and was partially camouflaged with large banana leaves.

"Looks like one of them A. I. D. trucks," Bob said.

"Probably got a flat. Looks like the front tire's gone," I noticed.

"Yeah, it's jacked up on logs," Bob said. "We'll check it out after we get security in place. Ya never know when someone might come down it. Let's get back to the platoon."

"Okay," I agreed. "Danh, you'd better stay here to keep an eye on things."

We then crept back to where Thach and Ly were waiting. They were both down on one knee, their weapons pointed toward our left flank. I squatted next to Thach and briefed him on the situation while Bob took the handset and called the Lieutenant.

"Fox Control, this is Fox Three. Over."

"Fox Three, this is Fox Control. What's the hold-up? Over."

"Fox Control, this is Fox Three. We've hit an east-west trail that's not on the map. Over."

"Roger, Fox Three. Let me know when you're ready to move. Over."

"Will do, Fox Control. Fox Three out." Bob turned to Thach.

"Get two men up the trail to the west." Thach nodded.

"Make sure they go at least seventy-five meters," I said. "We don't want any unannounced company."

He sent two Bodes up the trail and Stik Rader radioed that he was sending two men down the trail to the east. As soon as both outposts were in place it would be safe to cross. If a V.C. unit came rolling down the trail, I wanted as much advance notice as possible so we could organize an appropriate reception. If they were too many we would let them pass and call in a B-52 strike on them. A single strike covered an area measuring one thousand meters wide and three thousand meters long with evenly spaced craters pockmarking the impact zone. Nothing could live through it. If they were a small unit we would have time to set up a hasty ambush.

"Thach, you'd better put someone across the trail

too," I said. He motioned two Bodes forward to set up a listening post on the other side of the trail. One by one, they eased out of the jungle, looked this way and that, then darted across the open trail before disappearing again.

"What do you guys think?" I asked.

"I think we make contact soon," Thach answered.

"You Bodes have a sixth sense," I said.

It was true, I had seen it many times before. Whenever the enemy was near the Bodes could sense it long before we made contact. Whenever you saw them with their jade Buddhas in their mouths you knew that you were in for a hot time. They believed that by placing Buddha in their mouths they were closer to God and had nothing to fear. I also had that same gut feeling that large enemy units were operating in the area. The elements were all there: a triple-canopy jungle, an excellent water supply, and a major trail—all the necessary requirements for a large enemy base complex.

"Well, if the shit hits the fan, reinforcements are only a few minutes away," Bob said as we waited for security to radio that they were in position.

"But the cavalry doesn't always come when you need 'em," I added.

"You got that right. Remember Chi-Linh?"

"How could I forget? A whole American division was supposed to have been standing by when we locked horns with a couple of main-force regiments from the 9th Viet-Cong Division. Only no one showed up."

"Many good men die that day," Thach said. "My son only fifteen." His eyes were welling with water and he turned away in embarrassment, wiping his face with his sleeve.

I'd never forget the plane ride back to Trang-Sup after the battle. Kimh and I were in the back of a C-123 with wall-to-wall bodies. It was over 120 degrees inside and there weren't any body bags. Whenever the plane banked a pool of blood flowed from one side to the other.

Gazing at the disfigured remains of the dead, I found it hard to believe that so many good friends had died. Only in the heat of war could such meaningful relationships form so fast or end so abruptly.

There were naive moments when I had bought the delusion of invincibility and convinced myself that I couldn't be killed. Maybe it stemmed from mythical illusions of immortality so coveted by youthful men, but that planeload of bodies was a grim reminder of how mortal we really are. Still, I couldn't bring myself to let go of that unspoken bond, even in the presence of death.

"I'll never forget the sight of the wives crying when we got back." Bob lowered his head. "It was a sad time for everyone."

"Yeah, you could smell the incense burning and hear the women wailing for days," I said.

"Did you ever get the feeling that those conventional types were out to shaft us?" Bob asked.

"Feeling, hell! They don't like Special Forces and they don't give a damn what happens to the Bodes."

"You're probably right, old buddy," Bob said.

I remembered when we formed the M.G.F. back at Ho-Ngoc-Tao. We had to trade, steal, or scrounge everything, from weapons and ammunition to cots and food. When they wanted to arm us with World War II carbines one of the guys went up to an arms-supply depot and traded his tape recorder for two hundred new M-16's. When we needed food, I had a few Viet-Cong flags made from red, blue, and yellow cargo parachutes at a tailor shop in Bien-Hoa. Then I took them to the 25th Division at Cu-Chi, where a lieutenant at the supply depot agreed to give me anything and everything for a real V.C. flag. I even shot a few holes in them so they'd look like the real McCoy. Needless to say, the Bodes ate well at Ho-Ngoc-Tao. All of their meat came from the general staff's food locker.

My thoughts were interrupted by a Cambodian voice on the HT-1 radio. Thach held it tight against his ear and listened.

"It Kien. He in position one hundred meter up trail," he said.

"Tell 'im to hold his position until everyone gets across the trail," Bob told him. "We'll call when it's time to come in." About thirty seconds later Kien called back. Thach sprang to his feet with a worried expression on his face.

"Trung-si, one V.C. come down trail from west."

"Tell Kien to stay in place and to call if he sees any more," Bob ordered.

"I'll have Danh take him out with the Sten," I said. The silencer-equipped British Sten would allow us to knock him down without killing him. We hoped to take him prisoner without alerting the entire area.

"If he's just a point man, let him pass," Bob said as I turned to run back to Danh's position along the trail.

"One V.C. coming," I said, pointing toward the jungle to my left. "Try for a shoulder shot—we need a prisoner." Danh nodded. I was excited. If we could take a prisoner and convince him to help us, it could save a lot of lives. If he wasn't an officer or political cadre, there was a good chance that we could quickly convince him to reveal the size and location of enemy units operating in the area. Once convinced the Bodes weren't going to kill them, enemy enlisted men often became very cooperative. On the Black Box operation one actually volunteered to serve as our guide.

We backed off the trail for about a meter or two and positioned ourselves behind a large cypress tree. Danh lay on the right side closer to the trail while I took the left side. As he parted a clump of ferns so that he could have a clear field of fire, I brushed aside a tangle of dead branches and settled into a comfortable prone position. I could see what appeared to be a face moving toward us. It looked very white as it danced in and out of the patches of mottled greens and browns of jungle growth.

Glancing to my right, I could make out that Danh was ready: his finger nervously caressing the trigger of his weapon—his front sight blade slowly tracking the V.C. Just a couple of ounces of pressure on the trigger and the bolt would slam home.

I checked the selector switch on my M-16 and cautiously moved it from safe to full automatic. The dull click sounded unusually loud in the silence. Even though I didn't want to fire an unsilenced weapon, I would be ready just in case anything went wrong.

About twenty-five meters out I could see that the approaching figure was a Viet-Cong soldier wearing a blue uniform and a pith helmet. A brown rucksack was on his back and he was carrying an AK-47 cradled under his left arm. This could be close, I thought. If he's got a round chambered, it would only take him a split second to get off a burst. I sensed movement on the tree next to my head. "Oh, no," I thought. "Fire ants!"

At about fifteen meters, I could see what looked like a red and gold star embossed on the front of his helmet. The swarm of red ants was crawling over my left sleeve and onto my hand. The V.C.'s rifle was pointing our way. It seemed like he was looking right at us.

I took in a deep breath, let half of it out, and took up the slack on my trigger. The top of my front sight blade was aimed at the middle of his chest. The ants began to dig their fiery mandibles into my skin. Each bite burned like a white-hot needle. I could hear my heart pounding in my chest, but in spite of the pain, I couldn't afford to flinch.

At five meters the man in the pith helmet saw us. A look of terror suddenly flashed on his face. But before he could act, the bolt on Danh's Sten slammed home, "pffft." The bullet hit him with such force he looked like he had run into an invisible wall. His arms flew upward and he landed on his back with a dull thud.

We jumped to our feet as Danh moved cautiously forward with his gun trained on the body. I quickly brushed the ants off my arm, noticing the red welts on the back of my hand. The Viet-Cong soldier was lying on the trail with his body quivering and his mouth and left eye wide open.

Each of us grabbed an arm and began dragging him off the trail. Bob and Thach came running up and picked up his rifle and pith helmet.

"Is he alive?" Bob wanted to know.

"Can't say. I'll check as soon as we get him off the trail," I said as we dragged him back to where Ly was waiting with the radio.

"Looks dead to me," Bob said. I squatted next to the now-motionless body to check for vital signs.

"Let me check his pulse." His wrist was still warm, but there was nothing.

My left hand burned from the ant bites. I looked at the back of my hand and wrist and noticed that the welts were quickly growing larger and felt warm to the touch.

"He's dead," I said.

"He see us, Bac-si," Danh responded with a trace of apprehension in his voice. He was obviously concerned how I would react. "I sorry have to kill, but he see us."

"I know. Where the hell did you hit him? I don't see any blood," I said.

"Wait a minute," Bob said, leaning over. His thumb pried open the dead man's right eye. Red and white jelly filling the socket was all that was left.

"Right in the eye," Bob said. Looking closer, I could see that the bullet had entered the socket and somehow veered downward through the roof of his mouth, evidently lodging somewhere in his trunk. Thach patted Danh on the back. He seemed relieved by this and returned to his position on the trail.

As I stared into the dead man's face, I was surprised to see that it bore the same expression he had shown the split second before Danh squeezed the trigger. The look of wide-eyed terror was frozen in time. He must have died instantly. In a way he was fortunate. Dying is easy, I thought, it's the getting there that can be rough. I once saw a man with a smile on his lips looking up at the sky through maggot-filled eyes. Maybe he knew something we didn't.

"He V.C. message man from 271st Regiment," Thach responded after searching through his wallet and pockets.

"The 271st!" Bob said. "That's the same unit we mixed it up with near Chi-Linh."

"Yeah, it's one of the regiments attached to the 9th V.C. Division," I said.

Maybe this was our lucky day, I thought. We may just have nailed the dispatch courier who was carrying the news of our presence. Maybe the Frenchman in Quan-Loi wasn't working for the V.C. Maybe the three V.C. we'd made contact with earlier hadn't passed the word that we were in the area. There were a lot of maybes but no for sures.

The fact that the runner was alone on the trail was probably a good sign. I had learned from experience that whenever they were unaware of our presence they weren't security-conscious.

But even if we had been compromised there was still a good chance we could accomplish our mission. Although enemy troops in the area greatly outnumbered us, they were handicapped by poor communications, and from what I'd been able to figure out, they had radios at the regimental and possibly the battalion levels but nothing at the company, platoon, or squad levels. At these lower levels, they had to rely on runners to carry messages. Because of poor communications at their lower levels of organization they often found it difficult to respond quickly to targets of opportunity. Even if they were to find out that we were here we could conceivably pinpoint the location of their larger units and be out of the area before they could do anything about it.

Estimating the strength, capabilities, and what action the enemy might take was no simple matter. If you overestimated him you became overly cautious and failed to accomplish the mission; if you underestimated him, you became careless and paid the consequences. The one thing I knew for sure was that in the past few months there had been a major shift in the enemy's strategy. He now appeared willing to accept severe losses in order to achieve limited objectives. On several occasions he had made costly efforts to surround and overwhelm the M.G.F., which amounted to little more than suicidal expenditures of men. Thanks to the "never give an inch" attitude of the Bodes and effective air and artillery support, the enemy was unable to achieve his objectives and took heavy casualties in the process.

With Thach squatting next to me, I noticed that he was carrying a new pistol; a chrome-plated nine-millimeter Browning automatic with hand-carved ivory grips.

"Nice pistol you got there," I said.

He paused for a moment. "Yes, it very good," he answered.

"Pick it up in a Tay-Ninh barbershop?" I asked with a mock surprise in my voice.

"Yes, Bac-si." He knew that I knew that it was the same pistol taken from a South Vietnamese officer a few days earlier.

"When we get back you'll have to let me try it out."

"I do."

"Look here." Bob removed a plastic bag full of mail from the dead man's rucksack. "Looks like the mail's gonna be a little late."

"Might be some valuable stuff in there," I said as Bob continued to rummage through the rucksack, finding a box of cookies from a Saigon bakery. He gave the box to Thach and told him to pass them out to the troops.

"Better give the Lieutenant a call," Bob said. Ly handed him the handset. Bob relayed the news of the ambush and informed Lieutenant Condon that we would be moving out as soon as we checked out the deserted truck.

"Booby trap the body and the ruck," Bob told Thach. "Jim and I'll check out the truck."

"Okay, Trung-si."

Bob and I moved back to the trail. As we drew near, I could see Danh was sitting on his rucksack next to the same cypress.

"C'mon, Danh, let's check out the truck," I said. As the three of us walked down the trail, I felt naked and exposed. Although it was only a few meters to the truck, I knew that anyone who set foot on a trail was inviting sudden death.

"Looks like a V.C. freeway, doesn't it?" Bob whispered.

"Yeah, it probably runs all the way to Hanoi."

"This how V.C. bring supply from Kampuchea," Danh said. "American think supply come down Ho Chi Minh Trail, but they wrong. Chinese and Russian bring to Kampuchea in boat. Then V.C. bring to Vietnam in truck."

"You could be right," I said. When we reached the truck, I could see that it had been unloaded so that a tire could be removed. A large canvas-draped pile stood near the rear.

"Check out the load," Bob said. "I'll check the truck." Danh kept a watchful eye on the trail while Bob climbed into the cab and I pulled the canvas cover from the pile.

"It's definitely Russian-made," Bob said as he checked out the bed of the truck. "There's a plate on the dash with Russian on it."

"Will you take a look at this," I said in amazement. "I can't believe it! These are hundred-pound bags from the Continental Grain Company of New York."

"Are you kiddin' me!" Bob said as he jumped to the ground. "Why the hell is New York sending rice to Vietnam?"

"Got me. I didn't even know we grew rice in New York."

"Ain't that a bummer. We give 'em rice and the Ruskies give 'em the trucks to carry it."

"Nothing surprises me anymore," I said. "What d'ya think we should do with this stuff? There's too much to carry."

"I don't know. Wait a minute. You got any time pencils left?" he asked.

"Yeah, I've got two with eight-hour delays," I said.

"Great, I've got a couple of grenades. We'll bury 'em in the rice and they'll go off eight hours after we leave." I handed him the two time pencils and he screwed one of them into a grenade while I used my survival knife to cut three-inch slits along the seams of two of the bags. The musty smell of the burlap reminded me of a barn on a hot summer day. When I finished rolling up my right sleeve, he handed me the first grenade.

"She's all set and ready to go," he said.

I took the grenade and slowly worked it deep into the center of the hundred-pound bag. When he finished the second grenade, I repeated the process with the other sack.

"That oughta do it," I said as we pulled the tarp back over the pile. If Charlie didn't pick it up within eight hours it would be blown all over the area. If he picked it up both he and the rice would probably be blown up. Either way, we weren't sticking around for it to happen.

"What about the truck?" I asked. "It looks almost new."

"You're right," Bob said. He turned to Danh. "Hey, throw me one of your grenades."

Danh removed a grenade from his harness and carefully tossed it to Bob.

"You guys keep an eye on the trail while I hook this up to the engine," he said.

Danh and I moved to a sunny area several meters down the trail from the truck and stood guard.

"Boy, this dry heat feels good," I said as I removed my hat, closed my eyes, and faced the sun.

"It warm." The small ruby on Danh's front tooth sparkled in the sunlight. If this had been a different time and place I probably would have hung my sweat-soaked fatigues on a branch to dry and stretched out on the trail to absorb a few rays.

"Well, when we get back to Trang-Sup we'll have plenty of time to dry out," I said. Looking at my left hand, I could see that it was now taut and swollen from the ant stings. The back of it was as smooth as a balloon and my fingers felt fat. Bob closed the hood on the truck.

"Okay, she's all set." Bob jumped to the ground. "Whoever starts this thing'll get a hell of a ride. Okay, let's get back to the platoon."

When we got back, Thach had finished booby trapping the body and the rucksack. He had dragged the corpse to a spot that could be seen from the trail. If the wild pigs didn't eat the body, his friends would have no trouble spotting him. The body was rigged with a pull device connected to a Claymore mine. A hand grenade with the pin removed and rigged for instant detonation was placed under the rucksack.

While I gave the area a once-over, Ly finished booby trapping the dead man's ammunition. Using a pliers, he removed the projectiles from their shell casings. He then dumped out the powder, replaced it with detonating cord, and reassembled the bullets. If anyone fired the ammunition his weapon would blow up in his face.

Bob briefed Lieutenant Condon, then we moved back across the trail and headed north for about a hundred meters. While we waited for the rest of the company to cross the trail, I rubbed some cortisone ointment into my hand, hoping it would relieve the swelling. I didn't want to take any Benadryl because it made me drowsy.

As the last of the Bodes slipped into the jungle on our side, Bob gave the order, "Okay, Jim, everyone's across and security's in. Let's move out." Glancing to my right, I could see that the Recon Platoon was in position. Their lead man was about twenty meters to my right and ten meters to the rear.

I checked our position on my map, took a quick azimuth with my compass, and pointed Danh in the right direction. He gave me a thumbs up and we headed out in two parallel columns.

NEWS CLIPPINGS

Saigon. . . . . . 8AM 95°
The New York Times, July 18, 1967

Optimism of Robert McNamara, Defense Secretary, over progress in the Vietnam war, following a few days' visit to that country, is described by very well-informed military men on the scene as "phony." It is considered the standard operating "line" put out for political consumption.
U.S. News & World Report, July 21, 1967

Born: To Sen. and Mrs. Edward M. Kennedy, an 8-pound 7-ounce son, their third child; in Boston, July 14. Will he run for President? "He'll have to clear that with his uncle," quipped Teddy. "Bobby thinks every baby is his."
Newsweek, July 24, 1967

The war in Vietnam cannot be won by the U.S. It can only be won by the South Vietnamese. If South Vietnam refused to raise enough troops to win the war, why should the U.S. continue to pour troops into the war?
The Miami Herald, July 18, 1967

Your voluminous Vietnam issue accomplished three things: it convinced the doves that the hawks were flying into disaster, encouraged the hawks to try harder and left the majority of us sparrows circulating around in confusion as usual.
Coventry, Conn.   *Diana Wahmann*
Newsweek, July 24, 1967

Best Sellers
Fiction
1. The Arrangement, Kazan
Nonfiction
1. The Death of a President, Manchester
U.S. News & World Report, July 21, 1967

With the war budget up $5 billion (to $27 billion a year), a tax increase on the way and the Presidential campaign already rumbling into low gear, Mr. Johnson could neither accept the strategic and political risks of stopping the war on Hanoi's present terms nor the even wider risks of greatly enlarging it.
Newsweek, July 24, 1967

Mr. AIKEN. Mr. President, on Thursday, July 13, in announcing the decision to send more troops to Vietnam President Johnson told the American people that—
  We are generally pleased with the progress we have made militarily. We are very sure that we are on the right track.
Congressional Record—Senate, July 18, 1967

3

1015 Hours (10:15 A.M.)

The mid-morning heat was stifling as we threaded our way through the steamy tangle. Rivulets of sweat coursed through the oily repellent, stinging our eyes and blurring our vision as we struggled through the sweltering humidity, but so far no more enemy had been sighted.

I checked my army-issue Seiko. It was 1015 hours. I had a Rolex back at Trang-Sup, but always left it in my footlocker when I went out on operations because I didn't want the enemy to get it if I was killed or captured.

The Third Platoon continued to set the direction and pace while the Recon Platoon determined the distance between our two columns. In thicker terrain the columns closed the gap, and when the brush thinned out we moved further apart. At times the tangle was so compacted it was nearly claustrophobic. At other times it melted away so that you could maintain visual contact for thirty yards or more.

Following Recon in the right column was the Headquarters Section with Lieutenant Jim Condon and his radio operator, SSG Roger "Ranger" Smith. The Headquarters Section was followed by SFC Bill Ferguson, SFC Frank Hagey, and the rest of the Second Platoon. In the left column the Third Herd was followed by SFC Ernie "Duke" Snider's First Platoon—166 men in all.

Ten meters to my right, I could see the green scarves of the Recon Platoon. Each platoon wore different color scarves so we could more easily identify and control them when we made contact with the enemy. The Third wore red, the Second yellow, and the First blue. Watching Recon move parallel to us, I could see that SSG L. Brooks "Stik" Rader was taking the point. Stik was incredibly agile. Like Danh, he had that same feline grace which enabled him to slip almost imperceptibly through the thickest tangle. He was our Light Weapons specialist and prior to volunteering for the M.G.F. served with the A-Detachment at Dong-Xoai. He stood about five feet nine inches tall with brown hair and sharp, distinct features. He was by far the thinnest American on the team, but resilient and tough. His friends affectionately referred to him as "Stik." He knew his business and had a hard-earned reputation for being one of the best small-unit leaders in Vietnam.

As we continued on our northerly azimuth, the terrain changed from a dark, triple-canopied jungle to a bright, single-canopied area consisting mostly of bamboo stands and banana trees. Clumps of small green bananas hung from the trees, with monkeys scurrying across the ground and swinging almost playfully from branch to branch. After moving about fifty meters, I spotted what appeared to be a thatch roof about twenty meters distant. I raised my left hand to halt the column and sank to one knee. I had no way of knowing whether the roof formed the edge of an enemy base camp or a farmer's hut. Until it was checked out, I had to assume the worst.

"Pssst," I signaled Danh. When he turned, I pointed my M-16 to our left flank. He immediately went down on one knee. Bob came up and squatted beside me.

"What d'ya have?" he whispered.

"Looks like a hooch about twenty meters out to our left front."

"Any sign of movement?"

"No," I answered.

"Let's check her out."

Bob radioed the situation to the Lieutenant while I relayed the word down the line that we would be moving out on our left flank. Bob and I then removed our rucksacks and left them with Danh.

"Let's circle around and go at it from the rear," I said.

"Okay," Bob responded. "Let's go."

We moved out in a low crouch, clutching our M-16's for quick-kill, weaving through the bamboo and banana trees. Although we didn't make a sound, our presence startled the monkey colony, which chattered with nervous excitement. Their bulging eyes were riveted to our movements as if they were spectators to a mysterious event. Some appeared to be frozen in fear while others fled from our unwelcomed intrusion, breaking an occasional twig as they scurried away.

It took us a few minutes to work our way around to the right rear of the hooch. Once there I could see that it was a three-sided thatch lean-to, which stood about four feet high in the front. It was covered with fresh banana leaves the size of elephant ears. From where we were standing it looked empty, but appearances could be very deceptive. Both of us slowly sank to one knee, our ears straining for the slightest sound of movement. Suddenly, the air was filled with the rank odor of human feces. Both of us looked down and saw that Bob's knee had landed in the middle of a fresh pile of crap. He shot me a wounded "why me?" look. I had to restrain myself from laughing. There were no sounds coming from the hooch, so we rose to our feet and began inching our way forward. If someone was sitting inside we'd like to get the drop on him. Bob moved along its left side and I took the right. When we arrived at about a foot or two from its front, we both stopped. Bob gave me a nod and we jumped in front of the hooch with our weapons pointed inside—it was empty.

"Looks like a listening post," Bob said as he bent down to pick up a small, soot-blackened aluminum pot from its bamboo floor.

"Someone must have left in a hurry," I said. "Charlie wouldn't leave a good cooking pot."

I crawled inside the hooch and found a canteen, two

rolled-up bamboo mats, a green undershirt, and a khaki-colored Viet-Cong belt that had been stored near the rear wall.

"We'd better leave everything in place," I said.

"Yeah, don't leave any signs that we've been here," Bob added as he squatted and ran his fingers through a fire pit that had been dug about two feet in front of the hooch.

"Still warm," he said.

"Keep your eyes open," I said. "I'll rig the pit."

Bob stood up in front of the hooch, rested his M-16 on the roof, and watched for signs of the enemy. I knelt next to the pit and tied a piece of white string around a hand grenade. Using my knife I then dug a small three-inch-deep hole in the middle of the pit.

"Must be a hundred monkeys here," Bob commented.

"Probably waiting for the bananas to ripen," I said as I pulled the pin from the grenade and carefully placed it in the hole with the spoon facing up. Once in place I covered it with a little dirt, charcoal dust, and small pieces of unburned wood. If someone started another fire the string would burn, the spoon would fly off the grenade, and the explosion would kill or wound anyone within ten meters.

"How's that look?" I asked, smoothing the surface.

"Looks good," he said as he used a stick to scrape the crap off his knee. "Let's get back to the platoon."

I wiped my blackened hands on my trousers, picked up my weapon, and moved back to where Stik was talking with Thach.

"What did you guys find?" Stik wanted to know.

"Two-man listening post," Bob answered as Ly handed him the radio handset to contact the Lieutenant.

"Definitely used today," I told Stik. "They probably didi-mau'd when they saw us coming."

"What direction did it face?" Stik asked as Bob updated Condon.

"South," I said. "I'd guess it's guarding something up north of here."

"Probably a base area," Stik offered.

I pulled out my map and opened it as Bob handed the handset back to Ly.

"Condon says we've been on the same azimuth long enough," Bob said. "He wants us to bootleg east a few hundred meters and then head north again."

"Good idea," I said. "Setting a pattern can be dangerous to your health."

I turned to Stik.

"What d'ya think?"

"Sounds good to me. Just one thing. If we go further east we'll be moving pretty close to some open areas. I'd hate to get pinned down with our backs to one of 'em."

Stik was right. If we made heavy contact on one flank and had an open area on the other, our ability to maneuver would be greatly reduced.

"Okay, Stik, we'll watch it," I said as I checked my map. "As soon as we get past that clearing I'll follow forty-five degrees for about a half a klick and then go back on our old azimuth."

Stik gave us a thumbs up and headed back to his platoon. As soon as Bob and I got our rucks back on, I gave Danh the signal to move out. If we had been spotted by someone in the hooch there was a good chance they were now on their way to warn whoever was up ahead. If we stayed on the same azimuth the enemy could easily anticipate our route of march and set up an ambush. If we walked into a battalion-sized or larger horseshoe-shaped ambush, and they were able to catch us on low ground, they could cut us to pieces. If you set a pattern in this business it could be lethal.

Heading north again, we soon reentered densely compacted jungle. After a couple hundred meters of slow going we passed an open area on our right flank and began following a forty-five-degree azimuth. Now moving over relatively flat terrain we soon found ourselves in a forest of large three-story trees with little growth close to the ground. Except for being littered with rotting leaves the jungle floor was clear.

After negotiating our way through the great trees

for a couple of hundred meters we found an unused east-west trail whose once-busy ruts were packed with six-inch blades of grass. A few minutes past the trail we reached the bottom of the slope we had been traveling down and waded across a shallow stream whose stagnant water was covered with a crust of green algae.

After crossing the creek, we moved up a gradual incline. When we reached the top of a kidney-shaped hill, we changed directions and headed north once more. Looking at my map as I walked I could see that we were on some of the most elevated terrain in the area. It wasn't much of a hill compared to those we'd encountered on other operations, but for this area it was the high ground.

As we moved down the north slope of the hill, the foliage started to thin out again, so Recon increased the distance between the platoons to about thirty meters.

"Jim, hold it up," Bob hissed as he held the radio handset to his ear.

"Pssst!" Danh glanced over his shoulder as I gave him the hand signal to hold up.

I turned to Bob.

"What's up?" I asked.

"Stik's found some commo wires."

I gave Thach the signal to get down and he relayed it down the line.

"Jim, take a look at what he's got."

"Will do," I agreed as I slipped out of my ruck. "Be back in a few minutes."

I moved to my right until I hit the Recon Platoon. Most of the Bodes were down on one knee watching for signs of the enemy. Looking to my right, I could see Lieutenant Condon and Duke Snider moving up the line in my direction. The Lieutenant was a former enlisted man with extensive Special Forces experience. Before attending Officers Candidate School, he had served with the 77th and 6th Special Forces Group at Fort Bragg, the 1st Special Forces Group on Okinawa, and the 10th Special Forces Group in Germany. Prior to volunteering for the Mobile Guerrilla Force, he was assigned to one of the A-Detachments in Tay-Ninh Province. He had only been with us for a short time and this was his first mission as the unit commander. Although I hadn't known him long I had a feeling he would do well.

"Good morning, Lieutenant," I said. "How you doin', Duke?"

"Morning, Jim," the Lieutenant responded. "Where's Stik?"

"Just up ahead, sir," I responded, motioning with a nod of my head.

We moved a few meters more before we could see Stik, his radio operator, and the Recon Platoon sergeant standing near the southern edge of what looked like a clearing. As we neared their position, I could see that the clearing measured a couple of hundred meters wide and extended far to the north. The area was treeless, and its foot-long grass rippled gracefully in the morning breeze like a field of grain.

"Where are they?" the Lieutenant asked.

"Over here, sir," Stik responded as he led us about five meters into the clearing, stopped, and pointed to the ground. "We've got eight multicolored wires running east-west along the edge of the clearing."

"As far as I know, only battalions or larger use commo wire," I said.

"No shit," Duke responded sarcastically.

"Stik, get on the horn and get Hagey up here," Lieutenant Condon ordered.

"Yes, sir," Stik responded as his radio operator passed him the handset.

"Frank's our commo man," the Lieutenant added. "Let's have him check things out before we make a decision."

Looking out over the open area, I found that its serenity exerted a mesmerizing effect upon me. But the postcard beauty couldn't counter reality for long.

"Let's get back in the wood line," Stik advised, snapping me out of my momentary daydream.

"Yeah, they probably got this area staked out," Duke added.

As we reentered the tree line, one of the Bodes from the Recon Platoon pulled a machete from his scabbard and raised his hand to cut the wires. Duke grabbed his arm just as he began the downward swing.

"No, kid! You want to get us all killed?" he said. "You cut these and we'll all be in deep shit."

The Recon Platoon sergeant grabbed the young Bode by both arms, gave him a couple of firm shakes, and said something to him in harsh muffled tones.

"Look, sir, we'd better not hang around here too long," Stik said.

"I know," the Lieutenant responded as we turned to see Frank Hagey approaching our position.

"You wanted to see me, Lieutenant?" he asked.

"Yeah, Frank. We've got eight commo wires a few meters into the clearing that I'd like you to check out."

"Can do," Frank responded as he headed into the clearing and squatted next to the wires. After a minute or so he returned to where we were waiting.

"Well, what do you think?"

"Judging from the number of wires I'd say we have a regiment." Frank paused. "Maybe larger."

"That's what we thought," the Lieutenant answered.

"You know, there's been some talk that COSVN [Communist Party Headquarters In South Vietnam] may be located in this area," Frank added.

"C'mon, Frank, give us some slack," Stik quipped.

"Any chance of you tapping the wires?" the Lieutenant asked.

"Sure, if I had the equipment," Frank said. "But I don't have anything with me. How about getting something dropped in by the F.A.C.?"

"No, we don't have the time. We've got to find out who's talking to who and we have to do it quick."

"Yep," Duke added.

"Okay, Stik, you take your platoon and follow the wires west," the Lieutenant ordered. "The rest of you return to your platoons and stand by."

"We'd better get a F.A.C. up, sir," I said.

"Yeah, I'll get him on the horn. Let's get moving."

Frank and I headed back to our platoons while Duke, Stik, and the Lieutenant spread a map on the ground and continued comparing notes. When I got back to the Third Platoon, I could see that most of the Bodes were down in prone positions. The tension in the air was palpable. They had their jade Buddhas in their mouths—a sure sign that they were expecting something big. The sight of them caused the knot in my stomach to tighten. Bob, Thach, and Ly were sitting on the ground together looking at Bob's map. I knelt next to Bob and picked up a small twig.

"How's it look, Jim?" Bob asked.

"Stik found eight commo wires along the south end of the clearing," I said while using the twig to point to the location on the map.

The expression on Bob's face suddenly changed.

"Eight! Are you serious?" Bob inquired with an apprehensive look.

"Yeah, eight wires."

Thach sprang to his feet.

"I go talk to squad leaders," he said.

"Okay, Thach," Bob said. "What's the Lieutenant gonna do?"

"Stik's platoon is gonna follow the wires west while we hang loose," I said. "We'd better pass the word that Recon'll be out on our flank."

"Yeah." Bob folded his map and rose to his feet.

"The bodes look a little uptight," he added as he extended his hand to pull me to my feet. "Why don't you take a walk down the line and try to calm 'em down?"

"Okay. Once the first shot's fired they'll settle in."

"You know, it's a lot like a parachute jump," Bob added. "You're a little nervous on board the aircraft, but once you're out the door you lose any fear you might have had."

I'd started to move down the line when the morning silence was shattered by M-16 fire coming from the direction of the clearing. As if on cue, everyone instinctively flinched and flung himself to the ground with weapons pointed outward. After about two hundred rounds an ominous silence returned. I jumped to my feet and moved back to where Bob was monitoring his radio.

"What d'ya hear?" I asked.

"Nothing yet."

"I only heard 16's," I said.

"Yeah, I didn't hear any return fire. Maybe someone got spooked."

As I talked to Bob, Duke Snider and Chote, the First Platoon's interpreter, could be seen running in our direction.

"What happened, Duke?" Bob asked.

"Greased nine of those cats laying wire," Duke said as he used his sleeve to wipe the sweat from his face.

"What direction were they coming from?" I asked.

"From the east."

"Everyone okay?" I asked.

"Yeah, they didn't get off a round."

"What about Stik?" Bob asked. "Is he still gonna follow the wires?"

"Hell, they've already gone. We killed the nine after Stik moved out. I'd better get back to my people," Duke said as he and Chote headed back to the First Platoon.

"Hey, Bac-si," Danh called in a hushed voice.

I turned to see what he wanted, but before he could respond, the rhythmic cracking of AK's and M-16's erupted a few hundred meters northwest of our position, followed by the stutter of machine guns and the occasional concussion of grenades.

Bob grabbed the radio handset from Ly. I squatted next to him and could hear Stik talking to the Lieutenant with an urgency in his voice.

"They're all over the place. We're under heavy attack," Stik yelled, followed by a rush of static.

A few seconds later there was a heavy volume of fire on our opposite flank. The roar of automatic fire had reached a pitch where it was difficult to hear the radio. Just then Fergy broke into the conversation.

"Estimated company hitting the Second Platoon. Get a F.A.C. up quick. We're in deep shit over here!"

"The F.A.C.'s on the way, Fox Two," Lieutenant Condon responded.

"Fox Four, are you still there?" the Lieutenant asked.

"Roger, this is Four," Stik responded.

"Fox Four, you've got to come to us. If we move to you we'll all get caught on low ground."

"That's a Roger, Control. We're on-line and moving in your direction," Stik answered. "We've got wounded."

"Have I got everyone on the horn?" the Lieutenant asked. "Fox One, are you there?"

"That's a Roger," Duke responded.

"Fox Two?"

"Fox Two, here," Fergy answered.

"This is Fox Three," Bob added.

"Okay, we're on high ground with heavy contact on both flanks. I want you to set up a defensive perimeter," the Lieutenant ordered. "Fox One and Fox Two: make sure you link up your platoons on the southern end. Fox Two and Fox Three: position one squad from each of your platoons on the northern quarter of the perimeter until Recon breaks back in to fill the gap. Fox Three: send out one squad to help Recon reenter the perimeter. Any questions?" Condon paused. "Okay, stay off the air unless it's important."

Bob turned to Thach. "Let's circle the wagons. Move the first squad to the north side of the perimeter." Thach nodded. "Once Recon gets back in you can move 'em back here," Bob added. "Jim, you and I'll take the Second Squad out to link up with Stik."

"Okay, get 'em ready to move. I'll tell Kimh we've got wounded coming in."

I quickly moved down the line for about fifteen meters until I found Kimh.

"Kimh, Recon's got wounded. Let's get ready." I told him to set up a dispensary in a depression that was located about ten meters east of his location and then headed back up the line.

When I got back to Bob, he had the Second Squad ready to move and was talking to Stik on the radio.

"Fox Four, this is Fox Three. We've got one squad

moving in your direction. We'll set up a skirmish line
about fifty meters out and cover you coming in. Over."

"Roger Three; Four out," Stik responded.

The clatter of automatic fire punctuated by periodic
explosions continued on both flanks, but except for a
few stray rounds cutting through the leaves over our
heads, nothing was hitting our area.

"Let's move," Bob said.

Thach led the squad out of the perimeter and headed
northwest. Bob and I followed him along with Ly
carrying the radio, and ten members of the Second
Squad. Marching at a quick pace over the flat and
relatively open terrain, I gave last-minute instructions
to Thach.

"Three blasts on my whistle and we fall back halfway to the perimeter," I said. "Keep 'em on-line as
we move to the rear." Thach nodded. "The second
three blasts and we fall back all the way to the
perimeter."

"Okay, Bac-si."

When we reached the fifty-meter mark, Thach
stopped.

"Get them on-line, five paces apart," Bob ordered.

Thach deployed the first five men to his right and
the second five to his left. Bob and Ly took up a
position in a small depression and I hit the ground
behind a tree a couple of meters to their right.

"Here they come," Bob yelled. "Hold your fire."

Looking up, I could see part of the Recon Platoon
moving toward us through the scattered underbrush.
It looked as though a couple were being transported in
a fireman's carry. Their white bandages stood out in
the maze of greens and browns. As Bob talked on the
radio Thach took a prone position beside me.

"Fox Four, this is Fox Three, over," Bob said.

"Three, this is Four, over," Stik rasped over the
radio.

"Fox Four, you're about fifty meters out, over."

"Roger, Three. I've got a fix on you, Four out."

As Recon drew closer, the volume of fire reached a
fever pitch. Rounds began cutting through the brush

with a whine and thwacking into nearby trunks. On the far side of Recon's wounded, I could see the rest of the platoon leap-frogging through the brush to their rear. From this distance it looked like one squad was carrying the wounded while the other two took turns laying down a base of fire. One squad fired staggered bursts at the enemy while the second retreated about ten meters to the rear. Then the second squad laid down a base of fire while the first repeated the maneuver.

Closing to about thirty meters, I could smell the caustic fumes of CS gas and hear Stik yelling at his Bodes to keep on-line. About seventy-five meters on the other side of the Bodes, I could make out what looked like the khaki uniforms and erratic muzzle flashes from enemy troops moving toward us. I took a deep breath and slowly exhaled. "Here we go again," I said to myself as my system electrified from the familiar rush of adrenaline. I felt a little bit nervous— but I always did on the threshhold of a battle.

"Hey, Stik, over here," I yelled as the first of the Bodes carrying the wounded reached our position and flopped to their knees in exhaustion.

"Thach, tell 'em they've got another fifty meters to go!" I yelled.

Jumping to my feet, I rushed to the wounded.

The men were too spent to carry the wounded any farther, so I grabbed the nearest Bodes and helped them get the wounded on their backs. From what I could see, only one was seriously wounded. He had been hit in the upper leg and it looked as though the round had shattered his femur and severed his femoral artery. Someone had improvised a tourniquet from a green platoon scarf and a small piece of bamboo tied just above the wound. His trouser leg was soaked black with blood, but the wound appeared to have stopped bleeding.

Once the wounded moved through, I returned to my position behind the same tree next to Stik.

"You all right?" I asked.

"Yeah, give me some ammunition," he said, out of breath and drenched with sweat.

I reached down and pulled five magazines out of my B.A.R. belt and handed them to him.

"Caught 'em eating lunch." He inserted a fresh magazine into his M-16. "One of 'em spotted us and then a couple of platoons came right at us. Lucky we were on-line when they hit." He pulled his bolt to the rear and released it, slamming a round into the chamber.

"How many were there?" I asked.

Without looking up, Stik answered, "At least a company. I burned up five hundred rounds in no time flat. The Bodes kicked ass. But there were just too many. We couldn't shoot 'em fast enough.

"Keep moving," Stik barked to his men. "Keep moving."

The remainder of the Recon Platoon passed through our skirmish line—there was a short pause in the firing—then the Second Squad opened up on the pursuing enemy. Stik and I squeezed off a few well-aimed shots, but in this terrain the enemy was still too far out to hit.

Glancing to my rear, I could see that Recon was about halfway back to our perimeter. When I gave three long blasts on my whistle, everyone jumped to his feet and moved to the rear. Running with my back to the enemy was an uncomfortable sensation. I had the feeling that a round was about to crash into my back. Reaching the halfway point, we again hit the ground and resumed firing. In the shafts of sunlight that filtered through the canopy, the khaki-clad soldiers appeared to flash on and off as they darted in and out from behind trees and bushes.

I looked to my rear and checked Recon's progress. When I turned to resume firing, I saw that the enemy had disappeared from view. I could still hear the reports of a few AK-47's, but couldn't see anyone. Maybe their lead elements had outrun their main body and they were waiting for them to catch up, I thought. Whatever the reason, it gave us an opportunity to move again.

With a quick glance to the rear, I could see that Recon was almost back inside the perimeter. I gave a second three blasts on my whistle and everyone again jumped to his feet and ran to the rear. Reaching the perimeter, we caught up with the last of Stik's men.

The Recon Platoon sergeant didn't give his men a chance to rest. He immediately began deploying them along the northern quarter of the perimeter. Bob and Thach moved the Second Squad back into position in the Third Platoon's sector.

The firing on our flank of the perimeter had subsided to the point where you could only hear isolated rifle cracks or occasional staggered bursts, but there was still a constant crash coming from Ferguson's and Hagey's sector.

"Hey, Jim, over here."

To my right, I could see that Duke and Stik had set up behind a large fallen tree.

"Hey, Duke, what brings you back up here?" I asked as I took up a position between them.

"Just wanted to see if old Stik was still kickin'." He laughed.

"You know he's too ugly to get killed," I said.

"That's true. Musta temporarily lost my mind."

"Any word on Fergy and Frank?" I asked.

"They've got their hands full," Duke answered.

Just then, Stik took a look over the log and yelled, "Here they come again."

I peered over the rotting tree trunk to see large numbers of khaki uniforms moving toward us about seventy-five meters out. The Bodes immediately opened up with a ripple of M-16's, the "poing. . . whumph" of M-79 grenade launchers and the "ta, tow, tow, tow, tow, tow. . . . ta, tow, tow, tow, tow, tows" of the M-60's. The enemy was still too far away and most of the rounds were being absorbed or deflected by trees, branches, and vines before they reached their targets.

I looked to my left and could see that Thach was moving down the line trying to slow the Bodes' rate of fire. When the advancing enemy elements reached a distance of fifty meters, Stik, Duke, and I commenced firing. I was using tracer ammunition and carefully aimed and squeezed off each shot. Each crack sent a crimson streak into the foliage. My rifle was sighted in for one hundred meters, so I aimed a little low. When the top of my front sight blade was about belly-high on an enemy soldier I squeezed off a round. Firing with both eyes open, my right eye sighted the weapon and my left followed the luminescent line of the tracer's flight. Using tracer rounds gave me the advantage of tracking the exact trajectory of each bullet. If a shot was a little to the left or right of the target, I made a slight adjustment and squeezed off another round.

Following each round, I noticed that most of them ricocheted skyward or into the ground. The M-16 didn't have much brush-cutting capability. Having a high velocity but small caliber, the bullets were easily deflected by branches and vines.

When the V.C. were about forty meters out they suddenly changed tactics. Rather than trying to overrun us with a frontal assault they began to fire and maneuver. Each man ran forward four or five meters, hit the ground, fired a couple of rounds, jumped to his feet, and then ran forward another four or five meters.

With this change in tactics, I began firing three-round bursts. I could see that with each burst at least one of my rounds was hitting home. When the crimson streak hit an enemy soldier, he suddenly stopped and disappeared into the greens.

Judging from the way they continued to fire and maneuver, I concluded that they were pretty good—probably some of the best we'd ever encountered. As they closed the gap, Danh crawled up to the tree trunk next to me.

"I stay you, Bac-si," he said with a big smile.

I hoped he wasn't waiting for my heart. Moving at the front of the advancing enemy, I spotted what looked like an officer carrying an M-16. It appeared as though their assault was beginning to crumble and he was screaming frantically at his men to keep moving forward. I raised to one knee to get a clear shot at him, but before I could get off a burst, I felt a warm breath hit the left side of my head, knocking me to my butt in a sitting position. I was dazed and uncertain as to what had happened.

I felt something warm flowing down the left side of my face and neck. Stik turned and looked at me with a shocked expression—I'd been hit! I glanced to the left and out of the corner of my eye I could see bright red blood squirting out from the side of my head—was I dead?

I hesitated to touch my temple—I was afraid I'd find part of my head gone—but I forced myself to slowly raise my left hand and touch the wound. With warm blood spurting on my palm, I cautiously pushed my index finger into a small hole just over my temple. I felt a great sense of relief flood over me when I realized that part of my head hadn't been blown away.

"Stik, get me a battle dressing!" I yelled.

"Goddamn, Jim, I thought you were dead," he said. "I was waiting for you to fall over."

"Thanks, I need more friends like you," I said with a stunned smile as he removed a dressing from its wrapper.

Stik placed the dressing over the wound and I held it in place as he tied it to my head. I could feel warm blood flowing down my neck and chest. Looking out over the top of the tree I could see that we had broken the assault. Although there was still a lot of sporadic shooting, most of the enemy troops had taken up positions behind trees—a few were running to the rear.

"Get it tight," I said as he tied it in place. "You've gotta put on enough pressure to stop the bleeding." I was bleeding profusely but remained alert. I could clearly detect the metallic taste of blood in the corner of my mouth.

"I don't want to hurt you," he said.

"Don't worry about hurting me," I replied. "I've only got so much blood. If you can't stop it I'll be dead before dinner."

"It's tight, but you're still bleeding," he said with an

anxious look on his face. My collar, neck, and the left side of my face were covered with blood.

"You need help with that?" Duke yelled.

"No," Stik replied. "Keep an eye on Charlie."

"Danh, get an Ace bandage and two clamps out of the right pocket of my rucksack."

My ruck was only a few meters away, and Danh crawled over to it and returned with what I wanted.

"Okay, Stik," I said. "Take the dressing off and see if you can spot a bleeder. I think it cut one of my temporal arteries. Danh, get Kimh and tell him to bring his M-5 kit."

"You want me to try to clamp off the bleeder?" Stik asked.

"Yeah, if you can clamp the end of the artery Kimh can tie it off with surgical thread."

"I'll give it a shot," he said as he untied the dressing and looked closely at the wound.

"What do you see?" I asked.

"Looks like a small bullet hole," he said. "I don't see any bleeders. Just a round hole with a lot of blood gushing out of it. There's no exit wound either. The bullet's gotta be lodged somewhere in your head."

"Okay, let's try pressure again. If that doesn't work we're gonna have to open it up."

"You want to open it up out here?" Stik asked as he opened up another dressing with blood-covered hands.

"Are there any other options?" I asked as he placed it over the wound. "Get it as tight as you can make it. Don't worry about hurting me."

He tied it as tight as he could without ripping the dressing. I could feel the additional pressure on my skull as he tied off the bandage. Blood was still oozing out of the bottom half of the dressing.

"Now put the Ace on top of the dressing," I said.

Kimh and Danh returned to where Stik was working on me. Kimh turned pale when he saw that I had been shot in the head.

"Kimh, give Stik a hand with the Ace," I said. "Danh, you better get back up on the line."

Danh picked up his Sten and moved back to the

fallen tree, giving one last glance at me over his shoulder while Stik and Kimh applied the Ace bandage.

"As tight as you can make it," I said as they rolled the Ace around my head.

"Should I start an I.V.?" Kimh asked.

"No, not yet," I replied. "If you can stop the bleeding I won't need one."

When they finished wrapping it, Kimh covered the Ace with three-inch surgical tape. The bleeding stopped. I felt such a sense of relief that I let out a loud "Tay Yoo," a Cambodian battle cry. Danh turned and gave me a thumbs up as Kimh moved back down the line in the direction of the dispensary.

"You look like some damned Arab," Stik said with a relieved laugh. "If that bullet had been a hair to the right it would have blown your ugly head off."

"Up yours, Stik," I said with a weary smile.

"You feel dizzy, Jim?" Duke asked.

"No, I'll be all right."

"I'd better get back to my people," he said as he stood up and headed down the line in a low crouch.

"All you Marines have hard heads with nothing in between," Stik remarked before leaving.

NEWS CLIPPINGS

Prime Minister Air Vice Marshal Nguyen Cao Ky this morning said that during the past two years, he has never had any thoughts or committed any actions which are contrary to the best interests of the people and the nation.
Vietnam Press (Saigon), July 18, 1967

Dr. Benjamin Spock, noted pediatrician and one of the nation's most vocal spokesmen for peace in Vietnam, indicated Monday that he might be available as a third party presidential candidate next year.
Buffalo Evening News, July 18, 1967

The sharp dispute between General Westmoreland and Defense Secretary McNamara's Pentagon analysts revolves around the rate of enemy infiltration from North Vietnam.
Newsweek, July 24, 1967

June tourists: 99,410, a record high.
Honolulu Star Bulletin, July 18, 1967

The public and private comments on the Vietnam war have seldom been further apart in Washington than they are today. The official comments remain moderately optimistic; the private comments are much more solemn and even gloomy.
Courier Express (Buffalo), July 18, 1967

Doctor Zhivago *starring Geraldine Chaplin-Julie Christie-Tom Courtenay-Alec Guiness-Ralph Richardson-Omar Sharif-Rod Steiger*
Los Angeles Times, July 18, 1967

Mr. FINDLEY. Mr. Speaker, the strike at Colt Industries, which has halted all production of M-16 rifles so badly needed by allied forces in Vietnam, is a major scandal which actually has an adverse impact on our troops more immediate and more direct than the short-lived rail strike which brought such prompt action by Congress.

Congressional Record—House, July 18, 1967

With Mayor Daley of Chicago making a belated drive to take the 1968 political convention away from Miami Beach, which seemed to have a stranglehold on them, this is probably a good time to examine this quaint American folkway.

Los Angeles Times, July 18, 1967

Dear Abby: My wife and I are newlyweds. She wants to have a dinner party and invite all of her old boyfriends. All these fellows are still single. I told her I didn't think much of the idea.

Los Angeles Times, July 18, 1967

4

1315 Hours (1:15 P.M.)

The smell of spent gunpowder hung heavy in the moisture-laden air—so hot and humid it seemed at times almost suffocating to breathe. An unyielding sun tortured the jungle with its heat; still, I was grateful that we were mostly shaded from its rays.

I took advantage of the temporary lull in the battle to remove a canteen from my B.A.R. belt and take a long drink. In the stifling humidity, you sweated water like you were pouring canteens through a sieve. The exchange of fire had tapered off to a few sporadic shots. I surveyed the lay of our perimeter and noticed that only Danh remained at our firing position behind the fallen tree. He was lying in a prone position at the right end firing a round or two every few seconds. His British Sten must have run out of ammo because he was now squeezing off rounds from an M-16.

My hands and arms were coated with sticky blood which had caked with dirt, so I poured some water from my canteen and rubbed them clean. After drying off with my scarf, I pulled myself up to the fallen tree. No sooner had I eased my head over the rim of the moss-covered trunk when two rounds slammed into the rotting wood from only a short distance away, splattering wood and moss over the edge.

"Bac-si, V.C. very close," Danh called as he crawled up next to me.

He brushed aside some rotting leaves and twigs from the ground between us and smoothed the damp soil with his hand. Using a twig to draw a map he explained that the V.C. were spread out along our entire front. Some were as close as ten meters while others were as far away as a hundred meters.

"Many V.C.," he said.

"How many?"

"More one hundred, Bac-si."

"Okay, partner," I said. "Better get back to your position."

I removed a grenade from my harness and pulled the pin, let the spoon fly with a "ping," counted "One-one thousand. . .two-one thousand," then tossed it toward the V.C. sniper who had shot at me. Two seconds later it exploded with a loud "whumph!" I had no way of knowing if it had hit its target and I wasn't about to check it out.

"Hey, Bac-si, Trung-si Cole come," Danh called.

Bob, Thach, and Ly crawled up next to me. Ly rested his radio against the tree.

"You all right, old buddy?" Bob asked. I felt stable even though the slug was lodged in my head. At least the bleeding had stopped. "Thach told me you got hit and I got back as quick as I could."

"Yeah, I'm okay. Keep your head down or Charlie will take it off. He's only a few meters away."

"Our whole west flank's in the same boat. They're all pinned down," Bob added as he used his scarf to wipe the glistening beads of sweat from his face.

"We tied in with Duke?" I asked.

"Yeah, we're tied in tight with Duke's platoon and the Bodes are digging in along our side of the creek bed," Bob removed a canteen from his belt and drank as we talked.

"What'd'ya got here?" he wanted to know.

"I'd estimate a company pinned down across our front. They're as close as ten meters. In this terrain they don't have the men to overrun us and we don't have the troops to push 'em out."

"It looks like we've got a Mexican standoff." Bob paused . . . "We're gonna need air to knock 'em out of there. We can't keep this up much longer 'cuz we're almost out of ammo."

"Thach, could you get us an M-79 up here?" I asked. "They're digging in behind trees and we can't touch 'em with 16's."

"I get, Bac-si," he responded. "Bac-si, I give you," he said as he removed a small jade Buddha and a gold chain from around his neck. I was very moved by the gesture. I knew it had deep meaning to him.

"Thach, I think you should keep it," I said, trying to convey my gratitude.

"No, no, Bac-si," he insisted as he struggled to slip it over my head but couldn't quite fit it over the bandage. With grungy, dirt-covered fingers he managed to unclasp the chain and refasten the clasp around my neck.

"Thank you, my friend. I'll take good care of it."

"I get M-79," he responded, then scurried off through the brush to our left.

Cautiously peering out over the tree again, I spotted what looked like a squad clambering from right to left at about a hundred and twenty-five meters.

"Hey, Bob, look at that."

"Looks like they're wearing blue uniforms," he said.

"They got rucks on?" I asked.

"Yeah, think so. Yeah, they're carrying rucks all right. Wonder where they're headed?"

"Got me."

"Aw shit!" Bob said as he pointed at what looked like a number of platoon-sized units moving through the same area—they were all carrying rucksacks.

"I could be seeing things, but I'd say some of 'em are carrying mortar tubes," I said. "Wish I had a pair of binoculars."

"Probably a weapons platoon. I'd say we've got a battalion out there."

"Looks like we're in for a real knock down, drag out," I added.

"Trung-si, Thach come," Danh called.

Looking back over my left shoulder, I could see Thach and Kien crawling toward us. Kien was carrying his M-79 and wearing an ammo vest full of high-explosive rounds. He was also toting a couple of Russian RPG-7 rocket launchers.

"Where'd he get the RPG's?" I asked.

"He take from V.C." Thach smiled defiantly.

"How's his foot doing?" I wanted to know.

"Foot good," Kien said as he chewed on an old unlit cigar, rolling it with his tongue as he maneuvered it in the corner of his mouth.

"Hey, Thach, tell him I better not find out he's been stealing gold fillings," Bob joked as he pointed to his teeth.

"No, Trung-si," Thach responded with intense brown eyes. "He not do." Obviously he didn't catch the jest in Bob's words.

Thach positioned Kien at the left end of the tree while I removed my map and spread it out on the ground. As Bob and I discussed our situation, a confused roar of AK's, RPG's, frags, M-60's, M-79's, and M-16's resounded through the jungle, announcing an end to the lull.

"Look at this." I pointed to the map. "I don't think they'll come at us over the same ground again. I'd be willing to bet they hit us down at the other end of the platoon."

"Good bet," Bob said. "If they come through the thick stuff we won't see 'em till they're right on top of us."

"You said it."

"I'll tell you what," Bob said. "I'll leave Ly and the radio with you. I'm gonna move the M-60 and a few extra Bodes down to the other end. We'll see if I can set up a little reception for Mr. Charles. Why don't you see if you can find out what's holding up our air support?"

"Okay, I'll meet you back here."

Bob crawled off to the left. I told Thach that I was going to find the Lieutenant.

I crawled about ten meters in the direction of the center of the perimeter, and once out of the line of fire jumped to my feet and walked in a low crouch. Moving away from the Third Platoon, I could hear muffled automatic fire and explosions coming from those sectors of the perimeter covered by the First and Second Platoons. After walking another few meters through bamboo and scrub brush, I heard Condon's voice off to my left. Nearing the sound of his voice, I could see that he, SSG Roger "Ranger" Smith, and a couple of Bodes from the Headquarters Section had set up in a small depression that measured about five meters across. The Lieutenant was kneeling next to his PRC-25 and talking to the F.A.C. while Roger was sitting at his side with his map spread across his outstretched legs.

Condon keyed the mike a couple times, then spoke into the handset.

"Sidewinder, Sidewinder, this is Fox Control. How do you read me? Over."

There was a static hiss; then the F.A.C. responded.

"Fox Control, this is Sidewinder, I read you four by four. How me? Over."

"Sidewinder, I read you same."

"Trying to get the F.A.C. up here," Roger informed me as he cocked his head toward me. "You okay, Jim?"

"Yeah, I'm all right."

"You look like you had a fight with an ugly stick and lost."

"Fox Control, this is Sidewinder. Over."

"Ssshh, listen!" Roger hissed, pointing to the west.

Off in the distance I could hear the faint groan of an approaching O-1E spotter plane. Condon smiled as Roger placed his map on the ground in front of the Lieutenant and stood up. We're in business now, I thought.

"Sidewinder, this is Fox Control. If you follow a ninety-degree azimuth you'll come in right over us. Over."

"Roger, Fox Control. I'm on a ninety."

"Jim, as soon as I can get a slick in here I'll get you and the rest of the wounded out," the Lieutenant said with genuine concern in his voice.

"Don't worry about me, sir. I'm doing just fine."

"That round must have given you a pretty good whack," he added. "The side of your face is turning black and blue."

"Let me check your pupils," Roger said as he looked into my eyes.

"They look equally dilated?" I asked.

"Yeah, so far, so good. That round must have hit something else before it hit you."

"How's she look in your area?" Condon wanted to know.

"Well, sir, we've got a company pinned down in single canopy just to the northwest of us. They can't move and neither can we."

Condon's map and grease pencil were lying on the ground in front of him, so I squatted and, using the grease pencil as a pointer, showed him where Bob and I had seen a weapons platoon with mortars and an estimated battalion of infantry moving across our front.

"Bob and I figure they're gonna rush us through the thick stuff down at the southern end of the platoon."

"That's what I'd do if I was Charlie," Roger said.

"Sir, it's gonna take them awhile to set up their mortars," I said. "If we can get some air up here within the next few minutes, I'd like to put the first strikes in on the company that's out in front of us."

"You got it," Condon said as he studied his map. "If you can knock 'em outta there we'll shift some of your troops down to the other end of the platoon."

I nodded that I understood.

"If you can't hold 'em I'll reinforce you with the Headquarters Section," he added. "We gotta keep 'em outside the perimeter. If they break through we got big-time problems."

"Okay, sir. I'll relay that to Bob."

"Sir," Roger said, "if they're gonna set up mortars they're gonna need a clearing."

"Yeah, you're right. I'll have the F.A.C. keep an eye on the open areas."

"He's gonna have to watch that east-west trail," Roger added as he squatted and pointed to the trail that was located just a short distance south of our perimeter.

"Ya know Charlie'll use it to bring in reinforcements," the Lieutenant responded.

The drone of the F.A.C.'s engine grew louder as he approached.

"Sidewinder, this is Fox Control. I'll give you a 'now' when you're directly overhead. Over." The radio crackled to life.

"Roger, Fox Control."

"Here he comes." Roger smiled as we looked up. "Just a little more."

"Now!" Condon yelled into the handset.

"Okay, Fox Control. I've got ya."

Looking up, we could hear him circling overhead but couldn't see anything through the blanket of green foliage.

"You low on ammo?" Roger asked.

"Yeah, we need a resupply ASAP."

"What do you need?"

"Ah. . .M-16 and M-60 rounds, frag grenades, CS gas, and Claymores," I responded.

"Anything else?" he wanted to know.

"The H.E. rounds for the 79's are pretty much useless in the thick stuff. Any chance of getting some canister rounds?"

"I'll see what I can do," the Lieutenant answered.

"What kind of quantities we talking about?"

"Hell, we'll take anything we can get. I'm not worried about having too much."

"Okay, Jim, get on back to your platoon. I'll see what I can do."

"Yes, sir." Condon continued talking to the F.A.C. while I stood up and headed back.

As I neared the platoon, I could hear the distinctive "poing. . . , whumph!" of Kien's M-79 and two- and three-round bursts being fired by Danh, Ly, and Thach.

When I reached the fallen tree, I crouched next to Ly and made contact with the F.A.C.

"Sidewinder, this is Fox Three. Over."

"Fox Three, this is Sidewinder. Over."

"Sidewinder, I've got a company pinned down northwest of my position. Over."

"Roger, Fox Three. Can you give me smoke? I've got fast movers five minutes out. Over."

"Ly, gimme a smoke grenade," I said. He removed one from his harness and handed it to me. It was yellow smoke.

I pulled the pin on the grenade and tossed it about five meters out in front of our position. A few seconds later a caustic plume of thick yellow smoke enveloped the area and billowed sluggishly skyward.

"Wham!" Something hit me on the back, knocking me flat on my face. I spun around to see who had hit me—no one was there, but pieces of branches and bark were raining all around me like confetti. I looked up and could see hundreds of leaves floating slowly to earth through a pall of gray smoke. I wasn't hurt, but my ears were ringing.

"RPG," Danh yelled. "It hit top of tree."

The smoke grenade probably attracted the fire, I thought.

"Everyone all right?" I asked.

Ly had been hit by a falling branch, but other than that no one was hurt.

"Fox Three, this is Sidewinder. Are you still there? Over."

"This is Fox Three. Over."

"Fox Three, we've got a problem. I've got yellow smoke coming from two locations. Over."

"Damn," I said to myself. Had someone in the perimeter accidentally pulled the pin on a yellow smoke? Maybe the V.C. had intercepted our radio transmission and popped another yellow smoke to confuse the F.A.C.

"Ly, gimme another smoke," I said. He removed another and handed it to me. I read the label and saw that it was red smoke.

"Sidewinder, this is Fox Three. I'm popping another smoke. It's the same color as the socks of Boston's baseball team. Repeat, the same color as Boston's baseball team. Over." I hoped he was a baseball fan.

"Roger, Fox Three. I read you five by five."

I lobbed the grenade about ten meters off to my right front and waited. A couple of seconds later there was a muffled "pop" which released thick red coils of bright smoke in a low stream across the ground before curling upward through the jungle canopy.

"I've got you, Fox Three," the F.A.C. said. "The Air Force is up top. Where do you want it? Over."

Ly flashed me a big smile. "Number one, Bac-si, Soc-mow V.C."

"Sidewinder, this is Fox Three. I'd like heavy ordnance one hundred meters northwest of my position—repeat, heavy ordnance one hundred meters northwest of my position. Over."

"Roger, Fox Three."

"Sidewinder, this is Fox Three. If you bring 'em in on a two hundred and twenty-degree azimuth, they'll be flying parallel to our lines. Over."

"Roger, Fox Three."

I had a lot of confidence in the F.A.C., but didn't want the jets flying directly over our perimeter. If one accidentally dropped his ordnance a split second early, his deadly payload could land right on top of us. It wouldn't be the first time it had happened.

The F.A.C. swooped down low, dipping his nose toward the target followed by the "whoosh. . .pop!" of a phosphorous marking round, which blossomed into a graceful umbrella of molten white streamers. The fast burners would have no trouble pinpointing the target.

"Bac-si, Trung-si Cole come," Ly said. I looked over my left shoulder and saw Bob crawling toward us.

"How's it look?" Bob wanted to know.

"We've got fast movers up top," I said. "Condon's working on the ammo resupply."

"Good, the troops are getting low."

To our northeast, I could hear the hot roar of the first jet knifing in along the jungle's edge. My pulse rate picked up. You never could tell for sure where that first bomb would land.

"Get down!" I yelled.

The whine of the jet's engine rose to a bansheelike scream as it rolled in hot. About a hundred meters out, a daisy chain of orange-black fire balls flashed across our front—a second later the earth-rending concussion of 750-pound bombs pounded my eardrums as the force of the shock waves rushed over our position. I glanced over the log and saw billows of gray smoke drifting skyward.

"Sidewinder, this is Fox Three. Over."

"Fox Three, this is Sidewinder. Over."

"Sidewinder, you're looking good. Over."

"Roger, Fox Three."

Moments later, a second jet streaked in, shaking the jungle with violent seizures of fire and steel.

"I'm gonna start walking them in," I said.

"You know Charlie's gonna be forced to move on us," Bob said. "He's gonna be between a rock and a hard place."

"I know. It's either move or burn in place," I said.

Another load of heavy ordnance exploded across our front, sending slivers of red-hot shrapnel slicing through broad leaves, tree branches, and flesh. With each blast, the fluting wail of shrapnel punctuated the air overhead.

"Thach, pass the word we're bringing 'er in close," Bob directed. Thach nodded and crawled off to his left.

As Bob and I talked, a large piece of razor-sharp shrapnel whistled through the air and plowed into the base of a tree just a couple of feet from Bob.

"Look at the size of that sucker," he said. "Must weigh five pounds." It was hot and smoking.

"Sidewinder, this is Fox Three. Over."

"Fox Three, this is Sidewinder. Over."

"Could you give us napalm at fifty meters—repeat, napalm at fifty meters northwest of my position. Over."

"Roger, Fox Three. We aim to please."

A minute later I could hear another jet making its approach.

"Hot stuff coming in!" I yelled.

Using napalm always scared the hell out of me, so I imagined what it did to someone on the receiving end. If you weren't cremated, it killed you by sucking all the air out of your lungs to feed its insatiable fireball.

The jet roared over the canopy releasing its napalm pods which tumbled lazily end over end. There was a dull thud, a sickening "kawhooosh," and boiling, orange-yellow balls of liquid hell splashed through the jungle, consuming everything in its path. Even at fifty meters the invisible wall of heat hit my face with surprising force. The pungent petroleum smell of burning gas permeated the area. I could hear the screams of people in their death throes. They were agonizing human sounds which turned my stomach.

"Sidewinder, you're right on target. Over."

"Fox Three. . ."

"Here they come," Bob yelled.

The volume of fire up and down the line reached a deafening crescendo as dazed V.C. began running, stumbling, and pulling themselves out of the firestorm.

Bob, Kien, Ly, and Danh were firing as fast as they could line up their sights on targets while I crouched low and kept contact with the F.A.C.

"Fox Three, this is Sidewinder. Over."

The frenzied gunfire was so loud I could barely hear the F.A.C.

"Sidewinder, this is Fox Three," I yelled into the handset.

"Fox Three, this is Sidewinder. How we doin'? Over."

I started to yell again, but caught myself. "Why am I yelling? I'm the one who can barely hear."

"Sidewinder, this is Fox Three," I replied in a normal voice. "You've got 'em moving forward. Could you give me some twenty millimeter and C.B.U.'s? Over."

"That's a Roger, Fox Three. Where do you want it? Over."

"This is Fox Three. As close as possible. We need it now. Over."

"That's a Roger, Fox Three. It's on its way."

"Grenade!" Danh yelled. I hugged the ground. "Whumph!" There was a loud explosion a few meters to our right rear.

I dropped the handset, picked up my M-16, and looked out over the top of the tree. Just a few meters away a half-dozen V.C. were running at us in a crouched position with their weapons blazing. One was on fire and screaming. His khaki uniform was burned and most of his skin was charred a reddish black. I didn't have time to aim my weapon so I just swung it in his general direction, but before I could squeeze the trigger he fired a burst that lashed the air over my head. A split second later, I fired a long burst that caught him in mid-stride, blowing off his right arm and shoulder. The impact of the bullets spun him around and sprayed a stream of blood from his amputated arm like water from a hose. Then he just stood there in death shock, like a strange apparition staring at me. I pulled the trigger again, but nothing happened. Someone else got off a burst that lifted and twisted him upward before dropping him into a crumpled heap with his back against a tree trunk. He slowly slumped to the ground and sat there with his mouth and eyes gaping open.

Off to the north I could hear another jet closing fast.

"Get down," I yelled.

As the jet roared over our position its twenty-millimeter cannons screeched like the hinges on an enormous door that needed oil. Peering out over the tree, I could see a storm of rounds cutting across the ground, ripping through the foliage and remaining V.C. I picked up the handset.

"Sidewinder, this is Fox Three. Over."

"Fox Three, this is Sidewinder. How we looking? Over."

"This is Fox Three. Like a cow pissing on a flat rock. Over."

"That's a Roger, Three."

I removed the magazine from my M-16 and pulled the bolt to the rear. A shell casing was stuck in the chamber. "Cheap ammunition," I muttered to myself.

"Bob, take the radio, will ya?"

I gave him the handset and removed a pocket knife from my hip pocket. I tried to use it to pry out the shell, but the casing was stuck tight. I had a cleaning rod attached to my rifle with green tape, so I untaped it and screwed its sections together. Ramming it down the rifle's bore, I was able to dislodge the shell. I then reached into the center pocket of my ruck and removed a bottle of Hoppes #9 cleaning solvent and the rest of my cleaning equipment.

Another jet screeched across our front with the rasping sound of its twenty-millimeter cannons blasting away.

I opened the bottle of Hoppes, dipped my bore brush in it, and pushed it through my rifle bore a half-dozen times. The firing slackened to a few sporadic shots. Bob continued to talk to the F.A.C. Using my chamber brush and solvent, I then scrubbed out the chamber. The strong smell of the Hoppes was a pleasant change which reminded me of simpler times, hunting back home. As I scrubbed, black dissolved carbon dripped out on my hands, and I wondered where the reinforcements were. In the background I could hear Fergy and Duke requesting air support. After running a few cleaning wads through the bore and chamber, I wiped the entire weapon down with my silicone cloth and reassembled it.

"Sidewinder, this is Fox Three," Bob keyed the headset. "If you ever get up to Trang-Sup the Third Herd owes you a cold one."

"I copy that, Fox Three." The circling jets broke off and veered eastward.

Except for the tormented groans and cries coming from the killing zone, an uneasy silence descended over the Third Platoon's sector. The jungle in front of us had been ripped apart. The foliage hung in blackened shreds from the charred trunks of trees. Many had been stripped bare of their leaves and splintered like matchsticks. Blankets of bluish-gray smoke thickened and thinned in wispy, ghostlike patterns as they drifted across our front, giving an eerie, almost haunting feel to the battlescape. Here and there fires continued to burn. And over everything there hung the acrid scent of burnt cordite, charred flesh, and jellied gas.

NEWS CLIPPINGS

Secretary of State Dean Rusk said yesterday that one condition of terminating American raids against North Vietnam was a guarantee that the marines holding key positions would not be attacked by North Vietnamese regulars.
St. Louis Post-Dispatch, July 18, 1967

Joe Frazier and George Chuvalo finished their training grind yesterday at their upstate resort camps for their 12-round heavyweight bout in Madison Square Garden tomorrow night.
The New York Times, July 18, 1967

A year ago, Ronald Reagan was a political unknown. Today, he is a governor of the nation's biggest state— and rising fast in public-opinion polls for the presidency.
U.S. News & World Report, July 24, 1967

"Steve McQueen at his best!" The Sand Pebbles
Los Angeles Times, July 18, 1967

The ambassadors of the seven allied nations in the Republic of Vietnam will meet Tuesday "to strengthen consultation and cooperation among these nations," the Foreign Ministry said Monday.
The Korea Herald, July 18, 1967

Colt Ind. +3¾
The Wall Street Journal, July 18, 1967

Out of Robert McNamara's trip to the fighting front came a decision to slow the U.S. build up, resist Vietnam's becoming entirely an "American War." Wash-

ington's problem: how to get the South Vietnamese to carry more of the burden.
U.S. News & World Report, July 21, 1967

Barefoot in the Park—*A successful adaptation, by Neil Simon, of his Broadway comedy, well acted by Robert Redford, Jane Fonda, Mildred Natwick, and Charles Boyer. (Music Hall, 6th Ave. at 50th, PL7-3100)*
The New Yorker, July 22, 1967

If the United States followed the Constitution and Congress declared war, then the U.S. would be in a position to win the war in Vietnam, Brig. Gen. (Ret.) Richard B. Maoan said Monday night.
Courier Express (Buffalo), July 18, 1967

5

1415 Hours (2:15 P.M.)

A blazing afternoon sun caused the burnt-over expanse at our front to shimmer in the wavering heat vapors. Even under the partial sanctuary of the jungle canopy, the relentless heat bore down on us.

A hush had fallen over the battle, bringing a curious blend of relief and worried silence.

A short distance down the line and to our rear, Kimh had set up a makeshift aid station in a bomb crater that measured about a meter deep and eight meters across. With some of the overhead vegetation blown away, a brilliant shaft of sunlight reached all the way to its moist brown bottom. Penetrating the smoke and the mist, the rays illuminated the small clearing with an unearthly glow.

Nearing the rim of the crater, I could see that Kimh and the Recon Platoon medic were busy tending to a couple of wounded Bodes. The cratered earth around them was littered with blood-stained dressings, pieces of white gauze, empty syringes, and discarded penicillin bottles. The Bode from Stik's platoon who had been hit in the leg was lying on a poncho at the center of the crater. Kimh was hovering over him, tying a can of serum albumin to a four-foot section of bamboo that he had pounded into the soft dirt. The blood-volume expander flowed into a vein in the back of his hand through a thin plastic tube.

On the left side of the crater, a Bode from the Second Platoon was lying on his back with his head propped against a rucksack. The Recon Platoon medic was kneeling on the ground next to him, carefully covering his face with layers of white gauze. Stepping down into the depression, I rested my M-16 against a rucksack and knelt next to the Bode from the Recon Platoon. His lips were blue, and I could only see white slits through his half-open eyes.

"I gave him six hundred thousand units of procaine penicillin and a half gram of streptomycin," Kimh said as he knelt on the ground next to me. "The platoon medic gave him morphine when he was hit."

"Good." I could see the empty syrette attached to his collar. I checked the medical tag that was attached to his fatigue jacket. His name was Luc. The green tourniquet on his left leg was tied tight a couple of inches below his crotch. His camouflaged pant leg was caked with dried blood and dirt. A faint trace of fresh blood was still seeping through the coagulated crust.

"How's the other guy doing?" I inquired.

"Shrapnel wound."

"How serious?"

"It looks bad but it's not serious."

"Okay, I'll take a look at him as soon as we finish here."

I checked the flow of the serum albumin. White surgical tape held the tube and needle firmly against the back of his hand. There was no swelling. It looked good.

"He drifts in and out," Kimh said. "When he's conscious he asks for water."

"Don't give him anything," I said. "He'd just throw it up.

"Got a bandage scissors?" I asked as I felt Luc's pulse and watched the second hand on my Seiko. His wrist was cold and clammy and his pulse was running about 120 beats per minute.

Kimh removed scissors from his M-5 kit and handed them to me. Observing the movement of the wounded man's chest, I could see that his breathing was rapid and shallow. He was mumbling incoherently.

"Better check his blood pressure," I said as I used the scissors to cut through the bottom of his pant leg.

"About thirty minutes ago his systolic pressure was ninety-two."

"Check it again, he's gone into shock."

Kimh removed a blood-pressure cuff and stethoscope from his M-5 kit, rolled up the Bode's left sleeve, and wrapped the cuff around his arm. I finished cutting his pant leg up past his knee and all the way up to the tourniquet. I felt his now-exposed leg—it was cold and slippery with sweat. His light brown skin had turned a pale sallow color, giving the appearance of death.

On the inside of his thigh a small, dark hole outlined in black oozed bright red blood. It was about four inches below the tourniquet and halfway between his hip and knee. Below the wound his leg was cocked at an odd angle—a sure sign that the bullet had fractured his femur. I lowered my head close to the ground and found the exit wound at the back of his leg—it was a silver dollar-sized hole with small splinters of bone fragments embedded in the open flesh.

It didn't look all that bad, but this type of wound could be deceptive. When a fast-moving bullet tore through soft tissue, the shock often destroyed large amounts of the surrounding tissue. When this occurred, considerable amounts of blood could seep through the walls of small blood vessels and pool in the damaged areas. Death from shock was always a possibility.

"His systolic pressure is down to seventy-four," Kimh voiced his concern as he removed the stethoscope from his ears.

"Did you give him any epinephrine?" I asked.

"No."

"We're gonna have to stabilize his blood pressure. Give 'im 0.2 milligrams of epinephrine and get a normal saline I.V. going."

As Kimh prepared the injection, I placed four-inch squares of sterile gauze over the wounds, then covered them with surgical tape. Every time I touched Luc's leg he let out a hoarse groan from deep within his chest. Kimh didn't have any trouble starting the injection, but wasn't able to get the I.V. needle into his nearly collapsed vessel.

"Do a cut-down if you can't get it in."

"One more try," Kimh replied.

Using a thumb to hold a vein on Luc's left wrist in place, he finally worked the needle into it.

"You got it," I said.

With Luc's blood pressure dropping dangerously, we had to move fast. If we were unable to get it under control he would likely fall into irreversible shock and die of kidney or liver failure in a matter of minutes. From what I could figure, he had lost somewhere around a quart of blood before the tourniquet was applied. When he got hit and began to lose blood his vessels had automatically constricted to compensate for the loss. But now we'd reached the point where this defense mechanism was beginning to fail. I hoped the epinephrine would constrict his vessels again and increase his blood pressure.

"Whumph!" An explosion just a short distance south of the crater caught me unprepared. While working on the wounded, I often became oblivious to the fighting around me, but something that close had a way of snapping me back to reality.

"Open it up all the way," I said as Kimh adjusted the drip rate of the normal saline I.V. With the regulator opened all the way, the clear saltwater flowed into his veins.

"I'll splint his leg," Kimh said.

"Yeah, no telling when we'll get out of here. See if you can get someone to improvise a stretcher from a couple of ponchos and bamboo poles."

Kimh nodded.

Normally we carried out our dead and wounded in hammocks tied to bamboo, but in this case it was important to keep him as flat and stable as possible. His loss of blood contributed to the shock, but I was convinced that the primary cause was the excruciating pain. When Recon carried him all that distance without a splint, the sharp ends of his broken femur must have acted like a meat grinder on the surrounding tissue—I shuddered at the thought of the pain he must have endured.

"Should I loosen the tourniquet every thirty minutes, Bac-si?"

"No, don't let anyone touch it. He's already lost too much blood. Any more and we'll lose him."

If we were able to med-evac him to an American hospital within the next few hours they'd probably be able to save his leg. But with his artery severed and his femur broken, the chances of saving the leg grew slimmer with each passing hour. What concerned me the most was the possibility that the enemy would overrun our perimeter. If this happened, I knew that the Bodes wouldn't leave him for the V.C. I also knew that if we got into a running gun fight with the Cong there would be no way the Bodes could carry him on a stretcher. These considerations foretold painful decisions to come.

"Kimh, have you been sending the wounded back to their platoons?" I asked as he inserted safety pins to reassemble the wounded Bode's pant leg.

"If they can walk I send them back."

"Why don't you keep the next two or three here for security?" I suggested. "If Charlie gets inside the perimeter he'll blow your ass away."

He nodded that he would.

Kneeling next to the other wounded Bode, I said, "Okay, my friend, let's take a look at that face wound of yours."

I reached for the M-5 kit and placed it on the ground next to the Bode's wounded head while Kimh instructed the Recon Platoon medic to take Luc's blood pressure every fifteen minutes and keep an eye on his I.V.'s. Kneeling at the Bode's left side, I took his pulse and then removed the gauze from the left side of his forehead, revealing a deep red gash that went all the way to the bone, starting about a half inch below his hairline. When I removed more of the blood-soaked gauze, I could see that he had a second gash over his right eye. The two cuts came together between his

eyes, forming a perfect V. When Kimh finished with
Luc, he squatted on the ground to my right.

"His name is Ty," Kimh told me. "He says he was
with Sergeant Hagey."

Ty looked at me through worried brown eyes as I
peeled back the blood-soaked gauze. He mumbled
something in Cambodian, then grabbed hold of my
arm.

"He thinks he will die," Kimh explained.

"No, tell him it's not as bad as it feels. We'll sew
him up and in a month there'll be nothing left but a
thin red line."

Kimh explained what we were going to do, and it
seemed to relieve some of his anxiety. He was a good-
looking Bode, and the thought of being permanently
disfigured no doubt terrified him. Normally I didn't
suture wounds in the field because in most cases you
had to first surgically remove the damaged tissue surrounding the wound. Failure to do so would result in
death from gangrene. Facial wounds were an exception to this practice. It was generally advisable to sew
them up as soon as possible. My decision to close him
up immediately was also influenced by the possibility
of the V.C. overrunning us at any time. I figured that
if we had to fight our way out he'd have a much better
chance of surviving if his wound was closed. If he got
stranded in the jungle with his face torn apart, he'd
probably die of infection.

Removing the last layers of gauze from Ty's face, I
could see that the jagged rip continued down the right
side of his nose until it ended near the corner of his
mouth. It now formed a perfect Y. The once-light
brown skin of his face had swollen a deep purplish
black.

"Tell him we're gonna have to cover his eyes to
keep the soap out."

Kimh comforted him while I covered both of his
eyes with patches. Looking at his hands, I could see
his fingers digging into the dirt. It reminded me a lot
of my experiences in the dentist's chair. Once the
morphine took effect he'd relax.

"Did you give him any antibiotics?"

Kimh nodded and showed me where he had recorded it on the medical tag.

I told Kimh to ask him if Sergeant Hagey was all right. He told us that he and Frank had killed many V.C. and that Frank was outside of the perimeter somewhere near the southern end of the Second Platoon. He said that he hadn't seen Ferguson but thought that he was up at the other end of the platoon.

"Okay, let's clean him up and get to work," I said.

Kimh removed a plastic squirt bottle from the M-5 kit that contained a mixture of Phisohex and hydrogen peroxide. After shaking it up, he squirted some into the palm of my hand. The Phisohex had a fresh antiseptic smell that reminded me of our training at the U.S. Army Hospital at Fort Sam Houston, Texas. Rubbing my hands together made the white soapy liquid quickly turn brown with dissolved dirt and blood. Kimh then poured water from a canteen to rinse them clean.

"Hey, Kimh, tell him not to worry. In a couple of weeks he'll be back in Tay-Ninh raising hell again—I'll even buy him a buffalo steak at the Bamboo Club."

Ty forced a smile as I dried my hands with a surgical towel. Kimh then removed a sterile suture set from the kit which was wrapped in a green surgical towel. After removing the piece of tape that held it shut he placed it on the ground next to me and peeled it open. I checked its contents: two straight and two curved five-inch forceps, a straight razor, a surgical knife with extra blades, gut and black silk suture thread, general surgical scissors, an assortment of curved surgical needles, four eighteen-inch surgical towels, an emesis basin, and a pair of tweezers—everything I'd need to sew him up.

It was a hell of a place to try to maintain sterile technique, but we would have to do our best. When I thought about it, I was amazed how few wounds became infected in the tropical heat. The last one I could remember was a Montagnard from a village near Duc-Phong. After sewing up a gunshot wound in his ankle,

I told "Doctor Yen" he'd have to stay at the dispensary until I removed the stitches. That night he sneaked out of camp and returned to his village. About three weeks later, four Montagnards carried him back to the dispensary in a hammock. His ankle was inflamed with infection and half of the stitches had been ripped out by the swelling.

"Hand me a pair of seven and a half gloves," I said.

Kimh reached into his kit, opened a pair of paper-wrapped 7½'s, and laid them on the sterile field.

While I pulled the rubber gloves over my hands, Kimh dropped some sterile two-inch squares of gauze into the sterile emesis basin and then hung a bottle of normal saline from a piece of bamboo he had pushed into the ground next to Ty's head.

We were just about ready to operate when the popcorn-popping sound of rifles picked up along the Third Platoon's sector. The Cong were probably probing for weak spots. I could still hear the drone of the F.A.C. circling overhead, and every now and then the ground quivered from renewed bombing strikes.

"Flush it out with some saline," I directed.

With the end of the bottle's plastic tube about an inch from Ty's face, Kimh slowly opened the regulator and flushed out the wound. I looked at it closely. There was no sign of bleeding.

"Okay, let's sew 'er up," I said.

Kimh picked up the plastic squirt bottle and carefully filled the length of the wound with the hydrogen peroxide and Phisohex mixture. The hydrogen peroxide immediately began to bubble when it came in contact with the raw flesh.

After filling the wound with the soapy disinfectant, he squirted some on top of the two-inch squares of gauze and I gently scrubbed the length of the exposed wound. The morphine must have done the job because Ty didn't appear to be experiencing any more discomfort. He wasn't clutching the dirt any longer. When I finished with the wound, I worked my way further and further away from it until I had finally washed his entire face.

Kimh rinsed away the soap with normal saline after I finished the scrub. The white mixture flowed down Ty's neck and the side of his rucksack. When Kimh was through, he used a towel to dry the sides of Ty's head and neck and wipe the remaining soap out of his ears.

When he finished, I draped the wound with the four eighteen-inch towels that had been packed inside the sterile suture set. With his face wrapped, Ty looked half comical, like a nun with a green habit.

Kimh opened packages containing a 2cc plastic syringe and 23-gauge needle and dropped them both on the sterile field. I attached the needle to the syringe as he removed a bottle of lidocaine hydrochloride from the M-5 kit and wiped its rubber cap with a piece of alcohol-soaked gauze. He then held the bottle steady while I pushed the syringe's needle through the rubber cap and into the anesthetic. I then drew back on the syringe and filled it with the clear, pain-killing liquid.

After Kimh explained to Ty what we were doing, I carefully inserted the needle into the upper right corner of the Y-shaped wound. The injection of lidocaine caused the area around the needle to swell. Working my way down the right side of the Y, I injected the lidocaine about every quarter inch. When I finished the right side I did the left. This was normally the easiest part of sewing up a wound, but it was made difficult by the fact that 750-pound bombs were exploding all along the southern edge of our perimeter. Every time one of them exploded the earth convulsed. Finished, I pricked the upper right corner of the wound with the needle. Ty didn't move. He had an impassive look on his face.

"He numb," Kimh said.

I smiled. Between the morphine and the lidocaine, he probably wouldn't know if a tank ran over him.

I placed the syringe next to the emesis basin and picked up a curved forceps and a three-eighths-inch curved surgical needle. After clamping the center of the needle with the forceps, I threaded it with a piece of black silk surgical thread. To ensure that all the edges of the wound would line up properly I decided to put the first stitch in at the base of the V.

Gripping the flap of the V with the tweezers, I pushed the needle through the skin and into the underlying tissue. When it came out I pushed it into the flesh on the other side of the gash and out through the skin. Using the forceps, I then tied a tight surgical knot and cut away the excess thread with the scissors. It looked good—everything lined up perfectly. I was pleased with myself.

"Bac-si," a voice called. I looked up and saw Thach and Kien carrying another wounded Bode into the crater. Thach had a leg under each arm and Kien gripped him under his arms and around his chest.

"Bring him over here," I said. Kimh jumped to his feet and helped them.

"Lay him on the ground behind me." It was Lieu. "Damn it," I said to myself. I knew he'd never make it. We should have left him at Trang-Sup.

"He stand behind little tree to shoot at V.C.," Thach said, shaking his head.

Lieu withered on the ground as Kimh unbuttoned his fatigue jacket. An inch to the right of his navel there was a dark dime-sized hole, ringed by a small circle of fresh blood. There was no sign of external bleeding, but he was in a lot of pain. I wanted to help him, but couldn't contaminate my surgical gloves.

"I give him morphine," Thach said as Kimh and Kein rolled him onto his right side, his face grimacing in pain.

"Got an exit wound?" I asked.

"No," Kimh said as he searched Lieu's side and back for a second wound.

I was surprised. Bullet wounds of the stomach usually passed through the soft tissues and exited somewhere in the back.

Lieu continued squirming and kicked a shower of dirt on Ty's legs.

"Watch it! He's gonna contaminate everything," I yelled.

Thach and Kien tried to calm him down. I felt sorry

for him. He was only a kid and was probably scared to death—this one mistake could cost him his life.

Kimh slowly rolled him over on his back, covered his wound with a battle dressing, and buttoned his fatigue jacket.

The wound itself didn't look serious, but there was no telling what kind of damage had been done inside his stomach cavity. If the bullet had hit one of the main vessels he would die quickly. If it had ruptured his intestines he could die of infection. If we didn't get him to an American hospital his survival was a crap shoot. There were a lot of "if's."

"All we can do is try to control the pain and start an I.V.," I said. "If he's alive in thirty minutes he'll probably make it."

"I go now," Thach said.

"Tell Trung-si Cole I'll be back as soon as I finish here."

"Okay, Bac-si," Thach said as he and Kien headed back to the Third Platoon.

While Kimh endeavored to comfort Lieu, I continued suturing Ty's face.

Starting at the top right of the Y, I repeated the suturing procedure every quarter inch until finally putting in the last stitch at the base of the Y.

"How's that look?" I asked as I removed the patches from Ty's eyes.

Kimh leaned over. "It look good."

Kimh removed a signal mirror from his M-5 kit and handed it to Ty. He tilted the mirror a few times to examine the wound. He seemed pleased with our work.

"Tell him once the swelling goes down and the stitches are out he'll look great," I said as I covered the stitches with two-inch pieces of gauze and surgical tape.

When I finished, I removed the surgical gloves and took a long drink of water from my canteen. Kimh picked up a tube of opthalmic ointment and squeezed a little into each of Ty's red eyes.

"Hey, Kimh, you wouldn't have a cold Pepsi, would you?"

"I wish I did," Kimh said with a chuckle as he looked over at Lieu.

Suddenly the expression on his face turned serious.

"Bac-si, Thach feels very bad about Lieu."

"So do I."

"No, Bac-si. He is very sad. Lieu was afraid and he had to kick him and call him many bad names. Now maybe he will die."

"He was only doing his job," I said. "I'll talk to him."

After checking Luc's I.V., I squatted next to Lieu, and using Kimh to interpret, I promised that within a few hours we'd get him to an American hospital. We even managed to get a smile out of him when we told him that before he knew it he'd be eating hot American food and chasing beautiful nurses. Kimh laughed when he told him about the time he was med-evaced to the American M.A.S.H. hospital near Tay-Ninh.

Before leaving, I talked to Kimh about the possibility of hiding Luc and Lieu in some of the thick underbrush if it appeared we were going to be overrun. It would be risky, but there were no easy solutions. Kimh agreed and told me that he would draw a map of their location so that we could return after the battle to pick them up.

I was about ready to head back to the Third Platoon when a Bode from Duke's platoon dropped into the crater and said something to Kimh. Kimh told me that his name was Son and that a member of his squad had been shot in the head. After telling Son that I would go with him, I picked up my M-5 kit and followed him south through a maze of thorn-covered vines and tangled brush.

After about twenty meters of slow going we entered a sunny bamboo thicket with dense green bramble off to our right. As we wove our way through the thicket, dry pieces of dead and decaying stalks crushed beneath our feet. It was a strange war. Except for the melodic chirping and trilling of small birds overhead we were walking in solitude, while only a few meters away men were desperately fighting for their very survival.

"Whump, whump, whump . . ." An AK-47 opened up from behind a curtain of greens off to our right. I could see the bullets splintering a stand of bamboo just a few feet in front of me, and I had the strange, trancelike sensation that they were traveling in slow motion.

It only took me a split second to flick my selector switch to automatic as Son and I hit the ground behind a small hill. We hugged the ground as the AK continued firing with the brittle cracking sound of rounds chopping through the bamboo stalks around us. I considered throwing a grenade in the direction of the firing, but the wall of bamboo was just too thick—it would probably bounce back on us.

Son screamed something in Vietnamese and the firing stopped—it was silent again. I cautiously peered over the top of the mound, but all I could see was a mosaic of greens. Except for a smattering of gunfire coming from Duke's area, everything was still.

Suddenly I spotted movement—it looked like a white face. Firing a full magazine, I filled the air with tracers. There was a blood-curdling scream and the face disappeared. After I quickly changed my magazine, we jumped to our feet and rushed forward. I felt dangerously exposed, crashing through the bamboo thicket. I kept going even though I knew it was foolhardy. If he wasn't dead he had the clear advantage. What if it was a trick? What if there were more than one of them? With each step, my heart beat faster and faster.

A few meters into the thicket we found a Vietnamese soldier lying on the ground in twisted agony—his face and the front half of his neck had been blown away and loud guttural groans, blood, and scarlet foam poured from what once was his neck.

Son fired two quick shots into his chest and it was silent again. Son gathered up the dead man's weapons and web gear while I watched for any signs of movement—there were none.

"What did you yell?" I wanted to know. Son smiled.

"I Nguyen," he said, pointing to his chest. "I Vietnam, do not shoot."

We left the dead man where he'd fallen and continued in the direction of Duke's platoon. As we walked, I could hear the muffled whacking sound of choppers coming in from the south. Hopefully, they were bringing in reinforcements. As we reached the top of the hill the terrain thinned, and I spotted Duke's interpreter hunched over some bodies. Son and I ran forward and with a great sense of relief saw that they were enemy soldiers—they were wearing blue uniforms and pith helmets. There were about a dozen corpses scattered around the clearing, and Chote was checking them for anything of intelligence value. From what I could see most of them had been shot up pretty bad.

"Where's Duke?" I asked.

"Come, Bac-si." He motioned me to follow him.

When we reached the southern fringe of our perimeter I saw Duke kneeling behind a large fallen tree firing a captured AK-47. I squatted next to him and could see the backs of the retreating enemy about seventy-five meters away.

"Just returning his ammo to its rightful owners," Duke joked as he continued to fire. Looking south, I could see that for at least a hundred meters most of the foliage had been blown apart or burnt away. A few lingering hot spots were still smoldering, and the entire area was blanketed by a mantle of gray smoke and haze.

"How's it going, Jim?" he asked.

"Could be the calm before the storm," I said. "What did they hit you with?"

"At least a company, maybe more. They made two good runs at us," he said as he used his scarf to wipe the wetness from his face. "The Bodes held their fire until Charlie was twenty meters out, then let 'em have it with grazing fire and Claymores. We greased a lot of 'em, but some still got through."

"You're lucky they didn't roll up your flank."

"You're tellin' me. It was the weirdest thing I ever

saw," he said as he took a long swig from his canteen. "Once they broke through, they just stood there like they didn't know what to do next."

"That is strange. I figured 'em to be some pretty good troops."

"They just ran up the hill a ways and stopped. The Bodes caught 'em in a cross fire and blew 'em away. We got most of 'em, but there's still a few inside the perimeter."

"I know. We ran into one of 'em," I said.

"I'll tell ya, those sky jockeys did one hell of a job. They're my landscapers," he laughed, nudging his AK-47 toward the blackened jungle.

"Yeah, I don't think Charlie'll come through that area again."

"I'm gonna leave one squad to cover this area and move everyone else to cover the creek bed," he said.

"You know they'll hit there next," I said. "Hey, would you make contact with Fergy and tell him a Bode told me that Hagey was stranded outside the perimeter somewhere down on the southern end of his platoon."

"Sure, will do," he said as he picked up his radio handset.

"Bac-si," Son motioned for me to follow him.

"See ya later, Duke," I said as I stood up. He waved as he spoke into the handset.

As Son and I crept forward, we could hear the F.A.C.'s engine a couple of thousand feet above the canopy. The choppers that we had heard a few minutes earlier were now flying in what sounded like circular patterns a few hundred meters southwest of our position.

As we followed the southern edge of the perimeter, the Bodes were spaced five to ten paces apart and were busy taking advantage of the lull in the fighting. Some were digging holes while others were piling up pieces of trees in front of their positions. A few were feverishly cleaning their weapons.

About twenty-five meters down the line we were met by one of Duke's squad leaders. He led us to a

large cypress tree that was located just a few meters to
the rear of his position. Near its gnarled base I found
a wounded Bode lying in a fetal position on a blood-
covered poncho. I didn't know his name, but recognized him as one of the Bodes who had been with us
since Ho-Ngoc-Tao. He was a good friend of Danh's. I
assumed that his airway was partially blocked, because
every time he took a breath it sounded like he was
snoring. I laid my M-5 kit on the ground next to him.
Son told me that he and the squad leader would be on
the perimeter if I needed anything, and left.

I squatted next to the Bode and could see that he
was seriously wounded. Bloody saliva drooled from
the corner of his half-open mouth and pooled on the
poncho. The salty-sweet smell of fresh blood coating
the rubber poncho liner was repulsive. It had the same
smell as a body bag.

I looked him over and noticed that his jet-black hair
was matted with blood. Behind his left ear was a nickel-
sized bullet hole. In the shadowy tangle, smothered
under dim layers of twilight greens, I found it difficult
to see what I was doing. I needed to get him into a
sitting position, so I grabbed him under both arms and
dragged him off the poncho and propped him up against
the cypress trunk. The large ground roots formed a
perfect chair to cradle him in.

With him sitting against the tree in a semiconscious
state, I could see that the bullet had shattered the right
side of his jaw, passed through his mouth, then exited
behind his left ear. I couldn't tell if the bullet had
fractured or penetrated his skull. For his sake I hoped
that it hadn't. Jaw wounds were very painful and this
was no exception. I noticed that the platoon medic
had given him morphine and had attached the empty
syrette to his collar. Although morphine was our most
potent pain killer, it wasn't supposed to be used in the
case of head wounds because it tended to increase
pressure within the skull. It could also complicate his
breathing problems by further constricting his airway.

Using my pen flashlight, I checked his ears to see if
there was any clear cerebrospinal fluid draining from

them. It was a relief to see that there wasn't. When I checked his pupils, I found them both dilated and glazed with a fish-eyed look of shock.

When I tried to check his pulse, he started to gag and spit up blood. I stuck my finger into his mouth to make sure that it was clear and found it filled with what felt like pieces of bone and teeth. Putting my other hand under his chin, I pulled out pieces of a half-dozen or so teeth and the coughing stopped. If he was going to live, I'd have to figure out a way to stop the bleeding.

I was having trouble keeping him in a sitting position, so I straddled his legs and sat back on his knees. I tried to look inside his mouth, but found it too dark to see anything. In an attempt to get a better look at the damage, I pushed my pen flashlight partway into his mouth, and saw a mass of torn flesh, bone, and blood. It looked like the bullet had fractured his jaw, knocked out some teeth, ripped open his tongue, and gone up through the roof of his mouth before exiting behind his left ear. Most of the bleeding appeared to be coming from the hole in the roof of his mouth.

He was still having some difficulty breathing, but nothing life-threatening. However, I was concerned that his torn tongue could possibly swell up and constrict his airway. If that happened, I'd have to cut an emergency airway. My biggest problem right now was stopping the bleeding between the roof of his mouth and the exit wound. A pressure dressing wouldn't do any good, and I couldn't get inside the wound to tie off the bleeding vessels.

In an effort to get a better look at the roof of his mouth, I pushed the light a little bit deeper inside. He started to retch, his body jerked, and he heaved a warm bellyful of blood and vomit onto my face and chest. The taste of salty blood and the nauseating smell of vomit turned my stomach. The heat and humidity only intensified the experience. I should have known the probing would make him gag.

Shifting off his legs, I removed one of my canteens, poured some water into my cupped hands, and splashed it on my face. My scarf was covered with blood and vomit, so I untied it and tossed it away. Using about half a canteen of water, I then rinsed the front of my fatigue jacket. When I finished, I removed a green triangular bandage from the M-5 kit, dried my face with it, then tied it around my neck. After taking a couple of deep breaths and a drink of water, I was ready to go back to work.

When I looked at the wounded Bode leaning against the tree, I concluded that the only way I was going to be able to stop, or at least slow, the bleeding was to pack the space between the exit wound and the roof of his mouth with as much epinephrine-soaked gauze as possible. I figured that if epinephrine caused blood vessels to constrict when it was given intravenously, it might also cause the torn blood vessels to constrict when it came into contact with them. With the hole packed solid it might put enough pressure on the torn vessels to stop the bleeding.

I reached into my M-5 kit and removed a sterile suture set and unfolded it on the ground beside me. I then tore open a package of two-inch squares of gauze and dropped them into the stainless-steel emesis basin. Filling a syringe with epinephrine, I squirted it into the gauze. With a straight five-inch forceps, I then stirred them up to make sure that they were evenly soaked with the clear epinephrine solution.

I straddled his legs between my own to minimize movement. Then, holding his head against the tree with my left hand, I used my other hand to pick up a couple of two-by-twos with the forceps. I knew it was going to be a painful experience for him, but if it worked, it just might save his life.

With his head firmly against the tree, I slowly pushed the gauze into the hole behind his ear and carefully worked it deep into the wound—the deeper it went the more he groaned. When I thought that it might be getting close to the roof of his mouth, I stopped and, using my flashlight, took a look inside his mouth. There wasn't any sign of the gauze. After pushing it another quarter of an inch, I took another look and could see a little bit of the blood-soaked gauze and the silver tip of the forceps protruding through the hole in the roof of his mouth. With the first piece of gauze in place, I unclamped the forceps and removed it from his wound. So far so good, I thought to myself.

I picked up a couple more pieces of gauze and delicately worked them into the wound. Suddenly I sensed movement off to my right front. I froze. Was I seeing things, or was it another one of the V.C. who had broken through the perimeter? I debated whether or not I should make a dive for my M-16 a few feet away. But I decided not to move. With one hand over the Bode's mouth and the other holding the forceps, I scanned the dimly lit foliage for movement. I could have kicked myself for not keeping Son for security. After a long minute, I was convinced that there wasn't anyone there and resumed packing the wound. When the hole was packed as tight as I could make it, I covered the wound with a couple of dry pieces of gauze and wrapped his head with an ACE bandage. I looked back inside his mouth and was relieved to see that there wasn't any evidence of heavy bleeding.

When I finished, I turned his poncho over and, grabbing him under his arms, dragged him back onto it. I put him on his side with his face toward the ground so that if there was any more bleeding it would drain from his mouth. With that completed, I started a slow-dripping normal saline I.V. and gave him some penicillin and streptomycin. That was about all I could do for him. There were obvious limits to what you could do in the field. If he didn't lose any more blood, and if there wasn't any brain involvement, he'd probably pull through.

I then walked a short distance to the edge of the perimeter, and finding Son, asked him and another member of the First Platoon to carry the wounded Bode back to where Kimh could keep an eye on his airway.

While they cut a ten-foot section of green bamboo and tied a hammock to it, I filled out a medical card and attached it to the wounded Bode's jacket. After carefully moving him onto the hammock, they picked him up and carried him away.

Alone again, I began repacking my M-5 kit as I listened to the helicopter gunships tearing up the ground all along the eastern side of our perimeter. Chopper after chopper approached at tree-top level with the high-pitched "whirrr" of their machine guns, then beat away into the distance.

Under the relentless clamor of the chopper blades, I suddenly noticed that my ears had filled with a high-pitched ringing and the pressure in my head felt like it was going to explode. I didn't want to take anything that would dull my senses or put me to sleep, so I removed a couple of Darvon capsules from my kit and downed them with a drink of water. I then removed my signal mirror to take a close look at my dressing. There was no sign of any fresh bleeding, but everything to the left of my nose was stretched tight with edema and had turned black and blue. When I pressed my fingers against my face it felt like soft, spongy rubber.

NEWS CLIPPINGS

In Saigon American psychological warfare experts have drawn up a proposal to drop small transistor radios into Communist North Vietnam in order to get allied views across to the North Vietnamese people.
Eastern Sun (Malaysian Edition), July 18, 1967

A Band-Aid on a cancer. In the rare moments when he allows himself the luxury of despair, that is how Vice President Hubert H. Humphrey describes the Administration's urban development program.
St. Louis Post-Dispatch, July 18, 1967

Vietnamese Army, in reality, is deteriorating. Americans more and more are doing the fighting, of necessity. The trouble? Very incompetent leadership, an officer corps riddled by politics and a lack of ability.
U.S. News & World Report, July 24, 1967

Frank Robinson Fears He May Be Through For Season
Los Angeles Times, July 18, 1967

Vietnam Assembly approves ticket of Thieu and Ky.
Buffalo Evening News, July 18, 1967

COMBAT, 7:30 p.m. (7)
Los Angeles Times, July 18, 1967

The Americans inflicted heavy casualties on the North Vietnamese in two operations south of the demilitarized zone, U.S. High Command figures showed today.
The Guardian (Rangoon), July 18, 1967

Formation of a committee for Draft Resistance, a group

of 70 including folk singer Joan Baez, was announced in San Francisco.
Los Angeles Times, July 18, 1967

Sen. George McGovern (D-SD) will receive the third annual Estes Kefauver Award Saturday night from Californians for Liberal Representation at the Beverly Wilshire banquet. The award, to be presented by actor Robert Vaughn, is given to a legislator who speaks with "a courageous and independent voice in the vigilant pursuit of peace and justice."
Los Angeles Time, July 18, 1967

6

1535 Hours (3:35 P.M.)

The battle had seesawed around the perimeter for several hours. The only constant was the oppressive heat and humidity of an ever-watchful sun.

The time I'd spent patching up the wounded Bodes had removed me from the heart of the action, and I wanted an update on what was going on.

Not wanting to cut across the interior of our position, I decided to skirt along the southern edge of the perimeter before doglegging north. The scarves changed from blue to red as I reached the Third Platoon's sector. It felt good to be back with the Third Herd again.

The Bodes were still dug in along the east bank of the creek bed, firing pot shots and shouting catcalls and obscenities at the V.C. who, in turn, were sniping at them from the far bank. As I passed behind their positions, they waved and joked about my head. But I could tell from the broad grins on their faces that the little people were glad to see me alive.

About thirty meters into the Third Platoon's sector I found Bob, Thach, and Ly set up in a shallow trench located just a few meters east of the creek. It measured about ten feet long, two feet wide, and four feet deep. Bob was kneeling in the center of the trench with the radio handset pressed against his ear. Thach and Ly were to his right and were squeezing off well-aimed shots at enemy snipers hidden in the brush.

"Better keep down," Bob said as I jumped into the trench to his left and placed my medical kit on the lip behind me.

"Any word on my resupply?" I asked.

"Should be here in a few minutes," he said as he monitored the radio. "Can't do much till we get it. We're about out of everything."

"If they hit us now we'd be up the creek," I said.

Running out of ammunition and surrounded by the enemy had to be one of the worst feelings a person could experience. I wasn't that worried about being killed, but for some reason the thought of running out of ammunition scared the hell out of me. A few weeks earlier I had a nightmare about getting overrun. In the dream, I not only found myself out of ammunition but, as the V.C. closed in around me, I could only move in slow motion—like struggling underwater. I remember the Vietnamese screaming and firing and rounds spitting into the dirt all around me. I was fighting desperately to escape, when I bolted awake soaked in a cold sweat.

"Bob, can you think of anything worse than running out of ammo?" I asked as I rested my elbows on the ground in front of the trench and took up a good firing position.

"Oh, I don't know." He looked up and smiled. "Did you ever go into a public restroom to take a good shit and find there wasn't any toilet paper?"

"Yeah, you're right." I chuckled. Still, the specter of being overrun lingered in the back of my head.

"Bac-si, how Lieu do?" Thach asked with an anxious look etched into the lines of his face.

"If we med-evac him today he should make it."

We were all concerned about Lieu, but Thach's concern went much deeper. I could tell by the worry in his voice. I couldn't understand why he was so concerned about Lieu. Maybe there was more to it than I knew.

I glanced up and down the trench and noticed that it extended farther to my left but was congested with a tangle of leaves and vines.

"Let's make us some room here," I said as I lay my rifle on the ground, removed my K-Bar, and began cutting away the tightly packed vegetation. After slashing through four or five feet of growth, I hit the end of the trench and began tossing bundles of freshly cut foliage to the rear. I was scooping up one of the last armfuls of deadfall when I spotted something smooth and chalk-white partially submerged in the dirt and humus. I bent down to take a closer look when it hit me. It was a perfectly preserved human skull.

"Hey, Bob, look here," I said, displaying my discovery.

"What d'ya got?" he asked as he leaned over to look.

I picked it up and brushed off the dirt.

"A skull," I said.

"Think it's American?" he wanted to know.

"No, don't think so," I said, as I used my finger to pry dirt out of the eye sockets. "There's too much gold in his teeth. Probably an Oriental."

"Any other bones down there?" he asked.

I scraped the floor of the trench with my knife.

"No, nothing," I said. "You'd think there'd be part of a uniform or something. The pigs probably got 'em."

"Uh-huh, they can do a job on ya," Bob commented. "Hey, Jim, you sure this ain't a grave we're standing in?"

"Naw," I said as I rotated the skull in my hand and examined it. The possibility never crossed my mind, but the thought of setting up in someone's grave was a bit unnerving.

"Hey, take a look at this," I said as I handed him the skull. There was a perfectly round nickel-sized hole over the left eye and a large three-inch hole at the back of the skull.

"Looks to me like he took a round in the forehead." He handed the skull back to me. "Probably turned his brain to mush."

"He didn't feel a thing," I said as I stuck my finger in the hole.

"Lotta people could have died here," he said as he adjusted the squelch on the radio.

Looking at the skull, I found myself wondering who

he might have been. There was no way of knowing how long it had been buried, but my guess was that it had been there for many years. What a story it could tell—of past battles and forgotten dreams. Looking into the dirt-encrusted sockets, I had no way of knowing whether he had been friend or foe. I guess it didn't really matter now. For all I knew he could have died fighting the Viet-Minh, the French, or the Japanese—maybe he was Japanese. Maybe his remains would be the last returned home from World War II. When I thought about it, I realized that with our uniforms and flesh stripped away we all looked pretty much the same. We all return to dust. We all share the same last home.

Thinking back to when we first entered the area earlier that morning, I remembered wondering if we were the first human beings ever to set foot on this ground—now I knew that we weren't. There really wasn't anything new under the sun, not even here. Ours was at least the third battle to have taken place. The first was fought by those who dug the trench and the second by whoever called in the air strikes whose craters pockmarked the area.

There could have been more. It was hard to tell, the jungle had probably reclaimed many a hidden scar. For all I knew men could have been killing each other on this hill since the dawn of time. I thought to myself how intriguing it would be to return someday when the war had ended, as an archeologist. The thought of excavating the area also got me wondering if anyone would ever know of the men who had fought and died here. I knew it wasn't a Gettysburg or a Normandy or an Arlington, but it was a solemn resting place. No monuments would ever be erected in the solitude of this jungle, but somehow I felt that it was only fitting that they be remembered somehow, by someone.

"Hey, Jim." Bob's voice brought me back from my reflections. "You remember those two skeletons we found in that chopper over in Phuoc-Long Province?"

"Yeah, I wonder if they ever found out who they were."

"Sure they did," Bob said. "They keep everyone's dental records on file. They say no two people have the same teeth."

"Yeah. I've heard that."

That was a bizarre one. We'd been busting brush through thick jungle when right in the middle of nowhere we found what looked like a chopper in mint condition just resting on the jungle floor like it was on display. Examining the find, we could see two perfectly preserved skeletons through the Plexiglass. Still in their flight suits, strapped in at the controls, they looked as if they were still taking their job seriously. Everything was in such good condition that I half expected one of them to lift up his sun visor and say something like, "What took you so long?"

My thoughts were interrupted by the faint "thap, thap, thap" of a chopper approaching from the southwest.

"Fox Control, this is Swampfox. Over," a voice cracked over the radio.

"It's Major Gritz," Bob said.

"Bring it on in," I said, as I felt a surge of adrenaline recharging my body.

"Swampfox, this is Fox Control. If you follow a thirty-degree azimuth you'll come in right over us. Over," Lieutenant Condon radioed.

"Major Gri bring ammunition?" Thach asked.

"None too soon, old buddy." Bob beamed as he patted Thach on the back.

"Roger, Fox Control. Give me some smoke. Over," Gritz said.

"Swampfox, this is Fox Control. I'm throwing purple smoke. Over," Condon responded.

"Hey, Ly, put this in your ruck, will ya?" I asked as I handed him the skull.

"No, Bac-si," he said with a wide-eyed look, shook his head, then retreated to the far end of the trench. He was visibly shaken. For some reason it spooked him. Maybe it was some sort of superstition. Bob raised his eyebrows and gave a "don't ask me" look.

"Here, give it to me," Bob said as he extended his hand. "I'll take it back." I handed it to him and he reached to the rear of the trench and stuffed it into his rucksack.

The Bodes were a strange group. Things that would terrify the average American didn't phase them a bit, while things such as this could scare the hell out of them. I remembered the time on an earlier mission when one of the Americans killed a large python. That limp snake shook them up so badly they could barely function.

"How's the radio battery holding up?" I asked Ly.

"Good, Bac-si." He nodded.

"You got any extras?"

"Two."

"Good."

I wanted to change the subject as quickly as possible because I knew that fear could be contagious. If it got hold of him, it could spread like a wildfire around the perimeter. The resonant slap-thumping sound of the chopper blades grew louder as they neared our position.

"Heads up," I yelled as it passed by overhead. I looked up, half expecting a cascade of ammo crates to come crashing through the canopy.

"Whoomp, whoomp, whoomp . . ." The measured staccato of a Chinese fifty-one-caliber machine gun boomed away somewhere west of our position.

Hoping to get an azimuth on it, I grabbed the compass that hung around my neck and raised it to eye level, but when I glanced down to take a reading, I found that the glass was coated with dried blood and I couldn't read its numbers.

"We're taking fire," Gritz radioed as the chopper banked sharply and veered off to the northeast.

I used my fingernail to scrape off the dried blood, then took a quick azimuth on the machine gun.

"Swampfox, this is Fox Control. Did you make your drop?" Condon wanted to know.

"That's a negative, Fox Control. There's too much smoke down there to get an exact fix on your location. Give me a flare on my next pass. Over."

"Roger, Swampfox."

"He's gonna shoot a naval flare up through the

trees," Bob said as he continued to monitor the transmissions.

"If that doesn't work I could send up a few tracers," I said. "Hey, I've got a two-hundred-eighty-degree azimuth on that machine gun."

"Good," Bob said. "As soon as the F.A.C. gets back up we'll try to take it out."

"Here he comes again," I said as the pounding of the blades homed in from the northeast. "He'd better watch out for that fifty-one."

As the sound of the chopper grew louder, I crossed my fingers. If he stayed at tree-top level he'd probably make it. Any higher and he'd be blown out of the sky.

"Fox Control, this is Swampfox," Gritz radioed. "I've got your flare. Over."

"Roger, Swampfox."

"Whoomp, whoomp, whoomp . . ." The fifty-one opened up again on the chopper

"He's comin' in low and fast," I yelled under the din of the chopper rotor.

"Heads up," Bob yelled as everyone looked skyward.

The chopper was overhead and gone in a split second. As the "thap, thap, thapping" of the rotor blades faded into the distance boxes of ammunition tumbled through the canopy, snapping small branches. Up and down the line, the Bodes jumped to their feet and cheered. A few of the boxes slammed into the ground to the rear of the Third Platoon, but the others overshot our position and landed on the far side of the creek. If they were kicked out of the chopper doors right over the flare, the speed of the chopper must have thrown them forward.

Moments after they hit the ground, the volume of fire coming from both sides of the creek picked up again. A few enemy troops could be seen leap-frogging in the direction of the boxes.

"If we don't get those boxes it'll be all she wrote. You and Ly cover us," Bob said as he and Thach jumped out of the trench and sprinted across the creek bed in a zigzag pattern.

As they dodged in and out from behind trees, Ly

and I lay down a base of suppressing fire on the few
V.C. we could see. Although my tracers appeared to
be right on target, I couldn't tell for sure if I was
hitting them. I could see by the way Charlie was going
after the boxes he must have sensed that we were
running low on ammunition.

Bob only had a few meters to go before he reached
a box when a bright orange flash exploded at the base
of a tree just behind him. By the time the sound of the
concussion reached me, Bob had been picked up and
blown forward like a rag doll.

"RPG!" Ly yelled as we jumped to our feet.

The thought of Bob being torn apart by shrapnel
must have paralyzed me for a split second, but by the
time his chest hit the ground, I found myself rushing
toward him. When I reached the creek bed he had
rolled on his side and through a cloud of blue-gray
smoke was waving that he was okay. The blast had
bowled him over, but miraculously the shrapnel had
missed him.

When I saw that Bob was all right, I hit the ground
behind a large tree and continued firing. After squeezing off a few rounds, Ly sprinted past me. When he
reached Bob and Thach, the three of them began
searching the underbrush for more ammo crates. I saw
Bob pointing at something, and then the three of them
disappeared into the vegetation. About a minute had
passed when they burst through the curtain of green-
ery. Bob had a box hefted onto his left shoulder and
was firing staggered bursts behind him as he scrambled
back. Ly and Thach each had a box under their arms.

From my vantage point, I could see that they were
headed in the wrong direction. I jumped to my feet and
yelled to them, but they couldn't hear me over the
noise of the battle. I feared that if they continued any
farther to my right the Bodes down the line would
spot the movement in the underbrush and open fire.
We'd lost a lieutenant in a similar incident and I didn't
want a repeat of that tragedy.

As a last resort, I rested my M-16 against the trunk
of a tree and fired a fluorescent stream of red tracers

about waist-high a couple of meters in front of them. It caught their attention and they began running in my direction.

As they ran, I watched for enemy movement but couldn't see any. When they were almost back to my position, I spotted two blue uniforms coming out of the thick vegetation near where they found the boxes. I let them take a few steps into the clearing, then emptied a magazine. By the time the last casing flew free they had disappeared. I wasn't sure if I'd killed them or if they just dove for cover.

Once Bob, Thach, and Ly were safely back across the creek I fired a couple of more shots into the area where the two V.C. went down and ran to the rear. By the time I caught up with them, they were back in the trench soaked in sweat and gasping for air.

"Whew, that was close," Bob said, still trying to catch his breath.

"You okay?" I asked.

"Yeah, just a little sore. There was a loud 'pop,' and the next thing I remember was flying."

"I don't see how that shrapnel missed you," I said, shaking my head in amazement. "You sure you're not pulling a Frank Hagey on me?"

"Yeah, Jim, I'm sure I'm okay. Must be my lucky day."

Thach put his arm around Bob and smiled a big-toothed smile.

"Trung-si Cole number one," he said.

"Number one," Ly added as he raised his index finger.

"Hey, you guys did a great job," I said.

"Sure did," Bob added. "I appreciate it," he said as he bent over and kissed Thach's ear.

"Number ten," Thach quipped as he wiped his ear with his sleeve in embarrassment and rolled his eyes.

Bob, Ly, and I couldn't control ourselves and were laughing so hard that we could barely stand up.

"I open boxes," Thach grunted as he climbed out of the trench and began moving the boxes to the rear, trying to ignore us.

"Let's get serious," Bob said. "There's more out there. We're gonna have to go out again."

As I listened to Bob, it suddenly registered that something was wrong—his eyes had a glazed look. The concussion from the explosion must have hurt him more than he was admitting.

"You're not looking too good," I said. "You'd better stay here this time. Ly and I'll get what's left."

"Look who's talkin' about lookin' good," he said. "Look, there's one box in the area where we went the last time. I'll pick that one up and you check the area off to the left."

"Okay, let's do it."

As soon as we reached the far side of the creek, I broke off to my left front and clambered up a gradual incline, searching the jungle patterns for signs of the enemy and ammunition crates. Occasional shots muttered off to my left and right, but as far as I could tell no one was shooting at me. When I was about thirty meters into Charlie's turf, I noticed three soldiers running through the brush from right to left about twenty-five meters ahead of me. No sooner had I spotted their movement when one of them spotted me in turn. I fired at least a dozen rounds at them, then dove to the ground before they could return fire—I think I got two of them. Just as I hit the ground, a long burst of automatic fire stitched the ground a few inches to my right. As each round impacted, it kicked up chunks of moist soil, then settled back upon itself. I couldn't see where the fire was coming from, but it sounded like it was coming from somewhere in the trees.

I was on relatively open ground, so I quickly rolled a few meters to my left and took up a position behind a tree. The blood was pounding in my ears as I searched the branches for a sniper, but I couldn't see anyone in the sea of greens and blue sky patches in the canopy.

"Whump, whump, whump . . ." A second burst whacked into the trunk just above my head, pelting me with bark and pulp. But this time I spotted the orange muzzle flashes and the partial silhouette of the sniper half hidden in the branches of a large cypress about twenty meters in front of me. I quickly lined up my front sight blade on the shadow and fired what was left in my magazine. There was a scream, a figure tumbled out of the tree, and a body hit the jungle floor with a hollow thud.

After slipping a fresh magazine in and chambering a round, I rose to my feet and strained to see any movement in the bushes around the base of the tree, but it was too thick. I was about to move forward again when another shot was fired from higher up in the same tree. Without aiming, I sprayed the tree with tracers and then dove into some thick ferns further to my left. Figuring that I was already too far into enemy territory, I decided to crawl a little bit farther to my left and then start working my way back to the platoon.

After crawling several meters through a wall of rotting leaves and congested vines, I realized I was forming a molelike tunnel as I plowed forward. The mottled leaves were of every size and shape. Some were long and narrow, some heart-shaped, while others were two to three feet long and over a foot in diameter. They were bunched together in various stages of decomposition, filling the stagnant air with the moist compost smell of decaying matter.

Using my hands and my M-16 to part the leaves, I had moved about fifteen meters when my hand touched someone. The unexpected contact sent jolts of adrenaline stabbing into my system and overwhelmed me with such an icy fear that I cut lose with my M-16, sending a flurry of leaves flying in all directions. As the rounds blew away the layers of vegetation, I saw that it was a leg—but that was all. It had been severed just below the hip with a clean cut, its white bone protruding through the flesh like a shank of meat in a butcher shop.

By the time I inserted a fresh magazine, I'd regained my composure and detoured around the leg. I'd crawled a few meters more when I ran into freshly dug dirt. I paused and listened. I could hear something that sounded like whimpering up ahead. Finally it dawned on me—I was on the edge of a bomb crater.

From where I was lying, I could tell that the crying was coming from inside the depression. I couldn't see inside, but on the far side of the rim I spotted a box of ammunition lying on the soft dirt. The opposite rim of the crater came into view as I cautiously raised my head. I could see a pith helmet lying on the reverse slope but no sign of whoever was crying—he must have been just below me.

With my finger on the trigger, I peeked over the edge of the brim and saw the jet-black hair and shoulders of someone lying on his back. My first instinct was to squeeze a round into him, but the thought of taking him prisoner prevented me; besides, I had him cold.

With my rifle pointed at the top of his head, I slowly rose to my knees and called, "Dung lai!" If I remembered my Vietnamese it meant don't move! He didn't move but continued moaning and crying. I wasn't sure, but by the plaintive tone in his voice, it sounded like he was calling for his mother.

I extended my head over the crater's edge and my nostrils filled with the overpowering stench of death. I could feel the vomit rising in my throat as I fought back the urge to gag. The last time I'd smelled anything that bad was when a V.C.'s body was blown apart by a booby trap during the Black Box operation. I kept my rifle trained on his head while I scooted a little to my right, then slid on my rear down the inside slope. When I got even with him the sight of his wound took my breath away—everything from his waist down had been blown away. It looked as though someone had dumped a pile of Franco-American spaghetti down the slope beneath him. The blast had cut him in half, spilling his insides out on the ground. I'd seen a lot of bad wounds but nothing like this—I found it unbelievable that he was still alive.

He appeared to be only about seventeen years old. He had a boyish, clean-shaven face and a fresh haircut. He had a taut, waxen look on his face, but his brown eyes were alive and followed my every movement.

I considered applying a tourniquet but realized that

it wouldn't do any good. He was still breathing and alert, but he was really dead.

I looked at him with pity. He pleaded with me in Vietnamese—I think he was begging me to kill him. I nodded that I understood, moved closer, then raised my M-16 to his right temple. A couple of ounces of pressure on the trigger and he'd be out of his misery.

As he closed his eyes in anticipation, I couldn't help notice the large tears running down his dust-covered cheeks. A couple of minutes earlier I could have killed him in a heartbeat, but now I couldn't pull the trigger. He was just a boy lying there in his shattered manhood crying for his mother.

He opened his eyes and looked at me.

"Xin-loi." I told him that I was sorry. He was no longer the enemy, but a human being not so different from myself.

I removed a canteen from my belt and poured a little water on his lips. He didn't make any effort to swallow and let the water run down the side of his face into the dirt.

Although we had exchanged only a few words, I felt that something more had occurred, something deeper. You probably couldn't call it friendship, but it was intimate. Nothing like this had ever happened to me before. Whatever it was, I felt a strange mixture of joy and sorrow. Maybe we had touched something in common, had shared something.

"I've got to get that box back to the platoon," I thought as I removed my scarf. After pouring some water on it I used it to cover his eyes.

"Bac-si," a voice called.

"Over here," I yelled as I clawed my way out of the soft dirt, picked up the box of ammunition, and headed in the direction of the voice—it was Thach.

"You go too long, Bac-si," he said.

I followed him back toward the platoon and at the creek's edge we were met by Ly.

"I think V.C. sac mau you," he said as he ran his index finger across his throat and grabbed the box from me.

"Almost, my friend," I said.

The three of us ran to an area a few meters behind the trench where we found Bob filling his magazines.

"You get lost?" Bob asked as I knelt on the ground next to him.

"We'd better get some of this stuff over to Stik," I said. "His people are pretty low."

"Yeah," Bob said. "You get a count on the boxes."

Thach and Ly lined up the boxes on the ground in front of us while I made a quick inventory. From what I could see we had a total of twelve.

"We've got six boxes of M-16 ammo, two boxes of Claymores, two boxes of M-60, and two of M-79," I said.

"Good, that should last us a while," Bob commented.

"What do you say we send one box of 16's to Stik, one to Fergy and Frank, two to Duke, and we'll keep two?"

"Sounds good," Bob said as he rose to his feet. "They'll probably hit us and Duke next. Go ahead and evenly divide the rest among the four platoons."

"Okay," I said.

"You and Thach pass it out," he said. "I'm gonna give the Lieutenant an update."

As Bob and Ly headed back to the radio I began breaking open some of the boxes. Thach got a couple of men from each squad to carry the ammunition around to the other three platoon sergeants.

"We give one box to Trung-si Sau Lam?" Thach asked as he handed a box to one of the Bodes.

"Yeah," I laughed. "Give one to Sau Lam."

Trung-si Sau Lam was a nickname that the Bodes had given to Stik Rader because he worked them so hard during training back at Trang-Sup. My best guess was that it meant "Sergeant No Good." They liked Stik a lot, and it was their way of joking with him.

After Thach got all of the ammunition out to the platoons, Son came by to pick up his share of 7.62's for his M-60. I always tried to avoid eyeball-to-eyeball contact with him because he was the most cross-eyed person I'd ever seen—just looking at him was enough to make you dizzy. I never could figure how he did it, but he could lay down a base of fire like no one I'd ever known. Somehow it seemed to enhance his depth perception.

A few minutes later Bob returned, and he, Thach, and I sat on the ground filling the last of our empty magazines. When Bob leaned forward to pick up some ammo, I noticed that his rear end was soaked with a large splotch of blood.

"Hey, you've been hit," I said as I laid my M-16 on the ground, jumped to my feet, and squatted next to him.

"What?" he said in disbelief.

I grabbed him by the arm.

"You've been hit in the rear," I responded.

He turned to look and appeared shocked to see the blood. When he touched the area the palm of his hand turned blood-red.

"Take off your harness and drop your drawers," I said. "Thach, get me the M-5 kit."

Thach returned with the medical kit and set it on the ground next to me, just as Bob finished unbuttoning his trousers.

"What d'ya see?" Bob wanted to know as he dropped his trousers in a pile around his ankles. He looked pretty awkward standing half-naked in the jungle while I examined his buttocks.

From what I could see, he'd caught a piece of shrapnel in the right cheek—it didn't look too serious.

"RPG," Thach said as he looked at the quarter-inch gash in Bob's skin

"Yeah, looks like you caught a piece of the RPG after all," I said. "Does it hurt?"

"My whole backside aches, but nothin' that bad," he said. "What d'ya think?"

"Well, I'll tell you one thing. You won't be sitting down on the job for a while." I chuckled.

"C'mon, Jim, this is serious! What d'ya think?"

"Ah, it doesn't look bad," I said. "Most of the bleeding has stopped. It depends on how deep it went."

I gently pressed my finger against the wound, but couldn't feel anything hard.

"If it's lodged in the fat or muscle you shouldn't have any trouble with it."

"Good. Cover it up," he said.

"When we get back to Trang-Sup you're gonna have to have it X-rayed," I said as I covered it with a couple of two by two's and tape. "They may have to surgically remove it."

"We'll worry about that later," he said.

After I gave him shots of penicillin and streptomycin, he returned to the trench while Thach and I finished reloading the last of our magazines.

"Bac-si, I must tell you," Thach said as he grabbed my arm. The intensity in his voice surprised me. His face was a study of conflicting emotions.

"Tell me what?" I asked as I pushed a round into a magazine.

"I not tell anyone."

"Tell anyone what?" I asked, looking into his blood-shot eyes.

"Lieu, Bac-si. He is son of my sister."

"I didn't know." No wonder he was so shook up about him getting hurt.

"Her husband, he die at Dong-Xoia. Now maybe Lieu die."

"I'm sorry, Thach," I said as I put my hand on his shoulder. "We'll get him to an American hospital and he'll get the best treatment in the world."

"Thank you, Bac-si."

"Look, my friend, it's not your fault. You're the best damn platoon sergeant in Vietnam. If it wasn't for you, we'd all be dead. Every man in this platoon owes you his life."

I could see that his eyes were welling with tears.

"In the meantime Kimh'll keep an eye on him," I added.

"Okay, Bac-si," he said.

I snapped my ammo pouches shut and we both headed back to the trench.

NEWS CLIPPINGS

From left, the prisoners are Sgt. Isaac Comancho, Sgt. Kenneth Roraback, Sgt. Claude McClure and Sgt. George Smith. Comancho later escaped, Roraback was shot, McClure and Smith were freed.
Life, July 21, 1967

Sinatra—to any soldier with more than 18 months in service the name would have flashed to mind the great, golden-voiced holdover from bobbysox days—Frankee. But to more than 100,000 troops who ogled while the latest Sinatra stomped her boots at 17 different Vietnam sites, the word now has another reaction—Nancy.
Army Digest, July 1967

Official statistics show that the burden of fighting in South Vietnam has recently passed decisively to American troops. A study of casualty lists since the first of the year showed that while more South Vietnamese troops were killed in the first weeks of January, the situation is now reversed, even though government forces outnumber American troops by about 200,000.
Courier Express (Buffalo), July 18, 1967

Sides registering greatest proportionate upward progress this week.
1. Windy. . . .The Association
2. Can't Take My Eyes Off You. . . Frankie Valli
3. Light My Fire. . . .Doors
Billboard, July 22, 1967

President Marcos' trip to South Vietnam has assured a

continuing role for the Philippines to preserve freedom in the embattled nation, Manila newspapers said today.
Eastern Sun (Malaysian Edition), July 18, 1967

Sean Connery Is James Bond "You Only Live Twice"
The New York Times, July 18, 1967

Gustav Crane Hertz is the highest-ranking American to be taken prisoner by the Vietcong. His kidnapping in February 1965 drew only brief attention. But now, 30 months later, he is still missing and a growing cause celebre.
Life, July 21, 1967

Honeymooners—Kramden (Jackie Gleason) finds suitcase full of money and goes on a spree.
Buffalo Evening News, July 18, 1967

American C-130 transport planes carried 150 Congolese paratroopers to Kisangani in pursuit of an estimated 180 rebel mercenaries.
Los Angeles Times, July 18, 1967

7

1620 Hours (4:20 P.M.)

The midday heat had hovered in place for several hours, but now began its first tentative steps toward the night. Shadows were already lengthening as the sun arched into Cambodia. Across the jungle, sunlight angled through holes in the canopy, creating a mesmerizing effect as dust and haze danced through the light.

Everything in the Third Herd's sector appeared to be under control, so I told Bob that I was going to see if Fergy and Frank's platoon was experiencing any major medical problems. I had a gut feeling that Mr. Charles was getting ready for an all-out attack on our side of the perimeter and I wanted to be able to get back before they hit.

The Second Platoon was defending much of our eastern flank, so I just followed a ninety-degree azimuth across the interior of the perimeter until I spotted their yellow scarves. When I reached their side of the perimeter I immediately made contact with a couple of Bodes who were dug into a shallow fox hole. They told me that Fergy was set up just a short distance south of their position.

Moving down the line, I could see the results of the fighting that had taken place—enemy bodies, discarded ammunition boxes, and medical-supply containers littered the jungle floor. I had to step over many of the smaller trees in the area that had been toppled by high-velocity rounds. After moving about twenty meters, I spotted Fergy and his radio operator lying in a depression that measured about three meters across, ten meters long, and a half meter deep. The area was heavily shaded by large three-story trees and thick vegetation close to the ground. Fergy was the team's intelligence specialist. With his tall, lanky body, white skin, and sandy brown hair, he stood out like a sore thumb.

"Get down, J.C.," he yelled. "They'll get ya."

I immediately hit the ground and began crawling the last few meters. I couldn't help smiling when I saw that he had a large nylon American flag tied to a tree branch just to the rear of the depression.

"I ought to kick your ass," I said jokingly as I crawled into the depression and took up a position next to him. "Are you the one who developed the intel for this operation?"

"Hey, babe, don't blame me," he answered. "When we were back at Quan-Loi, some light colonel told Condon that it takes a long time to deploy a brigade."

"Think he was trying to tell us something?"

"No shit."

"Did ya get the ammo?" I asked.

"Yeah, but at this rate—"

"Whump, whump, whump . . ." The stutter of automatic fire interrupted us somewhere from the east. We hugged the ground as the rounds lashed the air overhead, bullwhipping through the foliage.

"Damn Cong!" Fergy snarled as we lay face-to-face in the dirt.

"Ya know, that flag's probably attracting fire like flies to a hog," I said.

"I'm sick of all this clandestine bullshit," Fergy said as he raised his head and fired a burst in retaliation. "I want those bastards to know who they're up against." He smiled. "If the shit really gets deep, I've got my beret in my rucksack."

"I've got mine too." I laughed with a feigned bravado in my voice."

"D'ya really?" Fergy replied, taken aback that I'd done the same thing.

"Yeah. It's in a plastic bag in the top of my ruck."

The machine gun stopped firing and we slowly raised our heads. Fergy pointed out that the firing was coming from a position about thirty meters east of us. The gun was firing from behind a tree stump that was located on the far side of a small clearing. With 'its bark stripped away, the stump looked almost white in the jungle light.

"Enough is enough," Fergy said. "I'm gonna try to take 'im out from the rear."

"Hold on," I said as I grabbed him by his ammunition harness. "Let's try something else first before you go off half-cocked."

"The brush is too thick to get at him with an M-79," he responded.

"What about air?"

"We've already called in two or three strikes on that area."

"We've got a couple of captured RPG's we could try," I suggested.

"No, there's only one way to do it," he said. "I'm gonna get a couple of Bodes to go with me."

"Okay, okay, but pop some smoke when ya get into position," I said. "We don't wanna grease your ass."

He nodded and crawled off to our right. As he crawled out of the depression another Bode from the Second Platoon dropped in, wincing in pain. He'd been shot in the ankle and the bone was shattered. While I checked his wound Fergy's radio operator began firing well-aimed rounds from a captured AK-47 at the area around the stump.

The bullet had passed all the way through both sides of the ankle. The nylon webbing of his jungle boot had turned black with caked blood and dirt, but most of the bleeding appeared to have stopped. I thought about removing his boot but figured I'd never get it back on again.

"Whump, whump, whump . . ." Another burst lashed the jungle overhead, but as long as we kept flat he couldn't hit us.

When the firing stopped, I removed a couple of battle dressings and an Ace bandage from my M-5 kit.

After giving him a syrette of morphine and loading him up with penicillin and streptomycin, I covered the entrance and exit wounds with the dressings and wrapped his ankle with the Ace. As soon as I got a chance, I'd improvise a bamboo splint that would extend a couple of inches below the heel of his boot. He'd probably be able to walk on it if he had to. It was a little awkward working in a prone position, but at least it kept us out of the line of fire.

"Bac-si," the radio operator called. I looked up and saw a knotted plume of red smoke billowing up in front of the white stump. I picked up my M-16 and took up a position next to the radio operator. Through the smoke, I suddenly saw the shadowy outline of figures moving behind the stump.

"Hold your fire," I said as I took up the slack on my trigger.

The frantic "whack, whack, whack . . ." of an M-16 opened up as two Bodes and Fergy bolted through the smoke and into the clearing. Once out of the smoke they hesitated for a second, then began running in our direction. It looked as though Fergy was carrying someone slumped over his shoulders.

I jumped to my feet, ran forward about ten meters, and took up a position behind a tree on our side of the clearing. If there was an enemy soldier anywhere along the edge of the clearing he'd have a clear shot at them.

As they scrambled toward me, I had the helpless feeling that they were about to be blown away.

"C'mon on, Fergy!" I yelled. "Move it, move it!"

"I got one," he yelled as he approached.

"You crazy bastard, are you out of your gourd?" I yelled as we ran the last few yards together.

"I didn't have time to go the long way," he said. "They're getting ready to come at us again."

When we reached the depression, he flopped the black-clad soldier on the ground next to the wounded Bode and then dropped to his knees out of breath.

"Whew! I'm not as young as I used to be," he gasped.

"You may be getting older but you sure as hell ain't getting any smarter," I added.

"Hey!" Fergy yelled as the wounded Bode began kicking the prisoner in the ribs with his good foot and screaming something I couldn't understand.

Fergy and I dragged them apart. I looked into the soldier's terror-filled face and could see that he was convinced that we were going to kill him. Fergy lit a cigarette and handed it to the prisoner, trying to calm him down, but the V.C. continued to follow the Bode's every move. His face and right shoulder were covered with blood, but other than that, he appeared to be in pretty good shape.

"What a break," I said to myself as I looked at his shoulder. He could provide us with some valuable information.

"I got to within five yards of him before he saw me," Fergy said. "I had to knock him down with a shoulder shot. He had a spider hole behind the stump, and every time we tried to take him out he just jumped into it."

"Who says someone else ain't gonna use that same hole?" I asked.

"I buried two toe poppers in it," he answered. "No one's gonna use it for a while."

"What happened to his face?" I asked. He looked a little worse for wear. His right cheek was red and puffy, one eye nearly swollen shut, and sticky blood caked in the clefts of his nostrils and upper lip.

"He wasn't all that enthused about comin' with me." Fergy gave a sardonic smile. "I had to butt stroke 'im."

I watched Fergy give the prisoner a drink of water and felt a great sense of accomplishment because, for us, it was a war of few prisoners. None of our men ever surrendered, and the few Viet-Cong we captured were usually wounded.

"Trung-si," the radio operated shouted.

A sting of prickly heat rushed up my spine when I turned to see a line of black, pajama-clad Viet-Cong coming at us from the far side of the clearing. Adrenaline shot into my system and my heart rate doubled as the ripple of muzzle flashes flickered through the scattered foliage. I threw myself to the ground, flipped the selector switch to full automatic, and sighted in on the onrushing tide.

Out of the corner of my eye I also saw the wounded Bode raise his M-16 in the direction of the prisoner, but before I could yell "no!" he fired. The round hit the V.C. in the back of the head and exploded through the front of his face in a crimson spray of blood, brain, and bone fragments. He was dead by the time he slumped to the ground even though his feet continued to twitch in nervous spasms.

I was furious and felt like smashing the Bode's head in, but the V.C. line was only twenty meters out and closing fast.

I lined up my front sight blade on the closest target and began firing two- and three-round bursts about chest-high. Out of the corner of my eye, I spotted what looked like a black baseball coming right at me. It quickly grew larger and a split second later passed a foot over my head and exploded somewhere behind us. It must have been a Chinese rifle grenade.

Above the roar of rifle fire and explosions I could hear screaming and yelling. Fergy yelled something at me, but with all the noise I couldn't understand a word.

When the enemy was only a few steps away I fired the last round in my magazine and let out a loud "Tay-yoo" as I sprang to my feet. Someone immediately ran into me with tremendous force and knocked the breath out of me. I fell backward and somehow landed on my chest with someone on top of me—it was a V.C. With all of my strength I twisted and hit him in the jaw with my elbow. He let out a grunt that followed the crack of his jaw. I rolled to my back with him on top of me and was shocked to see how old he was. He had a cracked, weatherbeaten face the consistency of parchment paper, yellow rotting teeth and a few scraggly white whiskers hanging from his chin. He clutched my fatigues at the shoulder, squeezing and twisting with his clenched fist, screaming at me in shrill Vietnamese as he desperately clawed at my throat with his other hand.

I couldn't reach his eyes, so I grabbed his Adam's apple with my right hand and tried to tear the windpipe out of his scrawny neck. He started to gag and cough a foul, fish-smelling breath into my face. I could feel him cutting the left side of my neck.

"A knife," I thought. "He's gonna cut my throat!" I let go of his neck, grabbed his right arm with both hands and pushed it away from my throat.

My God, his right hand had been shot off just above his wrist and a piece of sharp white bone extended through the bloody stump. He was trying to drive the bone into my throat!

"Whack!" A deafening shot exploded a couple feet from my left ear and the enemy soldier flew off my chest and out of my hands as if he'd been hit with a wrecking ball. I turned and saw that it was the wounded Bode who had fired the shot. Looking back to our front, I could see that the attack had been broken and that a couple of Bodes were already checking the enemy dead. I got to my feet and felt so dizzy I sidestepped and nearly fell back to the ground. I bent over to pick up my M-16 when I heard a raspy groan. The old V.C. let out a tired sigh and died. The quiet returned.

"You all right, J.C.?" Fergy asked, placing his hand on my shoulder.

"Yeah," I said as I bent over with my head lowered to the ground for a couple of seconds.

"Bac-si," the wounded Bode called in a soft voice. I turned and saw that he'd been hit again. This time it looked like a flesh wound about halfway between his left wrist and elbow. I removed another battle dressing from my M-5 kit, knelt next to him, and began tying it over the wound.

"V.C. number ten." He spat contemptuously.

I'd just finished working on his arm when I felt something warm sliding down the left side of my neck.

"My damned wound is leaking again," I said to

Fergy as I reached up and felt that some of my bandage had unraveled during the scuffle.

"You want me to put on a new Ace?" he asked.

"Yeah, will ya get one out of the kit?" I asked. I sat on the ground and began removing the layers of old bandage. I still felt a little weak. As I unraveled the Ace it released the pressure on the wound and I could feel fresh rivulets of blood draining down my neck and chest. As soon as I got it off Fergy knelt next to me and began applying the new one.

"Get it as tight as you can," I said.

I found myself looking at the old Viet-Cong papa san as Fergy wrapped my head. Staring into his lifeless eyes, I felt a sense of tragedy. Maybe it had something to do with him being an old soldier. He'd probably been fighting all his life, and it had come down to this. I also found myself wondering if he was still aware of what was going on around him. I knew he was dead, but who says that your brain and eyes stop working as soon as your heart stops beating?

"That should hold ya, J.C.," Fergy said as he finished trying the bandage.

"It looks like the swelling is getting worse," he added as he used his finger to gently press on the puffiness around my left eye. It was swollen completely shut. With Fergy finished, I picked up my M-16 and M-5 kit.

"You see Frank?" I asked.

"Not since we first made contact. Last I heard, he and the machine-gun section were down at the other end of the platoon," he said as he knelt next to his radio and picked up the handset.

"Well, I'm gonna see if I can find him," I said. "Will ya give Bob a call and tell him I'll be back in a little bit?"

"Sure, J.C.," he said. "If you see Frank tell him to get his ass up here."

"Okay, I'll catch you later, Fergy," I said as I headed off down the line.

"Hey, J.C." Fergy smiled. "Stop in anytime."

"Forget it. I ain't ever visiting you again."

Moving down the line, I could see that the Bodes were taking advantage of the lull in the fighting. Some were busy cleaning their weapons, fortifying their positions, or scarfing down some rations, while others were just stretched out on the ground taking a much-needed break.

I looked for Frank and I thought about the loss of the prisoner. At first I had felt disappointment and anger, but my anger passed as I came to realize that if the Bode hadn't killed him he just might have been able to change the outcome of the assault. If he'd been able to tie up just one of the four of us for a couple of seconds it would have reduced our fire power by twenty-five percent. As close as things turned out, it could have been the cutting edge between life and death for everyone involved.

When I reached the end of the Second Platoon's sector, my concern mounted when I couldn't find Frank. When the platoon scarves changed from yellow to blue I really became worried. A couple of Duke's Bodes told me that they hadn't seen Frank, so I backtracked until I hit the yellow scarves again. After talking to a few Bodes, I found one who spoke some English. He pointed south and told me that Frank was down by the creek. I checked my map and couldn't figure out what he was doing that far outside the perimeter. With all the enemy activity in the area, he could easily be cut off and captured. I sensed that his life was in grave danger.

Going outside the perimeter again wasn't something I relished doing, but with Frank without a radio there weren't any other options. After telling the Bode to pass the word that I was going out, I took a compass heading in the direction he gave me and started out. I took an azimuth because when I was ready to return I'd be able to take a back azimuth and, I hoped, reenter the perimeter at the exact same spot. It was easy to get disoriented in the thick jungle, and reentering the perimeter in another location could be lethal.

A few meters outside, I had entered a thicket of leafy bamboo when I heard a few shots farther south—it had to be Frank. The more I thought about the situation, the more anxious I became. I had no idea who was where or who was firing in that direction. For all I knew, there could be a hundred V.C. in between us. Zigzagging my way through the bamboo, I stopped and squatted every five or six paces and listened and watched for signs of the enemy or Frank. I didn't hear or see anything, but the firing increased to my north and west. It sounded as though they were probing Fergy's and Duke's area again.

The farther out I got, the more I thought the whole thing could be a trap. What if they had Frank surrounded and were just waiting for someone to come out for him? A cold fear of the unknown began to grip me. I could envision a large horseshoe-shaped ambush just waiting for me to walk into it.

"Don't let your imagination get out of control. Your imagination can distort reality," I told myself, as I remembered a night ambush where I had convinced myself that a small tree was an enemy soldier trying to sneak up on us. It was at times like this that your senses could begin to play tricks on you, conjuring up images in the back of your mind which only accentuated the uncertainty.

Only a few moments had passed, but it seemed like an eternity when I hit the bank of the stream. Most of it had dried up in this area, and its dark brown mud had cracked and curled in the hot air. The few still pools of water that remained were crusted with algae, over which hung a stagnant stench and swarms of blue-green flies.

I extended my head out over the creek bed. I looked to the left and saw that the concave ribbon of mud disappeared into a tunnel of tangled leaves.

"Whack, whack!" Shots from my right flank startled me. I quickly dropped to one knee and watched for movement. About thirty meters downstream, I spotted someone on the five-foot-high bank kneeling behind what looked like a large fallen tree—it was Frank!

I wanted to yell at him, but I risked the danger of giving my position away. The brush along this part of the creek was a solid wall of vines and thorns, so I carefully slid down the bank to the creek-bed.

I slowly worked my way in his direction, my footsteps cracking through the hard-shelled potsherds of the creek bed before sinking several inches into a creamy muck. Frank was busy watching whatever was going on on the other side of the log, and ducked when what appeared to be a grenade flew over his position. A second or two later it exploded with a muffled "whumph" in a pool of water behind him, showering him with mud and water.

When Frank raised his head over the top of the log, a second grenade flew over his head. He hit the ground for a second time. The instant it exploded, he again popped up and fired two quick shots over the top of the fallen tree.

"Whumph!" The force of the third explosion on the opposite side of the tree caught him in a firing position and hurled him backward.

"God, no," I said to myself as he flew spread-eagle through the air until landing on his back in the pool with a soupy splash.

I tried to run to him as fast as I could, but the creek's muddy suction slowed me to a walk. I knew he had to be dead or at least seriously wounded.

"God," I muttered to myself, "if he isn't dead he'll drown." Struggling forward, I had visions of Frank's wife and eight kids crying over his grave. What a tragedy—to survive so much only to die in a pool of slime.

As I got nearer, the waves quickly faded to a few ripples. In the middle of the stagnant pool, I saw his head. It was dead-still and looked like a white pool ball sitting in the middle of a green felt table.

Suddenly his shoulders rose above the green.

"He's alive!" I thought as he rose to his feet in the waist-deep water and staggered toward the bank. My sense of relief was overpowering and I let out a loud "Yaahoo!"

"You look like a drowned rat," I said as I reached the water's edge and extended my hand to pull him out of the pool dripping with green slime and mud, smelling like something that had crawled under the porch and died.

"He was a brave son of a bitch," he said, shaking his head. "He threw one grenade long and one short. The short one got me."

"You okay?" I asked him as I put my arm around his waist and helped him over to the bank.

"Sure, Jimmy," he said after sitting down on the trunk of a small tree. "Just let me get my breath for a minute."

Looking at him, I could tell that he was in a lot more pain than he would admit. His face was bright red from the blast. He was obviously disoriented, and his whole body was quivering in spasms.

"Here, take a couple of these," I said after removing two codeine tablets from my M-5 kit. "You'll feel better in a few minutes."

"What luck," he said as he swallowed the tablets. "If it wasn't for the water, I would have broken my back."

Suddenly, I realized that there weren't any Bodes up on the bank.

"Frank, where're the Bodes?" I asked.

"I had four," he answered.

"Where are they?"

"One got hit pretty bad and it took two to carry him back to the perimeter."

"What about the other one?"

"Well," he said while rubbing the back of his neck. "When the machine gun broke down, I couldn't get it working again so I had him take it to Stik to see if he could fix it. I don't know if he ever made it."

"You're tellin' me we're out here all alone?"

"Looks that way," he said as he leaned forward to stretch his back muscles.

"After Stik made contact up by the commo wires, the Lieutenant told Fergy and me to set up on the right side of the perimeter. We were putting the Bodes into position when Fergy got hit hard from the east."

"Where were you?"

"I was down on the southern end of the platoon when we got hit from the south. The platoon got divided into two sections in the firefight. After they broke contact, we got the platoon back together and I tied us in with Duke's people."

"Yeah, but how the heck did you get out here?"

"I don't know if it was luck or what, but as soon as I got everyone tied in they hit us again from the south. This time we really had our shit together. The Bodes were in position and our Claymores were out. I think the V.C. were surprised by the resistance and broke contact and started to run after just a couple of minutes. Well, as soon as they started to break, I took the machine gun and a few Bodes and counterattacked. We chased 'em all the way to the creek and I've been here ever since. We'd better get back up on the bank," he added.

I extended my hand and pulled him to his feet. Grabbing a few roots, we pulled our way up the bank. Once on top, I looked out over the fallen tree and was surprised at the view. From this position the entire area south of Duke's platoon could be seen. A few trees, small brush, and vegetation were scattered across the terrain, but for the most part, you had a pretty clear shot at anything that moved within a hundred meters or so. All along the blackened front, wispy tendrils of smoke curled upward from still-smoldering hot spots. The charred bodies of V.C. lay twisted and torn in the late afternoon sun.

"I've been putting flanking fire on 'em every time they moved on Duke's area," he said as he pointed over the top of the tree. "For a while it was a turkey shoot. They didn't spot me for a long time." He pointed to a blue-clad soldier lying on his side about twenty meters out. "That's the bugger that got me. I caught 'im in the chest just before that third grenade exploded."

"Whump, whump, whump . . ." An automatic weapon opened up from our left front. We ducked behind the tree trunk as rounds slammed into the wood, splattering chunks of bark over us. After the initial burst, we both popped up to return fire but couldn't find the target. Frank then discovered that he was out of ammunition.

"You see anything?" I asked as we knelt face-to-face against the tree.

"Yeah, they're in a small ravine about thirty meters out," he said. "You got a couple of mags?"

I reached down and unsnapped one of my B.A.R. belt pouches and pulled out five magazines.

"Here ya go," I said as I handed them to him.

"Thanks," he said, slipping four into his empty ammo pouch and one into his M-16. "Would you believe I fired my last two rounds into that guy who threw the grenades?"

Peeking out over the top of the log again, I spotted movement in the ravine and fired three quick bursts. Just as I ducked, they returned fire and I saw Frank out of the corner of my eye lob a grenade toward the ravine.

"Right on target," he said as he ducked. I slowly counted to "five one thousand," but nothing happened.

"Must be a dud," I said as we both looked and saw a gray cloud slowly filling the ravine.

"Did you throw gas?" I asked.

"Who me?" He laughed.

Both of us started laughing uncontrollably and sank to sitting positions with our backs against the tree.

"I think you really need an R and R," I said.

"Hey, Jimmy, what d'ya say we go to Hong Kong together?"

"Right now even Trang-Sup would be great," I said.

Looking at the front of Frank's fatigue jacket, I stopped laughing when I saw that it was perforated with small holes.

"Oh, no, he must have multiple chest wounds," I thought to myself.

"Frank, unbutton your jacket," I said as I knelt in front of him.

As he started opening the buttons, empty M-16 magazines fell out on the ground in front of him. His jacket was packed with them.

"I'm been sticking them in there so I wouldn't lose 'em," he said.

As they continued to spill out, I noticed that some of them were dented and the bluing scraped off from chunks of shrapnel.

"They must have absorbed the shrapnel from the grenade," I said.

"Yeah, must have," he said as the last one clinked to the ground.

With his shirt unbuttoned, I took a look at his chest. Much to my relief, it was just red with scrapes and bruises.

"Looks okay," I said, feeling for broken ribs. "How does it feel?"

"Like I got kicked by a mule."

"I think we're gonna have to send you down to Saigon for tests," I said. "You could have internal injuries."

When he started to button his jacket, I noticed that the upper part of his left sleeve was covered with dried blood.

"Wait a minute," I said, grabbing his forearm. "What's wrong with your arm?"

"Ah, just a flesh wound."

"Listen, Frank, you wouldn't bullshit a friend, would ya?" I asked him as I helped him remove his jacket. "You better let me have a look at it."

I saw that his shoulder was covered with a couple of blood-soaked four by four's and a few pieces of surgical tape. I pulled away some of the tape, lifted the gauze, and took a look at the wound. From what I could see, it was a fairly deep flesh wound. Fortunately, there didn't appear to be any bone involvement.

"What d'ya think, Jimmy?" he asked.

"As soon as we can get you back to a hospital it's gonna have to be debrided and sewn up, but right now let's just worry about getting you back inside the perimeter."

Things seemed a little too quiet, so as soon as Frank got his jacket back on, I took a look-see over the trunk. About seventy-five meters southwest of us, I saw what looked like at least a squad running in the direction of the creek in a crouched position.

"We'd better get out of here quick," I said. "Looks like they're gonna try to outflank us."

"They'll probably come down the creek bed," Frank added.

"Come on," I said as I picked up my M-5 kit.

I started to slide back down the bank, but stopped when I saw that he couldn't get up.

"Hey, buddy, let me give you a hand," I said as I grabbed him under each arm and lifted him to his feet.

"Just a little stiff," he said.

"I'm gonna recommend you for the 'Liar of the Year' award," I said as I helped him down the bank. We retraced my footprints back to where I'd first dropped into the creek bed, then turned left into the jungle. As I took a quick back azimuth with my compass we could hear the high-pitched sound of Vietnamese voices coming from the area of the downed tree.

"Don't stop," Frank whispered. "They're right behind us." I nodded and we picked up our pace. Moving first through the thick foliage and clattering bamboo, I kept us going in the right direction while watching for the Bodes. Frank was about two paces behind me, walking backward and watching for the V.C. trying to close the gap.

When we finally reached the far side of the bamboo, I felt some relief because I knew we were nearing our lines. I didn't want to startle the Bodes, so we stopped to watch and listen. I hoped they remembered that we were out here. Seeing Frank bent forward with a hand on one knee, I could tell that he was busted up more than he was letting on. I knew he hadn't fully recovered from hitting that mine on the Saigon-Tay-Ninh highway, and the grenade explosion wasn't helping matters.

Just then, Frank spotted a Bode and let out a loud "Wetsu."

"Wetsu," a Bode responded.

"We're home, Jimmy." Frank smiled as three Bodes ran out to meet us.

"Trung-si Hagey, Trung-si Hagey." They beamed as they grabbed him around the waist and patted him on the back.

"I think they're glad to see ya," I smiled.

"Not as glad as I am to see them." He beamed.

Once again inside the perimeter, a few more of Frank's Bodes gathered around him to welcome him back. As he talked to them, I thought of his comment about us making it home—I guess everything's relevant.

"Frank, I'd better get back," I said.

"Okay, Jimmy," he said as he shook my hand. "I'm gonna check in with Fergy. I haven't seen him since this morning."

"I guess I'll follow Duke's line around till I hit the Third Herd," I said. "It's probably the fastest way back—I'll see ya later."

"God and country." He smiled as he turned and headed north.

"Oh." Frank turned and looked into my eyes. "Thanks."

NEWS CLIPPINGS

According to U.S. officials the Communists have lost a total of 207,500 men in the war.
Buffalo Evening News, July 18, 1967

In a commentary today, the Hanoi daily Nham Dan condemned the U.S. imperialists for using B-52's to bomb both southern and northern parts of the demilitarized zone and the Vinh Linh area in the DRV on July 13.
The Guardian (Rangoon), July 18, 1967

New York police who ducked beer cans, eggs and milk bottles in their latest fight with the "hippies" must now see some merit to the slogan, "Make Love Not War."
Buffalo Evening News, July 18, 1967

The White House called on the National Liberation Front, the political arm of the Vietcong, and on North Vietnam, today to permit the impartial inspection of American prisoners and to return the seriously sick and wounded among them.
The New York Times, July 18, 1967

Pretty Miss Lynda Bird Johnson, in London for the first time and trying to see everything she can see, went shopping on Carnaby St. But she did not—repeat not— buy a miniskirt as some papers reported.
The Miami Herald, July 18, 1967

Robert Komer, the U.S. Pacification Chief in South Vietnam, said that the pacification program has been "very slow" but it should make considerably more progress in the future.
Sabah Times (Malaysia), July 18, 1967

Howard Hawks Presents John Wayne & Robert Mitchum in **El Dorado.**
Los Angeles Times, July 18, 1967

In Miami Beach, Secretary of State Rusk said peace might be achieved in Vietnam "if we could sit down with Hanoi."
The Wall Street Journal, July 18, 1967

Johnny Bench, who drove in the Buffalo Bisons' first run in Monday night's baseball 2-1 victory over Columbus, raised his batting average to .249. The super rookie leads the Herd in runs batted in (44) and home runs (15).
Buffalo Evening News, July 18, 1967

8

1710 Hours (5:10 P.M.)

The jungle was still hot and steamy from the day's bake. The relentless glare of the sun had only lost a touch of its intensity.

When I reached Bob, Thach, and Ly, I found them huddled behind a large moss-covered tree near the center of the Third Platoon's sector. Bob had his map spread out on the ground and was pointing to locations on it as he gave directions.

"Hey there," I interrupted. Bob looked up as I squatted between him and Thach.

"Hey, turkey, glad you made it back," he said as he put a hand on my knee.

"Yeah, I got tied up with Fergy and Frank. How's it look?"

He looked at the map and pointed to an area just west of our location.

"From what we can see, they're gonna hit us all along this side of the perimeter. Must be at least a battalion of 'em massing out there," he said as he moved his index finger along the map.

"Beaucoup V.C.," Ly said as he pursed his lips and shook his head.

"Ammunition almost gone," Thach added grimly.

"Great! What about another resupply?" I asked.

"A chopper's inbound now," Bob replied, "but I don't think it's gonna make it on time."

"How much time we got?" I wanted to know.

"None."

I jumped to my feet. "I'd better talk to Kimh about the wounded."

"Wait up, Jim," Bob said as he rose to his feet and tucked the map back into his hip pocket. "We're gonna have to split up on this one."

"How d'ya want to do it?"

"You and Thach take the northern half of the platoon and Ly and I'll take the southern end."

"Okay," I responded.

"Look," he added. "I'll keep the machine gun section with me. If your end gets hit hard we'll use it as a reaction force."

"Sounds good. What happened to the F.A.C.?"

"I think he went back to Quan-Loi to refuel. Should be back any time now."

"Any scuttlebut on reinforcements?" I wanted to know.

"Duke tells me the Lieutenant's trying to get the Mike Force in here."

"Well, we'd better get rolling."

"I'll see ya later," Bob called as Thach and I scrambled off to the north in a low crouch.

"Take care, guys." I waved.

"Mike Force come, Bac-si?" Thach asked as we walked up the line and watched for signs of the enemy off to our left.

"Let's hope so."

Even if reinforcements were sent in, I wondered if they'd be able to land anywhere in the area. There were a number of large clearings that would make excellent landing zones, but the enemy surely had them crisscrossed with automatic weapons. It was the oldest trick in the book: surround a unit and then ambush and wipe out the reinforcements on the landing zone.

As we worked our way up the line, Thach kept encouraging the Bodes while I tried to figure out why Bob had sent Thach and me to defend the northern part of our sector. He knew that the enemy would have to be crazy to come at us again over open ground. They'd have a much better chance of breaking through our lines if they attacked through the thick brush at the southern end of the platoon. Was Bob trying to keep Thach and me away from the worst of what was yet to come? I wouldn't put it past him.

When we reached an area close to the dispensary, I told Thach to get the troops ready for the assault, and that I'd join him after talking to Kimh.

"I do, Bac-si," he said as he continued north and I headed a few meters east to the crater.

Approaching the depression, I could see Ty sitting on its rim with his M-16 pointed in my direction. In the shaded greens and browns his bandage-covered face stood out like a flashlight in the dark—someone was going to have to invent green bandages.

Behind Ty I could see Kimh and a couple of our platoon medics working in what appeared to be a crater filled with our wounded. From my vantage point, the concave floor of the crater was carpeted with the camouflaged uniforms of wounded Bodes sprawled around the circular slope with arms and legs splayed at awkward angles. About a half-dozen glass bottles hung from bamboo poles with tubes running into the arms of those below. Scattered around the outside rim of the crater were scores of pieces of cardboard paper, discarded blood-stained dressings, and empty I.V. bottles.

"How's it going, Ty?" I asked as I reached his position and patted him on the back.

"Trung-si Hagey okay?" he asked as I checked his bandages for bleeding.

"Yeah, he's okay."

The areas around his mouth and eyes were the only parts of his face not covered by the mummified dressings. He still had a smile on his lips.

I was somewhat surprised by his concern for Frank, and guessed that he must have been the Bode who Frank sent to get his machine gun fixed—probably got hit somewhere along the way.

"Are you Trung-si Hagey's machine gunner?" I asked slowly.

"Machine gun." He nodded.

"Where's the machine gun?" I wanted to know.

"Trung-si Rader say no can fix," he answered.

I nodded that I understood.

Standing on the rim of the crater, I watched Kimh kneeling at Luc's side taking his blood pressure while a bottle of normal saline hung on a nearby pole and slowly dripped into a vein in his arm. I was relieved to see that his leg wound hadn't killed him.

I started down the slope of the saucer-shaped crater, carefully stepping over Lieu, who was lying on his back with his eyes closed and his mouth gaping open, with a shaft of sunlight dancing on his face through a hole in the overhead foliage. I wasn't sure that he was alive until I saw the white dressing on his stomach slowly rise then fall when he drew a labored breath. The fact that he was still alive was a good indication that the bullet hadn't severed any major vessels. Thach would be pleased with the news.

While looking at Lieu I thought that I heard the faint "thap thap thapping," of a chopper. I strained to listen for a few seconds until I was sure it was the telltale beating of an approaching chopper. I hoped it was the ammunition resupply.

"Kimh," I called. He appeared startled by my voice. Evidently he had been so involved in his work that he hadn't noticed my return.

"Bac-si." He smiled as he stood up and removed a clean white handkerchief from his breast pocket.

"How do you feel?" he asked as he rechecked my dressing.

"I've got some bad news, my friend, I'm afraid we're gonna have to hide the more seriously wounded."

"Why?" He looked at me with uncertainty in his voice.

"Our ammunition's almost gone and the V.C. are getting ready to hit us again."

The expression on his face turned cold as he removed his glasses and looked at me through tired eyes.

"V.C. will find them," he said as he used the handkerchief to wipe the greasy film from his lenses.

"Look, when they hit, they're gonna cut through here like a hot knife through butter. If we have to break out without ammunition the only thing that's gonna keep anyone alive is speed. If the stretchers slow us down no one's gonna make it and that includes the wounded."

"How long will they be left?"

"If we get the Mike Force in here and get resupplied we should be back right after first light."

He looked at the ground and replaced his glasses.

"Do it quick, Kimh. Once they get inside the perimeter it'll be too late."

He took a deep breath and sighed a weary groan.

"Okay, Bac-si."

"If you need me I'll be up on the northern end of the platoon," I said as I turned and carefully stepped over a few of the wounded. Near the rim of the crater I heard a loud grunt. When I looked I saw that it was the Bode from Duke's platoon who had been hit in the mouth. He was still lying in a fetal position with an I.V. hooked up to his arm, but he mustered enough strength to flash me a feeble thumbs-up. I returned the gesture, then continued on my way.

I found myself agonizing about the wounded as I made my way back to the perimeter. The thing that worried me most was the thought that the Bodes might kill them rather than risk letting them fall into the hands of the enemy. I was also worried about what Thach's reaction would be to leaving Lieu.

"Damn." I stopped and headed back to the crater. This was one of those problems that didn't have an easy solution. No matter what you did, it would probably cost lives.

"Kimh," I called as I approached. He looked and quickly ran in my direction.

"What is it, Bac-si?" he asked tensely.

"It's not gonna work," I said. "We've just got too many wounded to hide. Maybe two or three, but not this many—they'll find 'em for sure."

"What do we do, Bac-si?"

"Get the walking wounded back to their platoons,

then get the more serious ones on stretchers or hammocks, and have the platoon medics take 'em back to their areas. Tell 'em that they'll be responsible for 'em until we can get 'em med-evaced."

"I will do." He smiled. "Baci-si, I was much too afraid to hide them."

"You were right, Kimh. At least this way they'll have some chance of surviving. It may not be much, but at least it's a shot."

"I will get them ready to move," he said.

"Okay, my friend. Let's do it."

He nodded and began barking orders to the two medics who were working in the crater.

"Kimh," I called as I walked away, "as soon as you get everyone outta here come up to my position."

He waved and I headed back to the perimeter. I felt a great sense of relief about the wounded and our decision not to cache them. Furthermore, I thought, if we could hang on until it got dark we could break down into squad-sized units and work our way south to Quan-Loi or northwest to Loc-Ninh. There was no way Charlie could seal the entire perimeter—especially at night.

When I reached the perimeter, I spotted Thach giving last-minute instructions to the troops. Most of them had attached bayonets to their M-16's. As I headed up the line toward him an ominous foreboding settled over me. An oppressive silence had enveloped the line. The Bodes were too quiet. They were bunched in groups of two or three, some with looks of grim resignation, some with gaunt distant stares, others with strained tension etched on their faces, but no one said a word. All along the line, the biting stench of burnt flesh hung as a portent of imminent death and dying.

"Bac-si." Thach motioned for me to follow him.

We moved north for a few meters until we found Danh and Kien set up at both ends of the same fallen tree where we had fought earlier in the day.

"Many V.C. come," Danh said as Thach and I took up a position near the center of the tree and used our hands to clear the ground of spent cartridges.

"Bac-si." Kien pointed out over the top of the tree. Looking west through a broken haze of white, gray, and black smoke, I was shocked to see a long line of uniformed soldiers extended all across our front. Because of the distance and the blankets of haze, I couldn't tell if they were wearing blue or khaki-colored uniforms.

Watching the enemy move into position, I was nauseated by the gaseous stench of putrifying bodies. Enemy troops who had been torn apart or burned by bombs earlier in the day had been lying in the tropical sun for several hours and had already started to decompose. Just a few meters in front of our position sat the same khaki-clad soldier I had shot hours earlier—his mouth was still locked open with the same wide-eyed look of disbelief. The irritating hum of hungry flies buzzing about the dead only underscored the carnage.

As we waited for the V.C. assault, I found myself recalling a book about Shaka, the great Zulu chief. I was in high school at the time, and remembered wondering how his enemies must have felt with his regiments closing in on them—now I knew.

"They come," Thach said as he pulled his bolt to the rear and rested him M-16 on top of the fallen tree.

At a distance of about one hundred and twenty-five meters, I could see officers running up and down the line. It looked as though they were trying to get their men on-line and properly spaced as they advanced. When they closed to about ninety meters I could see that they were wearing blue uniforms, pith helmets, and webb gear. Most were toting AK's. They must have been the same troops we'd spotted moving across our front earlier in the day.

As I watched the blue line move forward at a slow walk, I removed the few full magazines I had left and placed them on the ground near my right knee. When I looked up again, I saw that the line had changed from a slow stride to a quick walk. As its pace picked up my heartbeat began to accelerate. Suddenly, a volley of heavy firing erupted somewhere south of our position. At about seventy-five meters out, the V.C.

broke into a dead run and began firing and screaming.
All along their line their muzzle flashes blinked on and
off like a hundred strobes.

"Here we go again," I said to myself as I wiped the
sweat from my palms for the last time, braced myself,
and took up a firm firing position. "Just a little bit
closer, a little bit closer," I mumbled to myself.

"Thooomp, thooomp, thooomp . . . !" The hollow
cough of V.C. mortars sounded from somewhere east
of our position, sending tingling shivers racing down
my spine. I glanced over at Thach and he flashed a
panicked "oh, no" look. There was something about
mortars that scared the hell out of me. It was probably
the unknown—the random, unpredictable pattern of
impact. Our only hope was that they'd explode in the
canopies of the larger trees and that most of the shrapnel would be absorbed by the foliage before it hit the
ground. Based on what I knew of enemy tactics, I
figured he was probably timing it so that the mortars
would start tearing us apart when their troops reached
about fifty meters—I knew these guys had their shit
together. With the enemy drawing near, I crouched
low and could hear their rounds cutting through vegetation and thumping into tree trunks.

At about sixty meters, the Bodes opened fire. I
lined up the top of my front sight blade on the chest of
one of the leading attackers. He was running zigzag,
so I aimed a couple of inches in front of his chest and
squeezed—an instant later he fell to the ground and
disappeared. With my left eye completely shut and my
right partially closed, I found that my field of vision
was becoming increasingly narrow. It was becoming
more and more difficult to get a fix on a target—a lot
like viewing the battlefield through a narrow pipe.

Just as I lined up my sights on a second attacker and
was about to pull the trigger, he was vaporized in an
explosion of fire and smoke. One second I could see
him running at me and a second later there was nothing there.

"Ssssshhhhh . . . karumph!"

"What the hell was that?" I yelled to Thach.

"Mortars," he shouted as gray-black bursts mushroomed to our front, tearing through the V.C. ranks with red-hot slivers of shrapnel.

I was almost paralyzed as I watched the rounds rip the assault to shreds. I couldn't believe my eyes. As the mortar rounds walked among the V.C., they cut down the nearest troops like a razor-sharp scythe cutting through sawgrass. Each explosion brought a bright orange flash followed by hot shock waves which rushed through the heavy air like expanding ripples on a pond. A second later, the deafening "karumph" pounded my ears like a bass drum.

After a minute-long barrage of mortar bursts, I could see the ghostly figures of blue-clad V.C. stumbling and staggering in confusion out of the patchy clouds of swirling smoke. Most of them appeared dazed and wounded, and the Bodes easily cut them down before they reached our lines.

When the layers of smoke began to dissipate, I could see that those who hadn't been killed were walking or running to the rear. I couldn't help thinking that some mortar commander was going to get his ass chewed on this one.

I wiped the layers of sweat and grime from the right side of my face and slumped to the ground in nervous exhaustion. I was replaying the turn of events, when Thach let out a loud "Taa-yoo," which startled me. I turned to see him jump on top of the fallen tree and start screaming and shaking his fist defiantly at the retreating V.C. Suddenly Danh joined him on the tree trunk and they both began dancing and singing:

> "Puc a puc a Ho Chi Minh
> Puc a puc a Ho Chi Minh"

Soon, gleeful Bodes all along the line jumped to their feet and started singing:

> "Puc a puc a Ho Chi Minh
> Puc a puc a Ho Chi Minh"

"What are they singing?" I yelled to Danh.

"We sing fuck Ho Chi Minh." He grinned, and continued dancing what looked like an Oriental jig.

"Hey, Jim." I turned to see that it was Bob, lugging a box of M-16 ammunition and two bandoliers of M-79 grenades.

"Did you see what happened? Buddha must be lookin' out for us," he said as he dumped part of the box on the ground and handed Thach the two bandoliers.

"You got that right. It looks to me like they overshot their target," I offered.

Thach leaped down from the log, grabbed Bob around the waist, and started dancing with him as he continued to sing.

"Hey, Thach," I said, "when we get back to Trang-Sup, you're gonna have to write down the words for me."

He laughed. "Okay, Bac-si."

"It could become a best seller." I chuckled as Danh and I knelt on the ground and began filling our empty magazines.

"Yeah, its got a good beat," Bob laughed. "Definitely Top 40 material. Maybe we can get it on *American Bandstand*."

"You get an azimuth on those mortars?" I asked.

"Yeah. As soon as the F.A.C. gets back we'll try to take 'em out with air," Bob answered as the dancing and singing died down.

"Hey, I'd better get back," Bob added as he scanned the battlefield. "They'll be back. You can count on it."

"Thanks for the ammo," I said as he headed back down the line in a low crouch.

"There's another load on the way," he yelled as he disappeared into the brush.

I was going to ask him if he wanted me to join him down at the other end of the platoon, but in all of the excitement I'd forgotten to bring it up.

While sitting on the ground filling the remainder of my empty magazines, I realized how really good I suddenly felt. The fear and exhaustion that I had experienced only a few minutes earlier were gone and I now found myself refreshed and ready to go. In some ways this day had been a lot like running a long distance race. There were times when you felt like you weren't going to make it and there were times when you felt as though you could go forever. Right now I was soaring.

"Bac-si." I looked to my rear and saw that it was Kien. He was carrying an American and two large, round Chinese Claymore mines.

"Where'd you get 'em?" I asked with excitement as he placed them on the ground next to me. He just smiled and continued to gum his soggy cigar butt.

"Hey, Thach. Tell Kien that cigars aren't good for his health." I winked at Thach as Kien thumbed the butt and spat tobacco juice at the ground.

Thach said something to him in Cambodian and they both busted up.

"What did he say?" I asked.

"Ah, he say if he worry he not join Mobile Guerrilla Force." Thach laughed

"No sweat." Kien nodded.

"Danh, come here. Let's get these mines out," I said as I handed one to him and one to Kien. "I'll run one out in the center. Kien, you put yours out to the left. Danh, you put yours out to the right."

They both indicated that they understood, so I took the American Claymore and my M-16 and crawled out over the top of the tree. After moving about ten meters, I reached the enemy soldier I had shot earlier in the day. He was still sitting in a rigor mortis position against the tree where he had died. His skin was gray now, and small black bugs were crawling on vacant eyes circled with dark hollows. As I crawled past him I gave him a push, and he slumped to the ground in slow motion.

Crawling with my face close to the ground, I noticed that most of the grass, bushes, vines, and small trees had been cut by lead or shrapnel. The smell of shredded foliage reminded me of a freshly cut lawn on a hot summer day.

A few meters farther out, I reached the top of a small hill and stopped. There was still a lot of firing going on, but I didn't think that anyone was shooting at me—at least I didn't see or hear any rounds hitting near me. Off in the distance I could see the enemy forming for another assault. I didn't pick up any movement in my immediate area, but I could hear voices and groaning coming from somewhere farther out. My best guess was that when the line had been staggered, some of the V.C. had sought sanctuary in the craters that pockmarked the bombed-over moonscape.

My Claymore came in a green cloth pouch with holes cut in its bottom so that its retractable steel legs could be extended and quickly stuck in the ground. After extending them, I looked out over the top of the hill, aimed it in the general direction of the enemy, then slowly pushed them into the soft mud. I tried to aim it so that its C-4 charge would propel hundreds of steel ball bearings parallel with the ground. I didn't want it to fire harmlessly over their heads or into the jungle floor. If it was aimed just right, it had a killing range of about fifty meters and could do one nasty job on troops in the open.

"Bac-si, they come," Thach yelled.

When I was satisfied that the mine was angled properly, I opened the flap on the bag and removed the firing device and "S" coiled wire that had been packed on top of the mine. Just a couple of feet to my left I noticed a small banana tree lying on the ground. It would make a perfect camouflage for the Claymore, so I snapped off a couple of its broad leaves and covered the mine. Holding the firing device and the "S" rolled wire in my left hand, I gradually worked my way back to my firing position, uncoiling it as I went. As the thin strand of wire unraveled, I kept looking up and around for any signs of enemy troops trying to infiltrate our lines through the scattered brush. When I reached the tree an automatic weapon opened up on me and I could hear its rounds slamming into the trunk only a couple of feet from my head. The Bodes immediately returned fire while I scurried back over the top of the tree and laid the Claymore's hand clicker next to me on the ground.

"Don't blow 'em until I blow mine," I called as I looked up and saw another long blue line moving at a slow gait across our entire front. I hoped they understood what I was saying, because the Bodes sometimes had a tendency to blow them too soon. If we could wait till the last possible second before detonation, we could do some real damage.

I remembered the time back at Duc-Phong when a local V.C. caught a company of Bodes with a Chi-Com Claymore. When it happened, the Bodes were in a single column just a couple hundred meters outside the front gate of the camp. Even though they were spread out in single file, it killed or wounded more than a dozen of them.

The enemy's advance through the mist and smoke that lay low over the battlefield reminded me of a locomotive slowly picking up speed through a veil of steam. At about seventy-five meters out, they broke into a full run and began firing and yelling as they charged to close the gap between us. Off to my left I could hear the distinctive "ta, tow, tow, tow, tow . . ." of our M-60 pouring out a steady stream of fire—Bob must have been in deep shit.

Although the ground in front of me appeared relatively flat, it must have had a number of draws and shallow ravines because, as the V.C. advanced, they would slowly sink from view. A few seconds later, bobbing waves of pith helmets would reappear and then a line of bodies would gradually rise into view.

"Hold your fire," I yelled.

For some reason the words of my drill instructor at the rifle range at Parris Island started running through my mind:

> "All ready on the left;
> All ready on the right:
> All ready on the firing line;
> Watch your targets;
> TARGETS!"

At about sixty meters the Bodes opened up. I too began picking individual targets and squeezing off rounds. I couldn't figure out why they persisted in assaulting us over open ground. With everyone armed with automatic weapons these types of frontal assaults were suicidal—their commander must have been a real meathead. It was going to cost him a lot of good men.

When the long blue line reached forty meters, the rifle cracking reached a roar. I could see the determined expressions on their faces. Their mouths were wide open and screaming as they ran. It was probably intended to scare the hell out of us, but I imagined that it also helped them counter their own fears. Glancing to my left and right, I could see that Kien and Danh were getting anxious to blow their Claymores. I picked up my firing device, and when the leading enemy troops reached thirty meters, squeezed the clicker. "Whaamm!" A split second later there was a second and a third explosion and leaves, branches, and enemy troops were blown back as though they had been hit by a tremendous force of wind. Through the dust and smoke of the backblast I could see that the mines had blown gaping holes in the enemy formation. The blast staggered their advance for a couple of seconds, but then the remaining soldiers surged toward us again.

I fired a whole magazine in a broad waist-level sweep across my front, spitting a brassy stream of casings all over the fallen log. I ducked to reload and started to look up when I saw a blue blur coming over the top of the tree. I fired a quick burst that might have hit him high, because he did a complete reverse flip as his head was knocked to the rear and his lower body continued forward. As he went flying by me, I looked to the rear to make sure he was dead and saw that he had landed on top of a Bode who was lying flat on his back. I couldn't see either of their faces.

I jumped to my feet and fired another long burst across my front and then turned and pulled the dead enemy soldier off the Bode. That's when I noticed that it was Thach. I turned back to fire the rest of what was left in my magazine, but couldn't find a target. There was still heavy fighting off to our left, but the enemy to our immediate front had vanished.

Looking back at Thach I didn't see any blood, but the dirt around his head appeared wet. He wasn't moving, but his eyes were following my movements and his chest was moving up and down as he breathed.

"Were you hit?" I yelled as I searched for a wound. He didn't say a word—just looked at me through sad, bloodshot eyes.

After searching his trunk for a wound, I worked my way up to his neck and head.

"Oh, no! It's his head," I said to Danh as he knelt on Thach's other side. "He's been hit in the head."

I knelt on his left side and carefully pushed my left hand under his neck, while slowly elevating his head. When I had enough room, I slipped my right hand under it. Oh, my God! I could feel his warm, dirt-covered brain resting in the palm of my hand—the back of his head had been blown away.

I looked at Danh. He didn't say a word, but I could see tears rolling down his cheeks. As I cradled Thach's shattered skull in my palms, Danh removed a canteen and rinsed the dirt from his brain. He then untied his red platoon scarf and spread it on the ground under Thach's head.

I felt a consoling hand on my shoulder. It was Kimh. He knelt on the ground to my right and removed a large battle dressing from his M-5 kit. As I held Thach's head, he gently applied the dressing over the wound.

Kimh finished with the dressing and we carefully lowered Thach's head onto the scarf. He grabbed my hand.

"Bac-si," he said in a soft voice, "I die."

I tried to say something, but was too choked up to utter a word. I took a couple of deep breaths and looked away, trying to fight back the tide of emotions.

"You'll be all right," I said as I felt my eyes pooling with warm tears.

"Bac-si, take me to my wife?" he asked.

I didn't know what to say to him.

"Kimh, get an I.V. going," I snapped.

He clutched my arm. "Let him die, Bac-si," he whispered in my ear. I looked into Kimh's battle-weary eyes and knew that he was right. Even if we were at Walter Reed Hospital he wouldn't make it.

"Are you in any pain?" I asked as he squeezed my hand and gave a long, fluttering sigh. There was no response, only blank, glassy eyes which stared back with a faraway look that made it seem as if they were looking right through you. I felt his neck for a pulse, but there was none.

"He's gone," I said.

No one said a word. For a long moment everyone sat in silence while I removed the gold chain and jade Buddha he had given me earlier and carefully refastened it around his neck.

"Goodbye, my friend," I said as I closed his eyelids and ran my hand through his hair in a final farewell.

With the firing to our south now reduced to an occasional shot, Danh and Kimh spread a camouflaged poncho liner on the ground next to him and then the three of us lifted Thach up and placed him on it. Watching Thach's body lying motionless on the liner, I found myself longing to talk to him—there were too many things that had been left unsaid.

Before wrapping him in the nylon poncho liner, I removed the chrome-plated Browning Automatic Pistol from his holster and handed it to Kimh.

"Give this to his wife."

"I will, Bac-si," he answered.

I unbuttoned Thach's breast pocket and removed the clear plastic bag that contained his wallet. I looked inside and found a folded piece of yellowed paper. When I opened it, I discovered that it was the write-up on a Bronze Star Medal we had presented to him a few months earlier. Even though it was wrinkled and stained I could still read the type:

By the direction of the President of the United States of America and the Commanding Officer of Detachment A-303, 5th Special Forces Group

**(Airborne) the Bronze Star Medal for heroism in
ground combat in the Republic of Vietnam is
hereby presented to . . .**

As my eyes followed the commendation, I remembered the day back at Trang-Sup when we presented it to him. Of course it hadn't been approved by the President, but it really didn't make any difference—it was his most prized possession. Whenever he went into Tay-Ninh, he wore it on his chest and went walking down the street with a peacock proud "kick my ass if you can" strut.

Looking further through his wallet, I found the actual medal pinned to one of its inside compartments. I thought it was the right thing to do, so I removed it and pinned it to his breast pocket. The red, white, and blue ribbon and the Bronze Medal looked clean and fresh against his dirt-covered camouflage jacket.

Looking at him lying on the poncho liner, I realized how lucky I was to have known old Thach. He was a special person. I knew that he would have given his life for me and that I would have done the same for him—he was my friend.

NEWS CLIPPINGS

It is the American soldier—not equipment or techniques—that is the heart and soul of the Army . . .
Army Digest, July 1967

The loss of more than 2100 planes over North Vietnam marked a big error and a heavy defeat of the U.S. imperialists in both the tactical and strategic fields.
North Vietnam News Service, July 18, 1967

Miss USA Sylvia Louise Hitchcock, who is a graceful blonde, was named Miss Universe of 1967 Saturday night.
The Guardian (Rangoon), July 18, 1967

The President's decision, arrived at after several days of anxious contemplation, was a typical Johnsonian compromise. There will be more American troops in Viet Nam at the end of the year than originally scheduled, but not so many as General Westmoreland wanted.
U.S. News & World Report, July 21, 1967

Carla Thomas, 25, daughter of a Memphis disk jockey, was recently voted the favorite singer of U.S. servicemen in Viet Nam, an honor won last year by the Supremes.
Time, July 21, 1967

What is clear is that Ho Chi Minh at least at one time regarded the Americans in his hands as "war criminals," covered by the 1945 Nuremburg Charter under which some Nazi leaders were tried and sentenced to death or imprisonment, and not as prisoners of a war protected by the Geneva Convention.
Look, July 25, 1967

*The **Dirty Dozen** is a cautionary tale, warning us of what can happen to conventional morality in time of stress.*
Life, July 21, 1967

U.S. artist Rockwell Kent defended Monday his donation of $10,000, part of a Lenin Peace Prize, to the Viet Cong women and children despite a U.S. prohibition of gifts to Vietnamese Communists.
Courier Express (Buffalo), July 18, 1967

6:30 Walter Cronkite
The Atlanta Journal, July 18, 1967

9

Even though the day was drawing to a close, the heat and humidity persisted. As the sun receded, the jungle greens beneath the canopy began to lose their color.

"Jim, let's go. Condon wants a meeting right away," Bob yelled as he and Ly ran up to where Kimh, Danh, Kien, and I were standing in somber silence around Thach's body.

"Thach's dead," I said. Kimh pointed to the poncho liner, and the expression on Bob's face changed.

"Give me a minute," he asked.

While he knelt next to Thach and whispered a few words, the five of us waited in a respectful silence. After a few seconds, he rose to his feet and used his sleeve to wipe his eyes.

"Let's go," he said as he, Ly, and I headed in the direction of the Bo-chi-huy (headquarters).

"Hey, wait up," a voice called. It was Duke Snider coming up the line. "I'm getting too old for this shit," he said as he joined us.

"What's going on?" I wanted to know.

"It's time to shit or get off the pot. If we don't move now everyone's toes'll be pointed skyward by morning."

"Charlie's probably waiting for reinforcements," I interjected. "If he's gonna hit us again, it'll probably be last light."

"There they are." Duke spotted Roger, Fergy, Frank, and Stik waiting for us. They were clustered around the Lieutenant while he knelt on one knee and talked into his handset.

"Let's go, you're holdin' up the show," Stik said as we walked into the depression and formed a circle around the Lieutenant.

"We got everyone?" Condon asked as he stood up.

"Yes, sir, everyone's here," Roger responded.

"Okay, listen up. I want to make this short. We just got word that reinforcements are on the way."

"Yeah, and the check's in the mail," Frank shot back cynically.

"We've heard that bull before," Fergy added, agreeing with Frank's sentiment.

"No," the Lieutenant reassured us. "The Mike Force is already airborne and on the way."

"All right! Let's get these Chinamen on the ground and get the hell outta here!" Frank patted me on the back and everyone cheered and smiled.

"Okay, let me lay it out for you. The F.A.C. tells me we've got a good-sized clearing a klick or so southeast of here. As soon as the Mike Force lands, they'll secure its perimeter and link up with us on the L.Z."

"Gotta think Charlie'll have it covered," Stik said while looking at his map.

"It's a chance we're gonna have to take," Condon responded. "The F.A.C.'ll work it over with TAC-AIR and gunships before the Mike Force lands. When we move we'll have gunships working our flanks and covering our rear."

"Well, it looks like it's now or never," Bob said.

"You've got that right," the Lieutenant agreed. "We gotta get the company resupplied and the wounded and dead out while we still have light."

"We don't have much time," Roger added.

"Sir, how d'ya want us to move outta here?" Frank inquired.

"Hell," Duke chimed in, "let's move just as we are."

"You got it." Condon paused. "We'll move out in two parallel columns with the Headquarters Section in between. On the right we'll lead out with the Second Platoon." He pointed to Fergy and Frank. "Duke, your platoon'll follow 'em out."

"Yes, sir." Duke blew his nose with his finger pressed against one nostril.

"You got enough demo left to booby-trap the area?" Condon asked him.

"Yes, sir. I'll keep 'em off our ass."

"Stik, your platoon'll lead out on the left and provide rear security. You'll be followed by the Third Herd."

"Sounds good," Stik said. "I'll assign one of my tail-gunner teams to cover our rear."

"Okay, sounds good. Jim, how d'ya want to handle the wounded?"

"Well, sir, let's keep 'em together right behind the Headquarters Section. We'll move 'em up here and follow you out."

"Okay," he agreed. "As soon as you get back to your platoons, have your wounded and dead moved here."

"Just one thing, sir," I added. "You've gotta keep the pace down. If we rough up some of these guys they're gonna go into shock and die."

"Don't worry. I'll keep it to a crawl."

"Gonna move 'em in hammocks?" Roger asked.

"Yeah, in hammocks and improvised stretchers. Four men on each hammock—two to carry and two to rest. We'll switch 'em every hundred meters or so."

"Yeah, we don't wanna run anyone into the ground," Frank added.

"Any questions?" Condon asked.

"Let's do it." Duke folded his map.

"Okay, get back to your platoons. We'll move out in ten minutes."

Everyone was really happy about what the Lieutenant had said and headed back to relay the good news to their platoons.

"How d'ya want to work it?" I asked Bob as he moved back through the trampled bamboo and brush.

"You take care of the wounded and I'll get the troops ready to move out."

Approaching the fallen tree, I could see that Kimh,

Danh, and Kien were crouched behind it trading shots with enemy snipers.

"I'll catch you on the L.Z.," he said as he and Ly broke off to our left and headed down the line.

"We go, Bac-si?" Danh asked as I knelt on the ground next to him.

"Yeah." I smiled. "The Mike Force is gonna secure an L.Z. about a thousand meters from here."

Picking up a small twig, I cleared a piece of ground and scratched out a simple map in the dirt explaining our plan for the breakout.

"I will tell the platoon medics," Kimh said.

"They've already got the word. Just get your gear up to the Bo-chi-huy. Danh, you and Kien get Thach ready to move."

"Okay, Bac-si," Danh answered.

When I finished giving directions, I moved down the line in a low crouch and found my rucksack lying where I had left it earlier in the day. Picking it up by one strap, I swung it over my right shoulder and headed back to the Bo-chi-huy. No longer packed with five hundred rounds of extra ammunition and half a dozen smoke and H.E. grenades, the rucksack was a lot lighter than before the battle.

Moving through the bamboo once again, I could hear the muffled drone of the F.A.C. overhead. Looking up through the trees, I caught a quick glimpse of the plane as it floated through one of the small holes in the overhead canopy. Outlined against a clear blue sky, it appeared like a large black bird drifting with outstretched wings.

Approaching the Bo-chi-huy, I could see that it was buzzing with activity. A mounting sense of urgency permeated the pre-dusk air. The Lieutenant was on the radio giving directions to F.A.C. and the platoons, while the Bodes from the Headquarters Security Section were busy getting their rucks on their backs and preparing to move out. From every direction, I could see the wounded being carried to the center of the perimeter like metal filings attracted to a magnet.

Just before reaching the Bo-chi-huy, I found a small clear area and dropped my ruck to the ground.

"Over here, over here," I yelled to the Bodes carrying the wounded. When they saw me, I raised my right arm over my head, and rotating it in tight circles, signaled them to come to me. When they neared, I could see that it wasn't going to be an easy trip to the L.Z. With heavy rucks on their backs, some of them were having difficulty carrying the extra weight of the wounded. The one thing I didn't want was a few of them passing out from heat exhaustion.

"Bac-si." Kimh arrived and lowered his ruck to the ground next to mine.

"Just a couple of things," I told him. "Make sure they keep the I.V.'s elevated at all times and that we have four men on each hammock."

"I will keep all of the I.V.'s together so I can watch them," he screamed as two fast movers roared overhead at treetop level. We looked at each other and smiled—it was a welcome sound.

"Okay, Kimh, you follow the Bo-chi-huy with the I.V.'s and I'll bring up the rear."

"Okay." As the wounded began arriving, he gave last-minute instructions to each of the porters. After most of them were in, I did a quick count and found that some of the hammocks only had two men assigned to carry them.

"Kimh, we only have two men on some of 'em."

"Kien went to get more," he reassured me as Danh arrived carrying Thach on his back. A couple of gunships were now hovering directly overhead, and I could feel the cool downdraft from their pulsating blades pushing its way through the tall trees. As their machine guns pounded away at suspected enemy positions, the wind from their rotors beat the canopy, stripping thousands of leaves from their branches which floated slowly to the ground.

"Where put Thach?" Danh asked.

"Just put him right here for now," I said while helping him place him on the ground near my ruck.

"Jim." Roger came running up to me. "Recon and

the Second Platoon are moving out. You ready to move?"

"Kien come," Danh said as he pointed north. Looking to my left, I could see Kien and about a half dozen Bodes moving in my direction at a slow run. I gave Roger a thumbs up.

"Two minutes," I said. "Keep it real slow."

When Kien arrived with the additional men, Kimh quickly assigned each of them a hammock. Keeping an eye on the Bo-chi-huy, I could see that the first of them were beginning to slowly snake their way southeast. As the column moved, the choppers continued to lay down fire ahead of them and on both flanks. If they did their jobs right we'd be moving through a lead corridor.

"Okay, Kimh, get 'em ready to move."

He yelled something in Cambodian and the Bodes carrying the lead hammock squatted and positioned the bamboo poles on their shoulders. When they rose to their feet, the hammocks slowly lifted the wounded Bodes off the ground. After giving them a tap on the rear they followed out the last Bode from the Bo-chi-huy.

"I will go now," Kimh said.

"Okay, you and Kien stay with the I.V.'s." They swung their rucks on their backs and headed out.

"I stay you," Danh said.

"Okay, partner." We stood together and watched the remainder of the wounded being carried out.

"Hey, if you can carry my ruck I'll carry Thach."

"Okay, Bac-si."

He already had his ruck on his back, so I leaned my M-16 against a nearby stump and picked up my ruck. While I held it tight against his chest, Danh slipped its straps over his shoulders. Once it was in place, I let it go and he bounced a couple of times to settle the weight of both loads. With rucks mounted front and rear he looked pretty well balanced.

"If you have a problem dump my ruck," I said. "Just make sure you get my hammock and beret out of it."

"No sweat." He smiled. "Can do."

Bending over to pick up Thach's nylon-wrapped body, I found that I couldn't pick him up.

"Can't get a grip on this slippery nylon." I struggled, looked around for some help—Danh was the only one left and he was carrying so much weight that he couldn't bend over.

"Damn," I said as I unraveled Thach from his nylon cocoon. With the nylon removed, I got him into a sitting position and tried to get him on my back. I didn't have the strength to pick him up.

"Must be getting weak," I said to Danh.

I grabbed Thach under his arms, dragged him a few feet, then propped him in a sitting position against a tree.

"Help me stand him up against the tree," I said, as I grabbed him around his chest and slowly worked his limp body to the trunk until he was in a standing position. Danh then moved to the rear of the tree and held him straight by grabbing hold of his collar and pulling him tight against the tree.

Once he had him tight, I was able to slide the left side of my neck down until I reached his stomach. I was then in a position to grab him behind his knees with my left arm.

"Let 'em go," I said.

When Danh released his grip Thach slumped forward, his dead weight folding across my shoulders.

"Good, Bac-si," Danh said, as I shifted Thach's weight to balance him on my shoulders. Once I had him positioned, I was able to grab his left wrist with my left hand. With my right hand free I picked up my M-16.

"We ready to roll?" I asked.

"We go."

Looking southeast, I could see that the last of the litter teams had already moved about thirty meters. From the sound of the gunships, I figured that their machine guns were pulverizing the terrain about three hundred meters southeast of us.

"Come on, partner. We'd better catch up," I said as he led the way out.

Taking one last look around, I could see that most of the brush, bamboo, and small trees had been cut to a height of about three feet. The whole area was strewn with empty ammo boxes and cartons and the plastic and cardboard containers that our medical supplies had been packed in. Within a few weeks the jungle would reclaim everything, and no one would know what had taken place here today. Looking out over the now-still perimeter, I suddenly detected movement about seventy-five meters northwest of our location.

"Psst."

Danh stopped about ten meters ahead of me and looked to his rear. I pointed my weapon in the direction of the movement.

"V.C.," he hissed as two uniforms came into full view.

From what I could see, it looked like the point element of at least a squad. They were probably trying to tail the Third Herd as they moved east.

Holding my M-16 with one hand and the butt gripped tightly in my armpit, I aimed in their general direction and squeezed off a long burst. Halfway through the magazine they disappeared and didn't return fire. I knew I probably hadn't hit them, but at least I'd slowed them down.

"Let's get outta here!"

We moved out at a quick pace hounded by an unseen enemy tailing close behind. When we entered the killing ground in front of what was the Second Platoon's area, I was awed by the extent of the carnage. The once-thick jungle had been ripped apart as though it had been hit by a tornado, and deep, moonlike craters pockmarked the earth. The area looked like the floor of a slaughterhouse. Bodies and severed limbs littered the ground, while pieces of intestines dangled from branches that had been stripped of their leaves.

When we reached the bottom of a gradual incline, we crossed a small finger-shaped hill where we ran into Duke and a few of his Bodes. They had come across what looked like thirty to fifty enemy rucksacks that were lined up in three neat rows. They must have belonged to some of the troops who'd hit Fergy and Frank's platoon earlier in the day. Duke was using his knife to cut the shoulder straps off each of the rucks, while the Bodes were dumping their contents on the ground.

"Don't have time to do a real job on these," he said as we approached.

From what I could see, they each contained a couple of blocks of dried fish, some uncooked rice, cooking utensils, a hammock and blanket, and a few personal odds and ends. I didn't see any maps or documents or anything else that would be of any intelligence value.

"Better get your butts outta here," I said. "Charlie's moving into the area."

"I'll be right behind ya," he said as he stopped to sample a piece of fish. "Whew, that shit's bad," he said, spitting out the half-chewed chunk of fish.

"You gonna booby-trap the area?"

"Yeah, don't touch anything. I already got a few things rigged to blow."

"Don't worry," I said as Danh and I continued on our way.

"Hey, Jim," Duke called. "Keep an eye open for Stik. He and some of his people are setting up stay-behind ambushes."

"Will do."

I was following Danh through the now-thickening jungle when I realized that we had lost visual contact with the rear elements of the column, but I figured they couldn't be too far ahead. Fortunately, the ground was damp and spongy. It wasn't difficult following their footprints through the trampled undergrowth.

As we continued east, the jungle began to thin and we soon found ourselves moving through a bamboo thicket. Without boots crunching through a carpet of dried and decaying bamboo, tall green stalks squeaked and clattered as they swayed in the early evening breeze. To our rear, I could hear the rumble of bombs from airstrikes Duke was calling in on what was once our perimeter. Off to the east I could hear the distinctive roar of jet engines rolling in hot and the resonant thunder of five-hundred-pound bombs. Further south, I could make out what sounded like a score of helicopter rotors popping through the heavy air.

"Mike Force?" Danh asked as he stopped and pointed south.

"Must be." I stopped for a couple of seconds to adjust Thach's weight on my back. Laboring to catch my breath, I realized that trying to carry Thach might have been a mistake. I had thought that once I had him on my back I wouldn't have any trouble, but I was now feeling completely drained of energy and every step was becoming more and more difficult.

Moving out again, we soon passed through the last of the bamboo and entered an area of waist-deep grass and scrub brush. Out in the open, without the shade of the canopy, the temperature seemed to shoot up a good twenty degrees. The glare of a low-slung sun hit my eyes and forced me to squint. The searing heat was doing a number on my wounded head.

As the sun beat down, my good eye burned shut with salty sweat. I could feel myself growing weaker as I struggled to maintain visual contact with Danh, but my vision was blurred. I was nauseated and dizzy. Suddenly, I found myself alone and disoriented and pushing my way through a wall of eight-foot elephant grass. The air was so choked with heat it was like breathing inside a plastic bag. A panicked sense of claustrophobia began to close in. I had to get out. Using all the strength and willpower I could muster, I parted the knife-like blades of grass which sliced at my skin. My pores had opened like a faucet. It felt as if I had stumbled into a sauna. My fatigues were soaked black with sweat and clung like wet rags to my now-reluctant body.

With the putrid taste of hot vomit rising in my throat, the surrounding greens and browns began to spin. Then everything went black.

When I awoke, I was flat on my back with Thach sitting next to me, his back resting against the wall of grass. For a second I thought he was alive, but then my eyes cleared and I realized that I was dreaming.

"Sorry, old buddy." I slowly rose to my knees and then to my feet. I don't know how long I had passed out. I removed a couple of salt tablets from my pocket and swallowed them with a long drink of water, realizing that I had probably lost more blood than I originally thought. If I'd been smart, I would have hooked myself to an I.V. and run in a bottle of normal saline.

After the water, I felt much better and thought that if I could work my way back to the main trail, I would either run into Danh coming back for me or Duke or Stik moving toward the L.Z.

"Bac-si," a voice called. It sounded like Danh.

"Over here."

A couple of seconds later, two Bodes came crashing through the elephant grass. It was Danh and Kien.

"Boy, am I glad to see you guys," I said as Danh grabbed me around the waist.

"I look to see you, Bac-si, but you go."

"Yeah, let's get moving. Let me get a couple of things outta my ruck and you can leave the rest."

He pulled the straps off his shoulders and dropped my ruck to the ground. After opening it, I removed my beret, my hammock, and my Olympus camera and stuffed them into empty pockets.

"Kien, give your ruck to Danh. You're gonna have to carry Thach." I could see that he didn't understand.

"I take Thach?"

Danh interrupted and said something in Cambodian to him.

"No sweat, Bac-si," he answered as he removed his ruck and helped Danh mount it on his chest. As soon as Danh had both rucks settled, he took a few steps back toward the trail. Kien couldn't resist removing the few cans of C rations I had packed near the top of my ruck.

"Let's go, Kien," I said as he stuffed them into his pockets and then picked up Thach in a fireman's carry. With everyone ready, we backtracked for a few meters until we hit the trail, then headed east again.

Within a few minutes, we moved out of the elephant grass into a flat, swampy area covered with soft mud and clumps of stunted grass that looked as though it might have at one time been used to grow rice. The clearing appeared to extend far into the distance and must have measured at least four hundred meters across. A few meters into the open, we crossed a small north-south stream. As we splashed across the four-inch-deep water, I could see the red tongues of tracer fire from at least a half-dozen choppers probing the tree lines on both flanks. At our distance, the choppers looked like angry dragon flies darting in and out as they raked the jungle fringe.

As I watched the aerial display, several bursts of M-16 fire broke the silence to our rear. Stik's tail gunners must have made contact with some V.C. trackers.

"Hey, Jim," a voice called.

I stopped and looked to my rear. It was Duke and his radio operator.

"Wait up," he yelled as I stopped and let Kien move past me.

"What d'ya hear?" I asked as he caught up and we walked together.

"Mike Force is on the ground." He smiled.

"They got the L.Z. secured?"

"Yup."

"China Boy, this is Fox Control." Lieutenant Condon's voice crackled over the radio.

"Fox Control, this is China Boy." It was the Mike Force. "Come to the yellow smoke. Over."

"There it is," I said as I pointed ahead to a yellow plume drifting against the blue sky. Looking to our left and right, I could see the camouflaged uniforms of the Mike Force standing in the wood lines on both flanks. Above them, choppers hovered protectively at treetop level with machine guns firing, and even higher in the sky was the ever-watchful F.A.C. drifting in tight circles.

After moving another two hundred meters, I could see that in the middle of the clearing the Bodes were setting up a circular-shaped inner perimeter that measured about a hundred meters across. Near its center, it looked as though most of the Americans from the Mobile Guerrilla Force were meeting with members of the Mike Force.

When we reached our inner perimeter, Duke and his radio operator broke off and headed for the First Platoon while Danh, Kien, and I headed toward the center. We found the Lieutenant, Roger, Fergy, Frank, and Bob talking to a couple of Americans from the Mike Force. Just to their right Kimh had all of the wounded lined up and ready to go.

"Everyone in?" the Lieutenant asked Roger.

"Stik's got one squad on a stay-behind ambush," Roger answered.

"Okay, listen up. If Charlie catches us out here on this L.Z. he'll kick our ass, so let's do what we have to do and get outta here. You platoon leaders make sure that your platoon sergeants get the ammunition and rations distributed. As soon as the dead and wounded are picked up, we'll move out in the same two parallel columns. Any questions?"

"How many choppers we got, sir?" I asked.

"We've got seven of 'em coming in one at a time. First one'll be on the ground in two minutes."

"How many wounded are there?" Condon wanted to know.

"About thirty have to be med-evaced, sir," I said.

"Okay, get 'em aboard as soon as the choppers land."

Bob and I ran over to where Kimh was waiting with the wounded.

"Everyone ready to go?"

"All ready, Bac-si."

"Okay. Get the most serious ones on the first chopper."

He nodded. "Okay Bac-si."

"Trung-si Donahue," a voice called from behind me. I turned to see that it was a tall, well-built Chinese Nung I'd met when the Mike Force was helping us build our camp at Duc-Phong.

"Chao-ong? (How are you?)," I said as I shook his hand. "Good to see you again. How's everything going?"

"Too much operation," he responded with a smile.

"Helicopter come," Kimh informed me as the Lieutenant popped a red smoke. Looking south, I could see the bulbous green hull of the Huey gliding in over the tree line, accompanied by the sound of slapping blades. A few seconds later, it hovered in with its underbelly flared up and its tube skids swaying as it kicked up a cloud of dust before settling about twenty meters from the wounded. As the rotors popped and thwacked, Kimh had the porters carry five or six of the hammocks to the left door. After directing the loading of the wounded, I talked to a member of the crew.

"You know where Trang-Sup is?" I yelled over the noise of the rotating chopper blades.

"Tay-Ninh Province. Near the base of the mountain."

"Good," I yelled. "The dead go to Trang-Sup and the wounded to either the Third Field Hospital in Saigon, the 24th Evac in Bien-Hoa, or the 196th's M.A.S.H. hospital near Tay-Ninh."

"The Viets go to Vietnamese hospitals," he barked back.

"Bullshit, these are Cambodians and they're going to American hospitals."

Bob must have overheard what was being said and joined the conversation.

"I'll tell you what," he yelled as he pointed his finger threateningly in the guy's face. "If I find out that they didn't go to an American hospital, I'll personally look you up. You got it?"

"Okay, okay," he said as Bob walked away. "That guy crazy?"

"That's right," I said. "Everyone on this team's crazy."

Kimh tugged on my sleeve. "All loaded, Bac-si."

I gave the pilot the thumbs up and everyone around the chopper ran in a crouch to where the rest of the wounded were lying on the ground. The Huey's blades screwed faster and faster as the pilot throttled down and the craft lifted a few feet off the ground. With a final surge of power, the chopper tilted forward, then climbed across the clearing, thrashing the tops of the canopy with its departing downdraft as it sailed over the tree line.

"I'll see you back at Trang-Sup, old buddy," Bob said as he shook my hand and put his arm around my waist.

"Yeah, take care of yourself. As soon as you get back, make sure you get your butt X-rayed and checked by a doctor."

"Ain't that bad."

"I don't know where I'll end up. If they send me outta country would you send my gear to me?"

"Don't worry. I'll take care of everything," he said as the second chopper touched down amid a flurry of wind that whipped the wounded-filled hammocks and caused us to shield our eyes. As Kimh supervised the loading, I could overhear Fergy yelling at Frank to get on the chopper and Frank yelling back that he wasn't leaving.

"Frank"—the Lieutenant grabbed his arm—"we need someone who hasn't been hit too bad to make sure the Bodes get taken care of. I want you to go."

"All right, sir, I understand."

"Damned Frank's a bullhead." Fergy laughed, shaking his head.

As Bob and I listened to the conversation someone grabbed me from behind and kissed my ear. It was Stik.

"Damn it, Stik. One of these days I'm gonna have to kick your skinny ass."

"That'll be the day. Hey, you take care of yourself. I'll catch ya back at camp."

"Chopper comin' in," Roger yelled as another Huey throbbed into the L.Z.

"Kimh, let's get Thach on this one," I called above the noise.

As the chopper touched down Kimh, Danh, Bob, and I picked Thach up and carried him out to the chopper. Once we had the wounded on board, we carefully slid his body across the chopper's metal floor.

"Hey," a member of the crew protested. "What's that slope doing with a Bronze Star?"

I exploded. "Listen, you fat fucker"—I shoved the muzzle of my M-16 into his belly—"that man's the best soldier you'll ever see."

"Take it easy," he said as he squirmed in his seat.

Bob grabbed my arm. "Come on, Jim, they're ready to take off."

"Don't let that sorry ass get to ya," he added as we ran back to where Kimh, Danh, and Kien were waiting with the next load of wounded.

"Keep 'em moving, Jim," the Lieutenant yelled.

"Yes, sir," I yelled back as the fourth chopper hovered in.

As soon as the chopper was loaded, Kimh ran back to where I was standing. While Frank and Roger helped load the fifth and sixth Hueys, I went over the company's medical needs with Kimh. Although no American medics would be left on the ground, I had complete confidence in his abilities.

"Jim," the Lieutenant called as he walked over and shook my hand, "last chopper's coming in. You and Frank make sure they take good care of the Bodes."

"Will do, sir."

"Goodbye, Bac-si," Kimh said as he and Danh grabbed my arm and shook my hand.

"Goodbye, my friends." I could feel myself being overcome by emotion. "You guys take care of Bob."

"No sweat." Kien nodded.

"Come on, Jimmy," Frank said as he grabbed my arm and we both ran in the direction of the waiting chopper. The dusk was beginning to choke out the last rays of light, filling the lower areas with pools of gray.

"Hey, J.C." It was Fergy. "You guys stay outta trouble, you hear?"

I gave him a thumbs up and Frank and I ran around to the right door of the chopper and climbed aboard. All of the seats and most of the floor space was already occupied, so we sat in the doorway with our feet dangling out of the chopper. The speed of its rotating blades quickly picked up as we slowly lifted off the ground. As it rose above the L.Z., I flashed everyone below a "V" while they waved back. Within a short time we began picking up speed and altitude, and before I knew it, the ground was slipping away as we pushed to the south.

As we rose high above the trees, the cool air felt clean and fresh as it blew through the open bay, ruffling my hair and tugging at my skin. To the west, a copper-colored sun slowly sank into a pastel haze, burnishing the matted jungle greens with an iridescent orange. It was good to be on our way, but somehow I felt bad about leaving.

As we floated south over the broccoli-topped jungle, I couldn't stop thinking about the guy who referred to Thach as a slope. The remark had angered me, but when I thought about it, I realized that he had probably been victimized by his own experiences in Vietnam. From my observations, most Americans only came into contact with two types of Vietnamese—those who were trying to kill you, and the pimps, prostitutes, and Saigon cowboys who were trying to take your money. Tragically, few had the opportunity to learn to know their other side.

It was a short, low-level flight back to Quan-Loi. When we landed next to the air strip, the last light of day had turned the sky a fiery crimson. Shortly after touching down, Frank and I were picked up by a dirt-covered jeep and driven to a nearby general-purpose tent.

The tent was divided into two sections, and while Frank waited in one end, I was taken to the other and told to have a seat on a stack of C ration boxes. A few minutes later an Oriental wearing what looked like camouflaged French army fatigues walked in and told me that he wanted to debrief me on the operation.

My first impression was that he was Vietnamese, but after talking to him for a couple of minutes, I realized that he was probably Filipino. His over-the-ear-length black hair was too long for someone in the military, so I assumed he must have been a civilian associated with one of the intelligence agencies.

In my discussion with him, I was able to provide a detailed description of enemy uniforms, weapons, and tactics, but wasn't able to give him any precise information regarding the identification of enemy units involved in the battle. I suggested that the Lieutenant or Fergy might be able to provide him with that information. A medic entered as we talked and took my pulse and blood pressure. When he left, a sergeant carried in about a half-dozen enemy weapons that we had brought out with us. My interrogator didn't say much about them, but I could tell that he was impressed by the fact that they were all factory new and excellently maintained. When he finished with the debriefing, he scribbled down a few comments in a small notebook and asked me to have Frank sent in.

I returned to the other end of the tent where I found Frank sitting on a stool with his pants rumpled in a heap around his ankles. Much to my surprise, I saw that he had also been hit in the leg. It was only a flesh wound, and a doctor was covering it with a dressing.

"Your turn on the hot seat," I said as he stood up and pulled up his trousers.

"Who is that guy?"

"Some sort of spook." I shrugged as he left.

"Sergeant Donahue?" the doctor asked.

"Yes, sir."

"Take a seat over here," he said, pointing to a stool next to the table. As soon as I sat down I heard the whine of a jeep transmission as it downshifted and pulled up outside the tent. A few seconds later Major Gritz strode in.

"Damn, Jim," he said as I rose to shake his hand. "Sit down, sit down." He laid his Swedish "K" submachine gun on the table. "I just got word that you and Frank had been hit. How serious is it?"

"Frank's got a couple of flesh wounds and possible internal injuries," I said as the doctor used a light to check my pupils and ears and then began to unwind the Ace from my head.

"If I'd known I'd have gotten you guys out earlier," he said as he watched the doctor, wincing slightly as the doctor tugged at the blood-caked bandage.

"Probably best that you didn't, sir. We only had eight Americans on this one."

"How's the rest of the team?"

"Well, sir, old Bob got some shrapnel in his butt. Other than that, they're in good shape."

"Good."

"You had us worried." I smiled.

"Why's that?" the Major replied, not quite sure of what I meant.

"When you flew in with that resupply we thought maybe that fifty-one caliber got ya."

"No." It was his turn to grin. "We came in so low he couldn't get a clear shot at us."

"This might hurt a little," the doctor interrupted as he placed my bloody dressing on the table and picked up a stainless steel probe. As he slowly worked it into the hole over my left temple, I gritted my teeth and gripped the edge of the table until my knuckles turned white. Watching the expression on Gritz's face, I hoped it wasn't any indication of the seriousness of the wound.

"What d'ya think?" Gritz asked him.

"Well, Major"—he paused, placing the probe on the table, then began applying a new dressing—"all I can tell you is that the projectile lacerated a couple of his temporal vessels and it's still in there."

"So where do we go from here?" Gritz wanted to know.

"Back to Saigon for further examination and surgery." Frank returned to the room. "Good to see ya, sir." Frank smiled as they shook hands heartily.

"Frank, I sure as hell hope you don't feel as bad as you look."

"I feel pretty good, sir. It could have been a lot worse."

"When you get back to Trang-Sup, I'm gonna restrict you to camp." Gritz laughed. "Every time you go out the front gate you get hurt."

"Seems that way."

"Look." Gritz picked up his Swedish "K." "As soon as I get the company back to Trang-Sup, I'll be down to see you guys."

"How much longer they gonna be in the field?" I asked.

"One day, two at the most."

A medic walked into the tent.

"Sir, the aircraft's ready to leave for Saigon," he told the doctor.

"See you in a couple of days, sir." Frank and I shook Gritz's hand, then followed the medic from the brightly lit tent to a jeep parked outside. I climbed into the back of the jeep and found that the tent's lights had ruined my night vision. I couldn't see a thing until the medic started the engine and turned on the jeep's headlights. Peeling away from the tent, leaving a cloud of dust, we sped down the runway toward the waiting C-130. While I hung on for my life, our headlights cut through the heavy evening air, splattering juicy bugs against the windshield. As we neared the waiting transport, we could see the prop blast from its outboard engines kicking up clouds of rust-colored dust, so the driver looped around to its rear before coming to a stop at the foot of the lowered ramp. With the smell of burning aviation fuel filling my nostrils, we climbed out of the jeep and onto the ramp. I looked up into the cabin of the aircraft and could see shadows moving in the red glow of its night lights.

"Hold it," a nurse yelled as she ran down the ramp. "Do you have any grenades, Claymores, or explosives?" she yelled over the roar of the engines.

"We're clean," Frank yelled back, raising his hands over his head.

"Need any assistance?" she asked as the three of us walked up the ramp.

"A cold beer would help," Frank said.

"I'll get you some orange juice." She led us to two

empty nylon seats on the left side of the aircraft and buckled us in.

"I think I'm in love," Frank yelled in my ear.

Looking around the cabin, I could see that they already had the Bodes and a few other wounded Americans on board. Some were strapped into seats on the other side of the aircraft, while others were tied down on stretchers. About a half-dozen nurses and medics were busy preparing them for take off. I was really happy to see that the Bodes were still with us. If they were going all the way back to Saigon, someone had probably made the decision that they were going to American hospitals.

Once the medical personnel had everyone secured, the hydraulic whine of the retracting ramp signaled our preparation for take off. The pilot taxied the lumbering C-130 to the end of the runway before swinging the nose around and coming to a complete stop. A moment later, the fuselage began to vibrate as the engines revved to a fever pitch. Suddenly we lurched forward and raced down the runway before leaping into the night sky above Quan-Loi.

We had only been airborne for a few minutes when a nurse brought us each a glass of orange juice. As we sipped, the steady hum of the engine lulled the Bodes to sleep. By the time we finished our juice, the cabin had cooled to the point where we were shivering uncontrollably.

"Can I get you a blanket?" one of the medics asked.

"Yeah, we're freezing our asses off," Frank said.

A couple of minutes later he returned with a blanket for each of us and a couple of cups of steaming coffee.

"Now that's service," Frank said as the medic wrapped one of the blankets around him.

Sitting in the soft glow of the cabin lights, we sipped coffee and watched the nurses shuttle among the wounded, checking their I.V.'s and dressings. As we watched, we talked about our feelings for the Bodes. In the afterglow of battle, it dawned on me how attached I had become to them and to Vietnam. I re-

membered going home on leave a few months earlier
and recalled how good it was to see friends and rela-
tives again, but I also remembered how much I missed
what I'd left behind. When my return flight touched
down in Bien-Hoa, I remember feeling that I was back
where I belonged—with my brothers-in-arms. Something rare had quietly taken place. A deep camarade-
rie had been formed which seemed to transcend
relationships half a world away.

As I sat reminiscing about other times and places,
my thoughts were interrupted when Frank's head
slumped to my shoulder—he was sound asleep. He
was still holding his half-full cup of coffee, so I removed it from his hand and placed it on the floor
under my seat.

A short time later the plane banked to the left,
giving me a clear glimpse of Saigon's night lights spar-
kling against the blackness. Banking again, the plane's
landing gear groaned as they were lowered and we
started our final approach.

A minute later its wheels touched down at Ton Son
Nhut with a screech, and the smell of scorched rubber
filled the aircraft. Halfway down the runway, the pilot
reversed the pitch on his props, forcing me to grab
hold of my seat as we abruptly slowed to a crawl.

Taxiing down the runway, our cabin's white lights
were turned on and the plane came alive with last-
minute activity as nurses and medics hurried to pre-
pare everyone for departure. I gave Frank a nudge.

"Hey, Frank, we're here."

"What?" he said, rubbing his eyes and squinting.

"We're in Saigon."

"Must have been dozing," he said as he yawned.

"Dozing, hell. You were snoring so loud they had to
issue everyone ear plugs."

He laughed. "Give me some slack."

When we finally came to a complete stop, the ramp
whined down, exposing a covey of ambulances with
their lights flashing. Seconds later one of them backed
up to the ramp, and a medic holding a clipboard
climbed up the ramp and began talking to one of the

nurses. When they finished talking, he walked over to where Frank and I were sitting.

"Staff Sergeant Donahue?" he asked.

"Yeah."

"Sarge, we've got a chopper waiting to take you up to the 24th Evac in Long-Binh."

"What about the Bodes?"

"The who?" he responded with a confused look on his face.

"The Cambodians," I said, pointing to the Bodes. "Where are they going?"

"Oh, well, it depends on their type of injury. Most of 'em will be going to the Third Field Hospital."

"Okay. That's all I wanted to know."

"You got an SFC Hagey on your list?" Frank inquired.

He ran his finger down his clipboard.

"Here we go. You're going over to the Third Field. It's right here in Saigon."

We both stood up and I put my arm around Frank's neck.

"Take care of yourself," I said.

"I won't be here long. As soon as I escape I'll be up to see ya. You want anything from the P.X.?"

"Two cheeseburgers with everything, a double order of fries, and a chocolate malt."

"You want it, you'll get it."

The medic led us down the ramp. The sultry night air hit my face with its warm breath along with the familiar Saigon smells of diesel exhaust and pungent Oriental cooking. As we exited the well-lit cabin, the night seemed especially calm and dark. A few airport lights stood out against the velvet backdrop with their subdued haloes glowing a misty white. When we reached the bottom of the ramp, they loaded Frank into one of the waiting ambulances. I walked a few meters across the tarmac to a medical chopper with its blades slumped at rest. Once I was strapped into my seat the pilot started the engine and within a couple of minutes we were floating high above Saigon on our way to Long-Binh. When we reached the Saigon to Long-Binh highway, we began following it northeast. A few miles up the highway, I noticed the outline of Ho-Ngoc-Tao on the left side of the road and it brought back memories of the days when we were there training the Bodes.

A few minutes past the camp, we banked and began our final approach into the 24th Evac. As we neared the ground, I suddenly realized that I had been here about a year earlier. A helicopter door gunner had suffered a serious sucking chest wound near Song-Be and on the flight back to the 24th I managed to keep him from drowning in his own blood by using a 50cc syringe to aspirate the blood from his lungs. Within a couple of minutes of landing they had him in the operating room with I.V.'s going and his chest opened wide. It was probably the most efficient emergency medical work I had ever seen, but the thought of them doing the same thing to my head had me worried.

As our chopper hovered over the landing pad and slowly set down, I could see four people waiting for me with a stretcher.

"Aw shit," I said to myself. "Here we go."

"Sergeant Donahue," one of them yelled under the slapping of the blades as he grabbed me under my arms and tired to lift me out of the chopper bay and onto the stretcher.

"Hey, I can walk," I yelled as I stepped out of the chopper and followed them into a nearby building. Once inside the Emergency Room, they took my M-16 and webb gear and gave me an envelope for my camera, beret, compass, watch, and wallet. I told them that if they didn't mind I'd like to hang on to my Montagnard bracelet—they didn't.

After having been in the jungle a few days, I found everything in the Emergency Room especially clean and sterile. From what I could see, about a half-dozen hospital personnel were busy treating three patients.

"Here, take everything off and put these on," a medic said as he handed me pajamas and a pair of slippers, then escorted me to a chair located behind a curtain. After removing my boots and fatigues, I dropped them on the floor and slipped into the P.J.'s.

They smelled as though they had just been laundered, and it didn't seem right to be putting them over the jungle filth I had accumulated. When the medic returned, he picked up my gear with a sneer and, clutching it at arm's length as if he were holding a dead rat, turned and left.

"Hey, don't throw them out," I said.

He gave me a "you gotta be kidding" look and kept on going.

A couple of minutes later, an SP-6 came in and asked me a few personal questions concerning my age, height, weight, allergies, etc. When he left, a doctor and nurse entered. The doctor checked my eyes, ears, nose, and throat, and when he left the nurse took my vital signs. I was a little bit surprised to see that my blood pressure was up to 146/74. Maybe it had something to do with my phobia about hospitals.

When she got everything she needed, she told me that a Dr. Beazley had ordered a hematocrit and a tetanus toxoid. She also let me know that when I was finished in the Emergency Room I'd be going to X-ray and then to the Operating Room. She also informed me that the surgeon had been an enlisted man during the Korean War and that his nickname was "Snake." A few minutes after she left, the same medic returned with a wheelchair and rolled me out of the Emergency Room and into X-ray—it was 0200 hours.

The X-ray tech wasn't there yet, so the medic helped me up onto the X-ray table and then left. Waiting on the cold, hard table, I felt out of place and began to shiver. For some reason I didn't like the smell of the room—there was something unnatural about it.

When the X-ray tech finally arrived, he quickly took several films of my head and then left. The medic returned a few minutes later, wheeled me into the Operating Room, and again left. As I waited alone in the dimly-lit room, my palms began to perspire as I envisioned the worst. The antiseptic smell of surgical soap and rubber only accentuated my nervous sweat. After a long wait, I was startled when a major walked in carrying a large envelope.

"Sergeant Donahue?" he asked as he turned on a couple of additional lights.

"Yes, sir."

He opened the envelope and removed some X-rays.

"I have your X-rays here," he said as he attached them to a viewing screen and turned on the light.

"How do they look, sir?"

"Take a look for yourself."

I wheeled over next to the screen and he pointed to a dark spot on one of the X-rays.

"You have something lodged in the area of your middle ear."

"Any evidence of a fracture or skull depression or anything like that?" I asked nervously.

"No, everything appears to be intact." He smiled.

"What a relief! I was worried there might be some brain involvement."

"No, nothing that serious," he reassured me. "The one thing we have to look out for in a wound like this is a blood clot between the skull and the brain—a subdural hematoma. We'll have to keep an eye on you for a couple of weeks."

"Sounds good to me. Is it gonna require general anesthesia?"

He slipped the X-ray back into the envelope. "No, I think we can handle it with a local. Let's get you on the table." After helping me lie down on the operating table, he turned on a bright overhead light, removed my dressing, and slipped on a pair of surgical gloves.

"I'm gonna give you a few small injections that might sting a little," he said while filling a syringe with one percent xylocaine.

"The doc's okay," I said to myself as he anesthetized the wound. I had a comfortable feeling that he was one of the best doctors I had come across. He had that special bedside manner that immediately put you at ease and instilled confidence.

When he finished numbing the wound, he told me he was going to open it up a little and then remove some of the devitalized tissue so that it wouldn't become infected when he closed it up.

"Do whatever you have to do, sir."

As he worked on the wound, we struck up a conversation. He told me that back in the States he was an avid hunter. I told him all about my experiences at Duc-Phong and with the Mobile Guerrilla Force. He remarked that as soon as I regained my strength he'd take me on a tour of the hospital and that he'd get me any medical supplies or equipment I needed.

In the middle of whatever he was doing, I saw him pick up a straight forceps and could feel him insert it into the wound. A few seconds later I felt something tugging in my middle ear. It wasn't a sharp pain, but I could feel a dull pulling sensation.

"Must have a barb on it," he said as he used the forceps to gently pull and twist. "There you go," he said as he pulled out a piece of blood-covered metal and showed it to me.

"It's the brass jacket from an AK-47 round," I said as he dropped it into my palm. "Must have gone through some bamboo before it hit me."

"Keep it as a souvenir."

"Thanks, Doc," I said as he closed my hand around it.

When he finished irrigating the wound, he closed it up with some 4-0 silk and applied a fresh white dressing.

"That should do it for now," he said as he sat me up and helped me back into the wheelchair. "How do you feel?"

"Little dizzy and nauseated."

"You get a few hours' sleep and you'll feel a lot better."

"Won't argue with that."

"I'll see you at ENT in the morning." He removed his surgical gloves.

"Okay, sir, thanks for everything." He turned off the overhead light and left the room. A short time later the medic returned and wheeled me out of the building and down a covered walkway.

"Ward Eight," he said as we turned left and wheeled into the building.

Entering the darkened ward, I could see there were

long rows of occupied bunks along both walls. About halfway down on the right, we passed a nurse who sat on the edge of a bed trying to comfort someone who was in pain. When we reached the last bed on the right, I was rolled alongside and the medic pulled down the sheet for me.

"In you go, Sarge," he said as he helped me out of the wheelchair and onto the edge of the bed. From where I was sitting, most of the wounded I could see appeared to be in pretty bad shape. The guy in the next bed had tubes running out of his mouth and nose and his shaved head appeared at least double its normal size.

"He's a captain with the 11th Armored Cav. His A.P.C. was hit by a rocket," the medic whispered before leaving. Watching the Captain lie there so near to death, I realized how fortunate I was.

"Bac-si," a voice whispered from the shadows.

I turned to see that it was Luc. Luc had been the Third Herd's platoon sergeant until he was shot in the stomach near Phuoc-Vinh. Seeing him for the first time since the Phuoc-Vinh operation, I was shocked by his appearance—he was skin and bone and looked like one of the walking dead. The skin that covered his protruding cheekbones was stretched tight and his eyes were sunk deep in their sockets.

"Luc, my friend," I said as he hugged me and then sat at the foot of my bed.

"Hospital number one. Have movie at night."

"Glad you like it."

"We same cowboy, V.C. same Indian." He smiled.

"How's the food?" I wanted to know.

"Much food, Bac-si, but not good." He pursed his lips in disdain and shook his head. "All food taste same potato."

"You mean to tell me they don't put nuoc-mam on the food?" I joked.

"No nuoc-mam," he said with a serious expression on his face.

"You look like you lost a little weight."

He lifted his shirt and showed me an eight-inch scar on his stomach.

"I have big operation," he said proudly.

"What's going on here?" a big blonde nurse interrupted.

"Just saying hello to an old friend."

"You'll have plenty of time for that in the morning," she said, extending her hand and helping him off the bed.

"I come back, Bac-si."

"Okay, Luc, see ya in the morning," I said as he and the nurse left, the sound of their voices fading into the night.

Alone in the now-silent ward, I rested my head on the cool, soft pillow and wondered how Bob and the Bodes were doing. In less than a breath, I was deep in sleep—it had been a long day . . .

NEWS CLIPPINGS

Both the U.S. and South Vietnamese commands reported scant ground activity yesterday in South Vietnam.
The Courier-Journal (Louisville), July 19, 1967

Epilogue

Though much is taken, much abides; and though
We are not now that strength which in old days
Moved earth and heaven, that which we are, we are:
One equal temper of heroic hearts,
Made weak by time and fate, but strong in will
To strive, to seek, to find, and not to yield.

—Alfred, Lord Tennyson

Bob Cole

In 1978 I decided that I was going to write a book about the Quan-Loi operation, and during the years that followed located all of the surviving American members of the team.

I reestablished contact with Bob when I ran into him at the July 1979 Special Forces Association Convention in Washington, D.C. It had been more than ten years since I had seen him and it didn't surprise me that he was still as soft-spoken as ever. Over a spaghetti dinner than night, I tried to get him to talk about the war, but it proved difficult.

When I finally got him to open up, he told me that he left Vietnam in 1968 and was assigned to the 7th Special Forces Group at Fort Bragg, North Carolina, where he taught small-unit tactics. Later that year he was transferred to the 46th Special Forces Company in

Thailand where he worked with the Thai Special Forces at Nampungdam.

Bob told me that he volunteered to return to Vietnam in 1969. When he arrived there, he was assigned to MACV-SOG's (Military Assistance Command, Vietnam—Studies and Observation Group) Command and Control North at Da-Nang. About halfway through his year-long tour at Da-Nang, he took a weekend R&R and caught a flight south to visit some old Vietnamese comrades who lived in Tay-Ninh. On his first night back in town, he took a couple of his friends to the Bamboo Club for grilled buffalo steaks and cold Beer "33." While eating dinner, he recognized a Cambodian who had fought with Fergy and Frank's platoon at Quan-Loi. The Bode joined them for dinner and told Bob that everyone who hadn't been killed or disabled was fighting in Cambodia. He also told him that my good friend Kimh had become a colonel in the Cambodian army.

Bob completed what was to be his last tour in Vietnam in 1970 and returned to the 6th Special Forces Group at Fort Bragg to retire as a master sergeant. He told me that as a retiree he found himself faced with a dilemma. He was originally from Brooklyn and couldn't decide whether to return there or remain in North Carolina. He decided to flip a coin. If it turned up heads he'd go back to New York and if it was tails he'd stay in North Carolina. Well, New York lost and Bob and his daughter Karen now live in Charlotte, where he works for the post office. In his spare time Bob enjoys fishing for trout and small-mouth bass in neighboring streams and lakes.

Bob's military awards and decorations include:
The Silver Star
Bronze Star Medal for Valor (2nd Award)
Army Commendation Medal for Valor
Purple Heart
Presidential Unit Citation
Meritorious Unit Citation
Good Conduct Medal (4th Award)

National Defense Service Medal
Vietnam Service Medal
Vietnam Campaign Medal (With 60 Device)
Vietnamese Cross of Gallantry (With Palm)
Combat Infantryman's Badge
Thai Fourragere
Thai Jump Wings
Senior Parachute Badge

"Bo" Gritz

While attending the '79 convention I also linked up with Bo. At that time he was staying at a friend's home in suburban Washington and invited me to stay with him while I was in town. The following morning we were up before first light doing push-ups on the front lawn, and by the time dawn cracked we were well into a long-distance run over the rolling suburban hills.

While working up a good sweat, Bo told me that he left Vietnam in 1968 to attend the Army's Chinese Language School in Monterey, California. When he completed language training in 1970, he received orders to attend the Command and General Staff College at Fort Leavenworth, Kansas. After graduating in 1972, he moved to Washington D.C. to become an aide to General William C. Westmoreland who, at that time, was Chief of Staff of the Army. Later that year, General Creighton W. Abrams replaced Westmoreland as Chief of Staff and Bo received orders to enroll in a full-time graduate program at the American University in Washington.

Upon completion of his graduate studies in 1974, he became the Commander of the 3rd Battalion of the 7th Special Forces Group in Panama. In 1976, he returned to Washington and the Pentagon to become the Chief of Congressional Relations for the Office of the Secretary of Defense.

In 1979, Bo made the difficult decision to retire from the Army so that he could devote full-time to the POW/MIA issue. He and his wife Claudia and children Michael and Melody now live on a small ranch (Sky Ranch) not far from Death Valley, California. Bo also has one son who is serving with the 82nd Airborne Division at Fort Bragg and another who is stationed in Korea. A few years ago he became a member of the Mormon Church and he now devotes much of his free time to church activities.

Bo's military awards and decorations include:
  The Silver Star (3rd Award)
  Legion of Merit (2nd Award)
  Distinguished Flying Cross
  Soldier's Medal
  Bronze Star Medal for Valor (8th Award)
  Air Medal (26th Award)
  Purple Heart
  Presidential Unit Citation
  Vietnam Service Medal
  Vietnam Campaign Medal (with 60 Device)
  Vietnamese Cross of Gallantry (With Palm)
  Gold Star of Cambodia
  Combat Infantryman's Badge
  Scuba Badge
  Pathfinder Badge
  Vietnamese Jump Wings
  Panamanian Jump Wings
  Honduran Jump Wings
  Colombian Jump Wings
  Master Parachute Badge

Frank Hagey

Locating the third member of the team was sheer luck. When I called the Vietnam Veterans' Outreach Center in Queens, New York, in April 1982 a familiar voice answered the phone. It was Frank. The last time I had heard his voice was on a hot summer day in August, 1967. Early in the morning on that particular day the Mobile Guerrilla Force boarded boats at the Special Forces camp at Ben-Soi for an operation called "Picnic."

After motoring down the Song Vam Co Dong River, we off-loaded on the north bank of the river approximately eight and a half klicks northwest of Ben-Soi. Moving northeast for a few hundred meters, we entered a fortified Viet-Cong base area and immediately made heavy contact with an undetermined number of V.C. While attempting to move one of the wounded Americans to safety, Frank was hit on the right side of his head by an exploding Chinese rifle grenade which caused extensive skull damage and left him critically wounded.

During our telephone conversation, Frank told me that after we loaded him on a med-evac chopper he received emergency medical treatment back in Saigon and was then sent to Japan and ultimately to Walter Reed Army Hospital. Once back at Walter Reed, they found that he had complete loss of hearing in one ear and partial loss in the other; he also had suffered paralysis of his left arm. While recovering from his wounds, he learned lip reading, and when some of his hearing returned he was issued hearing aids for both ears.

When he was released from the hospital, Frank returned to Fort Bragg and the 3rd Special Forces Group to continue physical therapy at Womack Army Hospital. After a year of therapy, he went back to Walter Reed to have a plastic plate attached over the hole in his skull. When he was reassigned to Bragg's 6th Special Forces Group, it was at that time that he received the traumatic news that he would no longer be allowed to remain a Green Beret. Because of his medical problems, he was told that he was being transferred to the 18th Airborne Corp's 50th Signal Battalion at Fort Bragg. Listening to Frank talk about the transfer, I could sense that it hurt him more than anything that had happened to him in the war—it was a wound that would take many years to heal.

Frank retired from the army as a 1st sergeant in July 1973. As a retiree, he worked in a Drug and Alcohol Counseling Program in Korea and later as a volunteer at the V.A.'s Vietnam Veterans' Outreach Center in Queens. Frank and his wife are now thinking about purchasing a farm in upstate New York.

Frank's military awards and decorations include:
 The Silver Star
 Purple Heart (5th Award)
 Presidential Unit Citation
 Good Conduct Medal (3rd Award)
 National Defense Service Medal
 Vietnam Service Medal
 Vietnam Campaign Medal (With 60 Device)
 Vietnamese Cross of Gallantry (With Palm)
 Combat Infantryman's Badge
 Glider Wings
 Master Parachute Badge

"Duke" Snider

Three months after making contact with Frank, I located the fourth member of the team. I was manning a Veterans' Information Table at the July, 1982 Special Forces Association Convention in Atlantic City, New Jersey, and I spotted someone wearing a cowboy hat, standing in the hotel lobby. When his voice bellowed across the room, I knew that it was the Duke

That night we sat in my hotel room talking, and he brought me up to date on what he'd been doing since 1967. During our conversation I could tell that it was difficult for him to recall those things he had been trying for so many years to forget. His wife Elizabeth later told me she was surprised that he would sit down and talk about it at all—he never had done so before.

As we reminisced into the early morning hours, Duke told me that when he completed his tour with the Mobile Guerrilla Force he was reassigned to the Special Forces Training Group at the John F. Kennedy Center for Special Warfare at Fort Bragg. In 1970 he again left for Vietnam, and this time was stationed with the B-Team at An-Loc. Later that year he returned to working with Cambodians when he was assigned to FANK (Forces Armees Nationales Khmeres) in Bien-Hoa.

Duke told me that while he was in Bien-Hoa he ran into his old friend Chote. The First Platoon's interpreter had become a captain in the Cambodian army and at that time was operating out of one of the camps in the Seven Mountains area of South Vietnam. After his tour with FANK, Duke received orders to report to the 75th Rangers at Fort Hood, Texas, and in 1973 was assigned to the JCRC (Joint Casualty Resolution Center) in Nakhon Phanom, Thailand.

Following the war in Southeast Asia, Duke returned to the States to serve at Fort Stewart, Georgia, and to attend the Sergeant Major Academy at Fort Bliss, Texas. After graduating from the Academy he reported to Fort Lewis, Washington, and then to the 10th Special Forces Group at Fort Devens, Massachusetts. Duke told me that the high point of his tour with the 10th was a nine-month mission to Liberia, Africa.

Duke retired from the Army in 1983 as the Command Sergeant Major of the 2nd Battalion of the 10th Special Forces Group. He currently works as an immigration inspector at Point Roberts, Washington, and lives in nearby Sumas with his wife Elizabeth, son Randal, and daughter Sharyl. His eldest son, Scott, is a law-enforcement officer. In his spare time Duke enjoys fishing for salmon, gardening, and the great Northwest.

Duke's military awards and decorations include:
   The Silver Star
   Meritorious Service Medal
   Bronze Star Medal for Valor (2nd Award)
   Joint Services Commendation Medal
   Army Commendation Medal for Valor (6th Award)
   Purple Heart
   Presidential Unit Citation
   Good Conduct Medal (6th Award)
   National Defense Service Medal
   Vietnam Service Medal (4)
   N.C.O. Professional Development Ribbon (5th Award)
   Army Service Ribbon
   Overseas Service Ribbon
   Vietnam Civil Action Medal (Unit)
   Vietnam Campaign Medal (With 60 Device)
   Vietnam Cross of Gallantry (With Palm—2nd Award)
   Combat Infantryman's Badge
   Vietnamese Jump Wings
   Master Parachute Badge

Roger Smith

On a cold November day in 1982, I was at my desk working on a report when the phone rang—it was Roger calling from California. After joking about Buffalo's weather, he told me that through the "old boy" network word had filtered down to him that I was putting together a book on the Mobile Guerrilla Force. Roger was very excited about the idea because he felt that a good nonfiction book could do a lot for the image of Vietnam veterans in general and Special Forces in particular. He also told me that he would send me copies of all of his Mobile Guerrilla Force photographs and would make a tape recording of everything he could remember about the Quan-Loi operation.

During our conversation, Roger informed me that he returned to the States in 1968 to serve as a radio operator with the 3rd and 6th Special Forces Groups at Fort Bragg. Later that year, he volunteered to return to Vietnam and serve a year with Detachment A-235 at Nhon-Co. In 1970 he was transferred to the 1st Special Forces Group on Okinawa, and in 1971 he again volunteered to return to Vietnam. During that tour, he served with MACV-SOG's Command and Control Central and operated out of Kontum with Recon Team Hawaii.

Roger was transferred to the 46th Special Forces Company in Thailand in 1972 and while there crossed paths with one of the Bodes who had fought with him and Jim Condon at Quan-Loi. The Bode had received a commission as a 3rd lieutenant in the Cambodian army and told Roger that he was on his way back to the war in Cambodia.

Roger received orders to report to Fort Bragg and the 7th Special Forces Group in 1974, and in 1975 he was transferred to the Special Forces Detachment in Korea. While in Korea, he served as the HALO (High Altitude Low Opening) advisor to the Korean Special Forces.

In 1980, he returned to the States to become an infantry 1st sergeant at Ford Ord, California, and after graduating from the Sergeants Major Academy in 1983 applied for an appointment as a warrant officer and reassignment back into Special Forces. Roger was appointed as a warrant officer 2 in 1984 and is currently attached to Operational Detachment A-175, 3rd Battalion, 1st Special Forces Group, Fort Lewis, Washington. He is the Executive Officer of the SCUBA (Self Contained Underwater Breathing Apparatus) Team.

Roger's military awards and decorations include:
  The Bronze Star Medal
  Meritorious Service Medal

Army Commendation Medal
Air Medal
Presidential Unit Citation
Good Conduct Medal
National Defense Service Medal
Vietnam Service Medal (7)
Armed Forces Expeditionary Medal
N.C.O. Professional Development Ribbon (5)
Army Service Ribbon
Overseas Service Ribbon (6)
Vietnam Civil Action Medal (Unit)
Vietnam Campaign Medal (With 60 Device)
Vietnamese Cross of Gallantry (With Palm)
Combat Infantryman's Badge
Pathfinder Badge
Scuba Badge
German Jump Wings
Republic of China Jump Wings
Thai Jump Wings
Republic of Korea Jump Wings
Vietnamese Jump Wings
Master Parachute Badge

"Stik" Rader

In February 1983, I put together a team of Vietnam veterans to make a parachute jump and seven-day, one-hundred-mile run across Death Valley, California. One of the first to volunteer was Stik Rader—he was as skinny as ever and looked every inch the long-distance runner. During the run, we passed places with names like Ubehebe Crater, Hell's Gate, Furnace Creek, and Badwater, and talked about Dong-Xoai, Song-Be, Trang-Sup, and Quan-Loi.

As we ran, Stik told me that when he returned to the States in October 1967 he became a foreign weapons instructor at the J.F.K. Center at Fort Bragg. In 1968, he volunteered to return to Vietnam and was assigned to MACV-SOG at Da-Nang and Long-Thanh. Upon completion of his tour, he volunteered for duty with the 46th Special Forces Company in Thailand, where he worked with the Thai Special Forces at Phitsanulok.

Stik was transferred to the 1st Special Forces Group on Okinawa in 1970. In 1971, he again volunteered to return to Vietnam. During this tour, he was assigned to MACV-SOG's Command and Control Central as a team leader with Recon Team Texas. In 1972, he returned to working with Cambodians when he was transferred to the FANK (Forces Armees Nationales Khmeres) Training Center in Phouc-Tuy Province.

After completing his last tour in Vietnam in 1973, Stik returned to the 5th Special Forces Group at Fort Bragg. In 1974, he left again for Southeast Asia and MAAG-LAOS (Military Advisory Assistance Group—Laos) and in 1975 again went to Thailand to work with USMACTHAI (Thai Advisory Group) in Bangkok. While in Bangkok, he ran into one of the Cambodians from the Recon Platoon at a bar on Pat-Pong Street. He told Stik that some of the Bodes from the Mobile Guerrilla Force had survived the Vietnamese, Prince Sihanouk, Lon Nol, and the Khmer Rouge, and that they were pressing on from camps located along the Thai-Cambodian border.

Stik completed his assignment in Thailand in 1976 and again returned to the 5th Special Forces Group at Fort Bragg. In 1977, he became an instructor and operations sergeant with the Georgetown University Army ROTC, and in 1978 attended the Sergeants Major Academy at Fort Bliss, Texas. After graduating from the academy, he attended the Army's Korean Language School in Monterey, California. When he completed language training, he was assigned to the 8th Army headquarters in Korea and in 1981 became the 1st Sergeant of the Honor Guard Company of the United Nations Command in Yongsan.

Stik left Korea in 1982 and was assigned as the Detachment Sergeant Major of the San Diego State College Army ROTC. In 1985 he asked to return to Special Forces. He is currently assigned as the Sergeant Major of Company A, 3rd Battalion, 1st Special Forces Group at Fort Lewis, Washington.

Stik's military awards and decorations include:
The Distinguished Flying Cross
Bronze Star Medal for Valor (5th Award)
Army Commendation Medal for Valor (3rd Award)
Purple Heart
Air Medal
Defense Meritorious Service Medal
Joint Service Commendation Medal
Good Conduct Medal (8th Award)
National Defense Service Medal
Vietnam Service Medal
Vietnam Campaign Medal (With 60 Device)
Vietnamese Cross of Gallantry (With Palm)
Combat Infantryman's Badge
Vietnamese Jump Wings
Thai Jump Wings
Republic of Korea Jump Wings
Master Parachute Badge

Jim Condon

In October 1986, the Department of the Army had informed me that they had located a James Condon who had served in Vietnam in 1967. They weren't sure that he was the same person that I had been looking for, but after many years of searching it was my first substantial lead.

That same afternoon I called a Dover, New Hampshire, telephone number and a woman with a southern accent answered the phone—it was Jim's wife Gail.

When she put him on the phone, I immediately sensed that nothing of any real importance had changed. He was still the same person I had known almost twenty years ago.

During our conversation, Jim told me that he left Vietnam in 1968 and was assigned to the U.S. Army Training Center at Fort Jackson, South Carolina. Later that year, he volunteered to return to Vietnam and served as a company commander with the 196th Light Infantry Brigade at Landing Zone Baldy.

In 1970, Jim received orders to report to the Infantry School at Fort Benning, Georgia, where he became an assistant operations officer in the Communications-Electronics Department. While stationed at Benning, he also graduated from the Advanced Infantry Officers' Course.

Following graduation, he joined the 1st Armored Divison at Erlangen, Germany, where he served as the company commander of a mechanized infantry company. In 1975, he was transferred to Ansbach, where he became the division's assistant civil-military affairs officer.

In 1977, Jim left Germany and reported to the 24th Infantry Division at Fort Stewart, Georgia, and while there earned a Bachelor's Degree in Human Resources Administration and a Master's Degree in Management.

Jim retired from the Army in March of 1980, and he and his wife Gail, son Jim, and daughters Katie and Pattie now live in Dover, New Hampshire. When I asked Gail how someone from Georgia ended up in New England, she told me that when Jim retired he closed his eyes and pointed to a spot on the map—it turned out to be Dover.

Jim's military awards and decorations include:
   The Silver Star
   Bronze Star Medal
   Army Commendation Medal (3rd Award)
   Presidential Unit Citation
   Good Conduct Medal

National Defense Service Medal
Vietnam Service Medal
Vietnam Campaign Medal (With 60 Device)
Vietnamese Cross of Gallantry (With Palm—2nd Award)
Armed Forces Reserve Medal
Combat Infantryman's Badge
Vietnamese Jump Wings
Master Parachute Badge

Bill Ferguson

The only member of the team who didn't make it home from the war in Southeast Asia was Bill Ferguson. Fergy was killed in action near Ben-Soi in August 1967. For his heroism exhibited on that fatal mission, he was posthumously awarded the Distinguished Service Cross, our nation's second highest award for valor. The citation reads as follows:

> **For extraordinary heroism in connection with military operations involving conflict with an armed hostile force in the Republic of Vietnam: Sergeant First Class Ferguson distinguished himself by exceptionally valorous actions on 13 August 1967 while serving as platoon leader of a Mobile Guerrilla Task Force on a combat mission deep in hostile territory. When another company of the same unit came under attack from a numerically superior Viet-Cong force, Sergeant Ferguson immediately volunteered to lead his men to their aid. Upon reaching the scene of the battle, he moved freely among his men directing their assault although exposed to withering automatic weapons fire. An enemy grenade seriously wounded him as he attacked a hostile position, but he refused medical aid and continued to press the of-**

fensive. With complete disregard for his own safety, Sergeant Ferguson directed deadly fire on the insurgents and hurled numerous grenades into their positions. He moved openly through the bullet-swept area time after time to inspire his men to greater efforts. He was mortally wounded while leading his men with dauntless courage in the face of grave danger. Sergeant First Class Ferguson's extraordinary heroism and devotion to duty, at the cost of his life, were in keeping with the highest traditions of the military service and reflect great credit upon himself, his unit, and the United States Army.

Glossary

Ace Bandage—Elastic bandage that was used to cover and add pressure to dressings and splints.

A-1E—Single-engine propeller-driven fighter/bomber.

Air America—C.I.A.-controlled airline.

AK-47—Standard automatic infantry rifle used by the Viet-Cong and North Vietnamese Army.

A.L.O.—Air Liaison Officer.

A.P.C.—Armored Personnel Carrier.

A-Team—Special Forces Operational Detachment that normally consisted of twelve men.

Azimuth—A compass direction.

B-52—Heavy American bomber. Also, a device used to open C ration cans.

"Bac-si"—Doctor.

B.A.R. Belt—Japanese-made ammunition belt and pouches originally intended to hold magazines for the Browning Automatic Rifle. The M.G.F. used them to hold M-16 magazines. Each pouch held five magazines.

"Beaucoup"—French for many. Often used by Vietnamese and Cambodian troops

Beer "33"—Vietnamese-brewed beer.

Benadryl—A strong antihistamine used to counteract an allergic reaction.

Betelnut—An opiate chewed by many people in Southeast Asia. It stains the user's lips red and teeth black.

Big Red One—1st Infantry Division (American).

Black Box—Top-secret electronic equipment carried on-board U-2 spy aircraft.

"Bo-chi-huy"—Headquarters.

Bodes—An abbreviation for Cambodians.

Body Bag—Rubberized bag with a zipper and carrying handles that was used to carry the dead from the battlefield.

Breaking Contact—The tactic of disengaging from contact with an enemy force.

Bush—The outer field areas where infantry units operated.

Canister Round—A 40MM M-79 Grenade Launcher round that was similar to, but larger than, a buckshot round that is fired from a shotgun.

C.B.U.'s—An abbreviation for antipersonnel cluster bombs.

C-4—High-explosive puttylike material. Small pieces would burn at a high temperature and could be used to heat water and rations.

Charlie, Charles, Mr. Charles—Slang expressions for Viet-Cong.

CH-47—Large American helicopter used to transport troops and equipment.

Chi-Com—Of Chinese Communist manufacture.

Chinese Nungs—Mike Force Troops who were of Chinese ancestry.

"Choa-ong?"—How are you?

Cholon—Chinese section of Saigon.

Chopper—Helicopter

Citroen—French made automobile.

Claymore Mines—Mines packed with explosive plastique and rigged to spray hundreds of steel pellets.

Commo Check—Radio check.

Commo Pad—Contained a list of the code names of all American members of the M.G.F. and the primary and secondary radio frequencies of all M.G.F. and supporting units.

C-130—Four engine medium sized aircraft used to transport troops and equipment.

C-123—Two-engine medium-sized aircraft used to transport troops and equipment.

C.O.S.V.N.—Abbreviation for Central Office of the Communist Party of South Vietnam.

C.P.—Command Post

C's—C rations, C-rats. Standard American field rations used in Vietnam.

C.S. Gas Grenade—Used by the M.G.F. to assist in breaking contact with the enemy.

Cut Down—Making an incision over a vein so that it could be elevated and an I.V. needle inserted. This procedure was used when the patient's blood vessels had collapsed due to shock.

Cycalo—Three-wheeled bicycle taxi with a large seat used to transport one or two passengers.

Detonator Cord—Detonation Cord for explosive charges.

Deuce-and-a-half—Two-and-a-half-ton truck.

Dien Bien Phu—Major battle in North Vietnam where the French were defeated by the Viet-Minh.

Dong Nai Valley—Formed by the Dong Nai River as it flows through War Zone "D."

"Dung-lai"—Don't move.

Dust-off—A medical evacuation flight by chopper.

Emesis Basin—A sterile basin used in the suture process. Also fit under the patient's chin and was used to collect vomit.

E.N.T.—Ear, Nose, and Throat.

Epinephrine—Injectable hormone that increases blood pressure by constricting blood vessels and stimulating the heart.

F.A.C.—Small single-engine Forward Air Control aircraft.

Fast Mover—Jet-fighter aircraft.

5th Special Forces Group Headquarters—Located in Nha-Trang. Provided leadership and support to the four C-Teams and other special-operations detachments located in South Vietnam.

Fire Team—An infantry unit that consisted of three to five men.

Five by five—Indicated that you were receiving a radio transmission loud and clear.

F.O.B.—Forward Operations Base.

"Fox Control"—Radio call sign used by 1st Lt. James Condon.

"Fox Four"—Radio call sign used by the Recon Platoon.

"Fox One"—Radio call sign used by the First Platoon.

"Fox Three"—Radio call sign used by the Third Platoon.

"Fox Two"—Radio call sign used by the Second Platoon.

Grazing Fire—When the trajectory of your bullets fly parallel to the ground and pass through the enemy formations at a level never higher than the chest or lower than the hips—the most deadly form of fire.

Greased—A slang expression for "killed."

Gunship—A Huey helicopter armed with machine guns and rockets that was used to provide close air support to troops engaged in ground combat.

Halazone Tablet—Water-purification tablet.

H.A.L.O.—High Altitude Low Opening. A technique of infiltrating an enemy-controlled area by parachute.

H.E.—High Explosive.

Hematocrit—A test that measures the percentage of red blood cells in whole blood.

Hemostat Clamp—Surgical instrument used to stop bleeding by clamping tissue or blood vessels. Also used to hold a suture needle when sewing up a wound.

Ho Chi Minh Trail—A complex system of trails and roads that ran south from North Vietnam through Laos and Cambodia. The system was used to transport men, equipment, and supplies into South Vietnam.

Hooch—Small house or structure constructed of bamboo and straw.

Hop—To hitch a ride on a helicopter or airplane.

HT-1 Radio—Walkie-talkie-type radio used by M.G.F. platoon sergeants and squad leaders.

Hueys—UH-1 Helicopter. Used to transport troops and equipment and to provide close air support.

Instant Detonation—To remove the four-second time-delay section from a hand grenade so that it will explode instantly when its pin is removed and spoon released.

Intel—Abbreviation for intelligence information.

I.V.—Intravenous injection of blood replacements such as normal saline, or blood plasma expanders such as serum albumin.

J.C.R.C.—Joint Casualty Resolution Center.

Kampuchea—Cambodia.

K-Bar—Marine Corps knife.

Khmer—Cambodian.

Khmer Rouge—Cambodian Communists.

Khmer Serei—Free Cambodians.

Klicks—Short for kilometers (1 kilometer = 1000 meters).

Kuomintang—Anti-Communist Chinese forces commanded by Chiang Kai-shek during World War II. After the Communist victory in China many of the Kuomintang forces retreated to Southeast Asia.

Lidocaine Hydrochloride—an injectable local anesthetic.

Listening Post—A one-, two-, or three-man post set up on the most likely avenues of approach to a base camp. Its mission was to observe and report on enemy activity.

Lon-Nol—Cambodian prince who, with U.S. assistance, overthrew and replaced Prince Norodum Sihanouk as the leader of Cambodia.

L.Z.—Landing Zone.

M-3 Kit—Small medical kit carried by M.G.F. squad medics.

M-5 Kit—Large medical kit carried by M.G.F. platoon and company medics.

MAAG-LAOS—Military Advisory Assistance Group-Laos.

MACV-SOG—Military Assistance Command, Vietnam—Studies and Observation Group. Conducted reconaissance and intelligence operations in South Vietnam, North Vietnam, Cambodia, and Laos.

Mags—Short for magazines. An M-16 magazine held twenty rounds.

M.A.S.H.—Mobile Army Surgical Hospital

Med-evac—Helicopter extraction of the sick, wounded, and dead from the battlefield.

Meprobamate Tablet—A mild tranquilizer that was used to relax muscles.

MIA/POW—Missing in Action/Prisoner of War.

Mike Force—Multipurpose reaction force whose primary mission was to come to the assistance of Special Forces units that were under attack or the threat of attack by larger enemy forces.

MK-II British Sten Gun—Silencer-equipped 9MM submachine gun that the M.G.F. used when the silent killing or wounding of an enemy soldier was required.

Mobile Guerrilla Force (M.G.F.)—A Special Forces-commanded unit that was assigned the mission of conducting guerrilla operations against Viet-Cong and North Vietnamese forces.

Moleskin—A cotton fabric used to cover blisters or areas of the skin that have been rubbed raw.

Montagnards—Hill people of Vietnam.

Morphine—Injectable high-potency narcotic pain reliever.

Morse Code—A coded communications system invented by S.F.B. Morse that was used by the M.G.F. when secret transmissions were necessary.

Naval Flare—Pen-sized signal flare used to signal aircraft.

Normal Saline I.V.—A sterile saltwater I.V. that was used to treat or prevent shock. Also used to treat serious cases of heat exhaustion or sun stroke.

"Number one"—Very good.

"Number ten"—Very bad.

Nuoc-mam—Strong-smelling fish extract used by Southeast Asians to add flavor to rice.

N.V.A.—North Vietnamese Army.

O-1E—Small single-engine propeller-driven Forward Air Control (F.A.C.) aircraft.

Orange Ground Panel—Reflective panel that was used to signal aircraft.

Penicillin—An antibiotic made from molds that is effective against certain classes of bacteria.

Pith Helmet—Helmet worn by some N.V.A. and Viet-Cong units.

Point—Lead man in an infantry column.

Policed—Term for "cleaning up."

P.O.W.—Prisoner of War.

Punji Pit—A camouflaged hole containing sharpened stakes in the bottom or sides.

PRC-74—Radio used by the M.G.F. Headquarters Unit to communicate by voice or code with someone beyond the range of the PRC-25 radio.

Prince Sihanouk—Neutralist leader of Cambodia

Project Delta—Special Forces unit that conducted secret reconaissance and intelligence-gathering missions.

Pull Device—A wire that if pulled would detonate a booby trap.

P.X.—Post Exchange.

Recon—Reconaissance.

R.O.T.C.—Reserve Officer Training Corps.

RPG—Enemy rocket-propelled rifle grenade.

Rucksack—The backpack carried in the field by M.G.F. troops.

"Saddle up"—An order for soldiers to put on their packs and move out.

"Sak sa bai?"—How are you?

"Sau lam"—Not good.

Scuttlebutt—Marine Corps/Navy term for rumors.

Serum Albumin—A blood-volume expander than increases blood volume by absorbing fluids from the area surrounding the vessels.

SFC—Sergeant First Class.

Shock—A state of acute circulatory insufficiency of blood. Usually caused by injury, burns, or hemorrhage.

Sky Spot—Computer-controlled airstrike that could be called in on known coordinates at night or during bad weather.

Slope—A derogatory term for an Oriental.

SP-6—Specialist Sixth Class.

Special Forces—American soldiers trained in unconventional operations. Activated at Fort Bragg, N.C., on June 20, 1952. They were first deployed to Vietnam in 1957.

SSG—Staff Sergeant.

Steing Tribe—A Montagnard tribe that lived in the northern part of the Third Corps Tactical Zone of South Vietnam.

Sterile Technique—To perform a medical procedure without contaminating the wound.

Subdural Hematoma—Blood clot between the skull and brain.

Swamp Fox—Radio call sign used by Maj. James Gritz.

Swedish "K"—9MM submachine gun that was manufactured in Sweden.

Systolic Pressure—A measurement of blood pressure.

Tail Gunner—Three- or four-man stay-behind ambush whose mission it was to boobytrap the trail left by the M.G.F. and to ambush enemy trackers.

"Tay yoo"—Battle cry of the M.G.F.

Tetanus Toxoid—An immunization against tetanus (lockjaw).

Terpin Hydrate—Liquid cough medicine.

III Corps—Third Corps Tactical Zone. Included the city of Saigon and extended from the northern Mekong Delta to the southern highlands.

Third Herd—The Third Platoon.

Time Pencil—A time-delay device that could be attached to grenades or Claymore mines. Once attached it would delay the explosion for a fixed amount of time.

Toe Popper—Small pressure-detonated booby trap intended to disable the enemy.

Ton-Son-Nhut—Large Vietnamese/American Air Force base located on the outskirts of Saigon.

Tracer—A bullet with a phosphorus coating designed to burn and provide a visual indication of the bullet's trajectory.

Viet-Cong or V.C.—South Vietnamese Communists.

Viet-Cong Province Committee—Provided leadership at the province level.

Viet-Cong Secret Zone—A well-defined enemy base area about which allied forces knew little or nothing.

Viet-Minh—Short for Viet Nam Doc Lap Dong Minh or League for the Independence of Vietnam. Organized by Communist and Nationalist forces during the Japanese occupation of Vietnam.

"WETSU"—Short for "we eat this shit up." Used as a password by the M.G.F.

White Dot Signal Mirror—U.S. Air Force-issued signal mirror that was used by the M.G.F. to signal aircraft.

White Phosphorous Round—Gave off a thick white smoke. Used by the F.A.C. to pinpoint the location of enemy targets when directing air strikes.

"Xin-loi"—Sorry.

Xylocaine—Injectable local anesthetic.

Index